Additional Praise for
Futuring: The Exploration of the Future

"I can't imagine how anyone could presume to teach a course in future studies, or engage in any professional activity that involves disciplined thinking about the future, without this book. It is an indispensable resource— one to be not only read but consulted many times over —by a respected pioneer in the field."

Walter Truett Anderson, president, World Academy of Art and Science

"A very valuable addition to the literature."

Theodore Gordon, retired president, The Futures Group

"*Futuring* is a comprehensive, skillfully assembled, eminently readable survey that should be useful to anyone seeking an overview of futures studies. Highly recommended.... I will definitely adopt this book for my class."

Peter Bishop, professor, University of Houston at Clear Lake

"*Futuring* ... is a sensible, down-to-earth, and thoroughly updated survey of the futurist enterprise.... For anyone who wants to know what futures studies are all about in their larger context, here is a practical guide, free of hype and jargon, that tells the whole story.... Ed's new book will be a significant milestone in the history of futures thinking."

W. Warren Wagar, professor of history emeritus, State University of New York at Binghamton

Futuring

The Exploration of the Future

Edward Cornish

World Future Society
Bethesda, Maryland
U.S.A.
www.wfs.org

Published by the World Future Society

The World Future Society helps individuals, organizations, and communities see, understand, and respond appropriately and effectively to change. Through media, meetings, and dialogue among its members, it raises awareness of change and encourages development of creative solutions.

Futuring: The Exploration of the Future

Manuscript Editor: Cynthia G. Wagner

Consulting Editor: Owen Davies

Production Editor: Sarah Warner

Business Manager: Jefferson Cornish

Cover Design: Lisa Mathias

Photos: Photos.com, Photodisc Inc.

Published by:
World Future Society
7910 Woodmont Avenue, Suite 450
Bethesda, Maryland 20814 USA
301-656-8274
www.wfs.org
info@wfs.org

Printed in the United States of America
First Paperback Printing: October 2005

Library of Congress Cataloging-in-Publication Data

Cornish, Edward, 1927-
  Futuring : the exploration of the future / by Edward Cornish.
    p. cm.
  Includes bibliographical references and index.
  ISBN 0-930242-57-2 (hardcover) ISBN 0-930242-61-0 (paper)
  1. Social prediction. 2. Forecasting—Methodology. 3. Social change. 4. Twenty-first century—Forecasts. 5. Decision making. I. Title.
  HM901.C67 2004
  303.49--dc22   2004000249

Dedication

This book is dedicated to everyone now working to ensure that today's young people and all future generations will have a desirable world to live in.

Special appreciation is extended to the members and friends of the World Future Society whose contributions of time and money have made this book possible.

Foundations who have made grants to the Society include the Nathan Cummins Foundation, National Science Foundation, the Library of Congress, German Marshall Fund, Gannett Foundation, Jenifer Altman Foundation, Deerfield Foundation, Mertz Gilmore Foundation, and others.

Individuals making major financial contributions include May Maury Harding, John Naisbitt, Barbara Marx Hubbard, Larry Smead, Jean Sinden, Robert W. Chernow, Roberto C. Dorion, Arnold Brown, Julio Millán, Andrew G. Verzilli, William E. Halal, Manuel Morales, and Jay Beckner.

Contents

Acknowledgements

It's impossible to acknowledge here the hundreds of people who have influenced my ideas about the future, but I must at least mention those individuals who contributed most directly to the preparation of this book.

Blake M. Cornish, my youngest son, got the project started by offering to help me revise my 1977 book *The Study of the Future*—a badly needed task that I had been too busy to undertake. Blake and I hoped that we could quickly revise the book to satisfy the professors who have pressed for a new edition, so he generously took time from his law practice to work on the revision. Blake put a great deal of thought and energy into this task, but it became increasingly clear that a simple updating would not suffice. Futuring had changed too much since the earlier volume, and my own thinking about the future had also changed. A new book was essential, but I couldn't write quickly what was required. Worse, I found that I had to do a lot of rethinking of my former ideas. Blake had to return to his law practice, but he made many useful contributions to the project. Among many other things, he made extensive contributions to the sections on futuring methodology and history, and also conducted a very useful survey of what professional futurists are actually thinking and doing.

For several years, I labored on by myself, whenever I could find a few free moments. As a manuscript began to take form, I felt a keen need for a good editor.

Owen Davies, a long-time collaborator of Marvin J. Cetron, had long impressed me with his exceptional talents as a writer and book editor, and Marv persuaded Owen to give me a hand. Owen's extraordinary literary judgment proved invaluable. He let me know when he thought the text was not working, so readers have been spared many tedious paragraphs and several whole chapters that did not fit well with the rest of the book.

Cynthia G. Wagner, managing editor of *The Futurist* magazine, handled the final editing of the manuscript after I revised the text in response to Owen's suggestions. Cindy's meticulous final editing and thoughtful suggestions resulted in innumerable improvements.

Sarah Warner, the World Future Society's electronic media coordinator, did the editorial processing and typesetting of the book, contacted reviewers, and performed many other essential tasks. She proved indispensable in getting the book ready for publication.

George Anthony Cornish, a marketing writer and my eldest son, provided a wealth of ideas, especially on making the text more engaging for readers. Jefferson R. Cornish, business manager of the World Future Society and my second son, handled most of the publishing tasks, such as preparation of proof copies for reviewers, contracting for printing and mailing, general marketing, and much more.

Lisa Mathias, art director of *The Futurist*, designed the cover art for the book as well as the charts and diagrams.

Other Society staff members assisting the project were Clifton C. Coles, Susan Echard, Tanya Parwani-Jaimes, and Anne D. Silk.

Reviewers and consultants included:

Walter Truett Anderson, Rajah Ikram Azam, Richard L. Barksdale, Wendell Bell, Clement Bezold, Jérôme Bindé, Peter Bishop, Arnold Brown, Lester R. Brown, Irving Buchen, George Bugliarello, James E. Burke, Marvin J. Cetron, Robert L. Chartrand, Joseph F. Coates, Vary T. Coates, Jose Cordeiro, Robert M. Cornish, James A. Dator, Frank Davidson, Hugues de Jouvenel, Robert de Voursney, Howard F. Didsbury Jr., Victor C. Ferkiss, Leon Fuerth, Glenn Garelik, Theodore J. Gordon, John J. Gottsman, William E. Halal, Kenneth W. Harris, Olaf Helmer, Hazel Henderson, Glen E. Hiemstra, Barbara Marx Hubbard, Kenneth W. Hunter, Rolf Jensen, Anthony J. Judge, Miriam F. Kelty, Richard D. Lamm, Robert Lamson, Harold A. Linstone, Timothy J. Mack, Michael Marien, Eleonora Barbieri Masini, Julio Millán, Stephen M. Millett, Graham T.T. Molitor, John Naisbitt, Burt Nanus, Ruben F.W. Nelson, Amy Oberg, Perry Pascarella, Dennis C. Pirages, John Renesch, Arthur B. Shostak, Richard A. Slaughter, David Pearce Snyder, Stane Stanic, Stephen F. Steele, Allen Tough, W. Warren Wagar, Edie Weiner, Ian Wilson, John Young, Peter Zuckerman.

Preface

Most of us know better than to drive down a highway at eighty miles an hour without looking at the road ahead. But when it comes to steering our careers and businesses, we hardly ever consider what's coming toward us; we often wind up in a nasty "crash" that we could have avoided if we had exercised a bit of foresight.

Foresight is a skill that we can learn, and it may provide more important benefits than almost any other skill we can acquire. Foresight enables us to anticipate many of the risks and opportunities that could confront us in the future, giving us time to decide what to do before we crash into them. Foresight can also help us to develop worthwhile and achievable long-term goals, along with reasonable strategies for attaining them.

However, foresight today is more than an intuitive skill, practiced with more or less success by individuals according to their inclinations, talent, and experience. In the last few decades, it has grown into a coherent body of techniques and knowledge, known by such terms as *futuring*, *futurism*, or *futures studies*. Thanks to the work of many creative pioneers, these techniques are now used systematically by companies, government agencies, "think tanks," and professional futurists around the world to anticipate an endless variety of problems and opportunities. We, too, can learn these skills and techniques and practice them systematically to improve our careers and our lives.

This book aims to give readers a basic understanding of futuring, and of the future in general. Knowing how to think about the future is becoming increasingly urgent as the pace of change in our world accelerates. To make wise decisions about our careers, finances, and general planning, we need to know how our world is changing and what we may expect in the future.

Having an understanding of the future does not mean, of course, that we will be able to predict it in detail. Our ability to forecast most future events is extremely limited. Yet what we *can* know is critical for our future success. We cannot make wise choices if we do not understand current world trends and their likely consequences for ourselves and the options we have for achieving our goals.

Thus, the goal of futuring is not to predict the future, but to make it better. We have enormous opportunities to improve our future, and we also can avoid many potential problems if we are willing to look ahead.

Sadly, many people today believe that it is pointless to think about the future because you cannot do anything about it. They are quite wrong. This book explains why and discusses many examples of people who showed extraordinary ability to create new futures for themselves, often overcoming adverse circumstances in their lives.

Thinking ahead is more important than ever before due to the rapid pace of technological and social change. In the past most people lived in the community in which they grew up, and they simply followed the life choices of their parents. A farmer's son was almost certain to be a farmer, his daughter a farmer's wife.

Today, however, we are overwhelmed by the options available to us. We can choose to live almost anywhere in the world. We can build careers in fields that may not have existed when we entered school—and see them disappear in a few years as new technologies come along to replace them. The Internet alone provides immediate access to a global marketplace with millions of people selling us things, organizations offering job opportunities, government agencies explaining their services, universities describing their faculty and courses, and innumerable experts and others interacting with each other—and with us. People and organizations now have ways to create futures for themselves that are far richer and more exciting than could even have been imagined a century ago.

This remarkable expansion of human possibilities is just one reason we need to improve our skill in making choices. Another is the shrinking of our world. As modern communications knits us into a single "ecosystem," we are buffeted by forces that could not have affected us a decade or two ago. The turbulence in the world economy propagates around the globe in days or weeks; a stock market slump in New York is felt in Tokyo and Singapore within minutes. The clashing value systems of our globalizing world are as much to blame for riots in Venezuela and terrorist attacks in New York.

Thanks to these and many such developments, foresight has become the great need of our times. We must think ahead if we are to cope with the hurricane-force changes now bashing at every aspect of life—our work, our homes, our education, our health, our amusements, our environment, even our religions. Fortunately, we are not the first to recognize this need.

The New Look of the Future

Serious thinking about the future was long blocked by the belief that the future is unknowable and beyond our control. People who spoke about the future were regarded as dreamers, charlatans, or just fools; sensible people focused on their immediate business. But World War II, atomic bombs, rockets, computers, and other momentous events forced thoughtful people to ponder the future impacts of the awesome technologies that were appearing. Military and government leaders as well as cutting-edge scholars began to think harder about what could happen in the future and to look for better ways to anticipate what might lie ahead.

These "futurists," as they began to be called in the 1960s, recognized that the future world develops out of the present world. Thus, we can learn a great deal about what may happen in the future by looking systematically at what is actually happening now. The key thing to watch is not events (sudden developments or one-day occurrences) but trends (long-term, ongoing shifts in such things as population, land use, technology, and governmental systems).

At the RAND Corporation, the first "think factory," Herman Kahn and his colleagues developed the scenario technique as a way to explore future possibilities in ways that were organized and disciplined but still very creative. Kahn's work deeply impressed military and political leaders of both the United States and the Soviet Union, who recognized the horrendous consequences of future thermonuclear "exchanges" that could kill hundreds of millions of people. Kahn's work should have won him the Nobel Peace Prize; instead, he was widely vilified and provided a model for the weird atomic scientist in the movie *Dr. Strangelove*. Today, the scenario technique is widely used by government and business groups striving to understand the possibilities of the future and the options that they have for dealing with them.

In recent years, futurists have steadily refined their methods and techniques, and there is an active futurist community supported by a number of newsletters, journals, and a magazine, *The Futurist*. Today, we can even see the possibility of a genuine science of the future—not a natural science like physics or biology but a social science like sociology or economics.

We will not, of course, be able to know for certain all that will happen to us in the future. However, developing our futuring skills will sharpen our ability to assess the probabilities, anticipate consequences, and choose ever-wiser courses of action that can lead us to the best possible future.

Edward Cornish
President, World Future Society
Editor, *The Futurist*
Bethesda, Maryland, U.S.A.

1

Explorers of the Future

We are all time travelers on a journey into the future. However, we are not tourists accompanied by a guide who can tell us just what lies ahead and will keep us safe and comfortable. Instead, we are explorers in an unknown and dangerous region that no one has ever seen before us.

Our fellow explorers express many different opinions about what lies ahead. Some of them foresee a marvelous paradise—a time filled with wonderful new technologies that will keep us all well-fed, healthy, and happy. Others among us warn of doom in one form or another: an ecological catastrophe, a new ice age, a collision with a comet, or any of an endless variety of other threats, some more plausible than others.

In our personal lives, we become keenly aware of the unknown in our future when we start college, take a new job, open a business, or move to a new town. We never can be sure what will happen to us, but the great explorers of the past would advise us that we have a better chance of succeeding if we prepare ourselves as well as possible.

The explorers who ventured into Earth's once-unknown regions have a lot to teach us about how to face the unknown. Like us today, the great explorers heard many different opinions of what to expect in the unknown regions they were entering: Pessimists warned of monsters and dragons; optimists imagined cities of gold and fountains of youth.

Though those explorers are not here to advise us personally, we have accounts of their expeditions, and from these we can deduce the lessons they would have offered for our journey into the unknown future.

The Lessons of the Great Explorers

Reading accounts of great expeditions, we notice that the explorers prepared very carefully for their journeys. Their success depended on having the right equipment, the right supplies, the right teammates, and the right training at the moment of need.

So the first lesson of the great explorers is: *Prepare for what you will face in the future.* Lack of preparation invites disaster. That may seem obvious, yet many people today see no point in preparing or even thinking about the future. "Let's not worry about the future until we get to it," they say. The great explorers would have no use for such a person: Only a reckless fool would imagine that problems will sit patiently waiting until we find it convenient to receive them. Quite to the contrary, problems may rush upon us at the worst possible moment, and our very survival can depend on how well we have prepared for them.

Good preparation can work for us today as we plan how to cope with what we have to face. The well-prepared student does well on examinations; the well-prepared job applicant gets hired. Most of us may think we have learned this lesson long ago, but we often seem to forget. The great explorers knew that forgetting *anything* in their preparations could be fatal.

A second lesson is implied by the first: *Anticipate future needs.* The great explorers took great pains to identify their likely future needs so they could know what to prepare for. They knew that if they failed to anticipate future needs the consequence might be fatal. So they tried to envision long before their expedition's departure all the different situations they might encounter. Today, as explorers of the future, we also need to anticipate what we may face so that we can be ready for it.

But how can we predict our future needs when we are going into the unknown? The great explorers faced the same dilemma, and they used their common sense to deal with it. They recognized that the "unknown" region was not *absolutely* unknown: Something was known about the area close to the unknown regions, and there were vague reports, rumors, educated guesses, and speculation about what lay in the blank areas of the map. The information might be very vague and untrustworthy, but the great explorers used it if they had nothing better.

Any map that might be relevant was treasured, however crude it might be. Meriwether Lewis, secretary to U.S. President Thomas Jefferson, prepared for the famed Lewis and Clark expedition (1804-06) by studying every available map of the Missouri River frontier; Lewis even interrogated one of the map makers to glean whatever bits of hearsay might not be reflected on the map. At the time, maps had almost no information about most of the territory that the expedition would be exploring, but whatever there was, Lewis got it. By the time the expedition set out, he knew all there was to know about the Missouri River and what lay to the west of it. This error-prone knowledge enabled Lewis to make excellent preparations for the journey, with the result that the Lewis and Clark expedition became one of the great triumphs of American history.

So the third lesson of the great explorers is this: *Use poor information when necessary.* Obviously, we want to use the best available, but when required to make decisions we must not disdain information just because it may not be adequately detailed or may contain errors. Sea captains during the Renaissance sailed around the world using maps that were not only crude but fanciful. The great explorers knew that when you are lost any sort of map may be a godsend.

Many people today think that we can know nothing about the future. They are 99.999++ percent right in the literal sense, but quite wrong in the practical sense: Almost everything we don't know about the future has little practical importance to us, whereas the little that we can know is extremely important, because it can help us make better decisions. Our business with the future is to improve it, not to predict it—at least not infallibly.

We explorers of the future must be practical and realistic. For our expedition to succeed, we must make the most of whatever knowledge we can acquire about what lies ahead. We can't afford to be ivory-tower perfectionists, insisting that information about the future be absolutely precise and accurate, laboratory tested, peer reviewed, and certified by a report approved by a blue-ribbon committee of geniuses. Imperfect knowledge can still provide highly useful guidance for our careers, our businesses, and our investments. It can even save our lives: Millions of people are alive and well today because they learned that they would likely suffer and die if they continued to smoke; armed with that knowledge, they forced themselves to stop smoking. Those foresighted individuals acted on the basis of imperfect evidence. Waiting for additional proof has already cost other millions of people their lives.

Using imperfect knowledge of the future can be essential if we are to act while events are still fluid—before they have hardened into realities that cannot be changed. As General Colin Powell once said, "If you can tell me with a hundred percent certainty that we are going to be bombed, it is too late for me to do anything about it."

Inventing the Future

Even the best-prepared explorers encounter problems that they are not prepared for or that are inevitable risks of their ventures. For the great explorers of the past, the weather was often the main risk. In 1914, the polar explorer Ernest Shackleton set out to cross the Antarctic continent, but his ship became trapped in ice and drifted for ten months before being crushed by the pack ice. At that point, the expedition was a total failure, and Shackleton was trapped in a seemingly hopeless situation. But with stunning resourcefulness, Shackleton managed to keep his men's hopes alive while he and five others sailed 800 miles to the island of South Georgia to get help. His success in saving every one of his men made him an "explorer's explorer," honored for successfully devising and executing an extraordinary Plan B when Plan A had failed.

So we have a fourth lesson from the great explorers: *Expect the unexpected.* An unexpected event is not necessarily bad; it may be a great opportunity. But in either case we want to be ready to deal with it effectively. Many young people today prepare for a career, but not for a career disaster or an unusual opportunity outside their expected career path. Out of the blue, they might be offered a job doing something very exciting in another country. Or they might unexpectedly lose a job and not have any idea what to do next.

In the early 2000s, almost all telecommunications and Internet corporations collapsed or downsized radically, so thousands of workers accustomed to high-paying jobs found themselves with no paycheck but big mortgages and children to feed. The newly unemployed desperately needed to replace their lost income, but they could no longer get jobs in their depressed industries. Many of these people had never anticipated being in such a predicament, and they had no idea what to do next.

In any such crisis, it helps to have resources—both tangible and intangible. Tangible resources include our physical possessions—clothing, automobile, etc.—plus any financial assets that can be used to acquire physical assets. Intangible assets include our experience, skills, and attitudes, as well as our networks of colleagues, friends, and relatives. In Shackleton's desperate ordeal, the bond between him and his men proved to be a priceless intangible asset. For us today, our reputation for trustworthy dealings with our creditors and associates can be an important intangible asset.

Other intangible resources that can help us deal with the unexpected include a good understanding of our changing world, intellectual tools for thinking ahead, and methods for assessing our options. These resources help us to cope with the unexpected because they enable us to think more knowledgeably and creatively about our options. If we work to develop these tools, we will have acquired useful skills for coping with unexpected challenges.

Gaining Power Over the Future

The fifth lesson of the great explorers is: *Think long term as well as short term.* For the great explorers, many years might pass between their first dream of leading an expedition and their return home. Columbus spent years traveling from city to city trying to get funding for his expedition across the Atlantic. During those years, he often had little to sustain him except his own vision of what could be accomplished. He faced one rejection after another before Queen Isabella finally provided the money.

Foresight empowers us for future achievements, and foresight that extends well into the future can be especially empowering because we can do so much if we work for years toward a distant goal. Over time, an acorn can grow into an oak, and an infant can grow into an adult human, but there is no way to do either overnight. On the other hand, near miracles can be accomplished if we have a long-term goal and keep working at it. And "long term" does not have to mean a thousand years from now. Extraordinary things can be achieved in a remarkably short time.

"Almost *anything* can be done in twenty years!" asserts Earl C. Joseph, a systems scientist and thinker. His statement may seem like a wild exaggeration, but consider this: From the moment that President Franklin Roosevelt gave the order to build the first atomic bombs, it took only four years to do it, even though it had never been done before and many experts *insisted* that the task was impossible. When President John F. Kennedy ordered NASA to put a man on the moon, it was done in only eight years. In each case, the U.S. government decided to do something extraordinary that had never been done before.

The goal was envisioned and judged feasible and desirable, strategies and plans were carefully developed, and the project was executed through intense effort. Both projects required careful studies of technological capabilities and the development of a clear vision of something important that might actually be achieved. After that, things were done that astounded the world.

You don't have to be a government to achieve a remarkable feat, but you do generally need to think and work on it for a substantial period of time. This requires envisioning a goal that you are willing to work for a long time to achieve. Alan Hald, a young Arizona banker, envisioned a new goal for himself in 1975 while attending a World Future Society conference. At the meeting, he encountered the editor of a new magazine for computer hobbyists. At the time, nobody but governments and big businesses could afford to build a computer, but that situation was about to change drastically, and Hald suddenly had a vision of the future of computers. He returned to Arizona in great excitement to talk to his partner about starting a business in computers. With that vision and lots of determination to realize it, their business (MicroAge) grew into America's largest microcomputer distributor, serving dealers around the world.

About the same time, Bill Gates and Paul Allen also developed a vision of the future of computers, which led them to business success. Within twenty years of developing their vision, they had become two of the richest men in the world.

Hald, Gates, and Allen thus joined Christopher Columbus, Meriwether Lewis, and Ernest Shackleton in demonstrating the power of having a long-term perspective on the future. If we are thinking long term rather than short term, we can be much more productive, and the eventual results of our efforts can be extraordinary.

Productive Dreaming

Thinking long term is easier if you have a dream to sustain you; in fact, it may be difficult not to slog through years of unrewarded labor and discouragement without a vision. And that brings us to the sixth lesson of the great explorers: *Dream productively.*

The great explorers were basically *doers*, not armchair adventurers fantasizing about great deeds. What counted with them was the actual achievement of their visions. Dreaming or fantasizing was a means to that end. The great explorers dreamed their ships across the seas long before sailing them. In their imaginations, they tested their mettle against snake-infested jungles, blazing-hot deserts, cruel mountains, and merciless ice floes. By exploring future possibilities in their imagination, they could anticipate their future needs realistically and prepare for what lay ahead of them. This was *productive* dreaming—one type of futuring.

For the great explorers, dreaming was not idle reverie but research—a mental exploration of what lay ahead. By fantasizing about future events, they could explore alternative goals and strategies and thus develop and select *worthwhile and achievable goals, as well as imaginative but realistic strategies for reaching* the goals they selected.

In productive dreaming, ends and means tend to be considered together: If you want to achieve something, you need a valid strategy for getting it. Likewise, if you cannot devise a reasonable strategy for getting to a certain goal, you probably should consider a different goal. Why choose to fail?

The trick of dreaming is not to get lost in idle reverie but to think creatively about the future and what we can do to accomplish worthwhile goals. Once we have a valid and compelling vision of what we want to achieve and how it can be done, we can focus on converting the dream into reality.

Setting Out on Our Expedition

The seventh and last lesson of the great explorers is: *Learn from your predecessors.* The great explorers always wanted to learn about previous expeditions in order to know how to mount their own and avoid the errors made by others. We can never succeed if we have to make every mistake for ourselves. For that reason, this book about the future puts heavy emphasis on what we can learn from the past.

Now, here they are, the seven lessons of the great explorers:

- Prepare for what you will face in the future.
- Anticipate future needs.
- Use poor information when necessary.
- Expect the unexpected.
- Think long term as well as short term.
- Dream productively.
- Learn from your predecessors.

Why are these lessons so imperative at just this moment in history? Because, as we will discover in the next chapter, we are poised on the edge of the greatest transformation that humanity has yet had to face.

2

The Great Transformation

The most important thing happening today is not reported in newspaper headlines or television broadcasts, yet it is far more important than most of what is reported. This mega-event is the global transformation of human life, and it affects everybody everywhere. The news media ignore it because they cannot take a picture of it or explain it in a sound bite. Scholars also rarely discuss it because such a colossal and complex event does not fit any of the narrow specialties within which professors work.

But we can sense that something extraordinary is happening to us if we begin to take stock of the unprecedented changes that have been occurring in human life and of the speed with which changes are coming. Thinkers who ponder the meaning of global events often speak of some kind of big social process being at work—a revolution or a wave of change or the emergence of something new—but what is really going on remains a mystery. Where are all these changes leading? What do they mean?

Authors of ponderous books dealing with big issues have struggled to find ways to describe what's happening and what it means, but the complexity of it all seems to defeat them. Michael Marien, who surveys books and articles dealing with human society and its future, believes that we can best think of our times as "the Era of Multiple Transformations." True enough, we can see that our technology, economy, and social institutions are all undergoing enormous change. Yet it is hard to avoid noticing that the changes are intricately interconnected: Technological changes are linked to economic changes, which are linked to environmental changes, etc. With so much inter-linking of the changes, we must be dealing with a super transformation that incorporates all the others.

Let's call this phenomenon—whatever it really is—the Great Transformation. We can describe it as the current metamorphosis of human life as we now know it, and we can add that it affects not only humans everywhere but also the natural world around us. It is central to our mission as explorers of the future, because the Great Transformation is the process whereby our future is being created.

Our Experience of Change

We begin to sense the existence of the Great Transformation as we notice the rapid changes in our lives: new technologies, new buildings, new lifestyles. It is not simply that human life is changing, but that it is changing extremely fast.

We can confirm the speed of this shift by comparing our world today with the world as it was in the recent past—say on August 6, 1945, the day an atomic bomb was exploded over the Japanese city of Hiroshima. Before they heard about the atomic bomb, people assumed that the world would return to "normal" as soon as the war was over; after the atomic bombing, they knew that things would never again be the same.

The premonition of drastic change has been validated by subsequent events, though not in the way people most feared. Rather than waging more atomic wars, the world focused on economic development. The production of goods and services has soared to levels that people back then would have viewed as impossible, if not unimaginable. During the same period, the world's population has more than doubled, giving our planet today billions more people than it ever had before the twentieth century. Meanwhile, more than 100 new nations have appeared, so that the world now has about four times as many independent countries as it had in 1945.

More or less unconsciously, we have adopted new values and lifestyles. Things viewed as right in 1945 are now seen as wrong, and vice versa. Divorce, scandalous back then, is now quietly accepted, but segregation of the races, acceptable in 1945, has become scandalous. And, of course, advances in technology have brought innumerable new tools to ease our daily lives. In 1945, horse carts were still delivering milk and ice to homes in New York City, and nobody had an air-conditioned home, a computer, or even a television. If you had electricity and a flush toilet, you were lucky: Beyond the great cities, kerosene lamps were in general use, along with privies and chamber pots. You could also be thankful if you had a telephone; only a minority of Americans did, and they would almost never call long distance, because it was so expensive. If somebody died, a message would be sent by telegraph. Automobiles were scarce, and there were no superhighways to drive them on; you were fortunate if you lived near any sort of paved road.

The world is different now. Since 1945, we have reshaped the planet to fit the desires of the automobile driver. Engineers have paved highways through jungles and across tundra. Tunnels now connect France with England and Sweden with Denmark, and there is talk of building a bridge-tunnel to link Europe with Africa at the Strait of Gibraltar.

As population swells and economies expand, these forces, too, have changed the world. Forests and meadows have disappeared under office buildings, shops, factories, and parking lots, and we have been gobbling up the earth's resources. To get water, we have drained lakes and rivers; to get coal, we have leveled mountains; to get iron and copper, we have dug up the landscape, creating huge, moonlike craters. This physical transformation of our world is a visible expression of transformations occurring in all aspects of human life.

Many of these changes have altered our own nature. With our cell phones, we can chat with people across the world instead of our neighbors next door; our internal horizons are broader as a result. Whereas our grandparents lived psychologically on farms and spoke the language of horse travel, we now think in video and speak computerese. Perhaps most important of all, we are transforming ourselves as we use surgery, drugs, and whatever else we can find to become thinner, taller, stronger, better looking, smarter, and sexier.

Hyperchange

The speed of change after World War II caught the attention of Max Ways, editor of *Fortune* magazine. In 1959, Ways estimated that the pace of change had become "perhaps fifty times as great as the average pace of previous centuries." Ways picked up the theme again in a 1964 article, "The Era of Radical Change," in which he identified four categories of social change: gradual change, revolution and major disruption, rapid change, and radical change. Ways argued that the period from 1800 to 1950 was one of *rapid* change, but about 1950 an era of radical change had begun. However, he was writing in the 1950s and early 1960s—an era that we today regard as a period of stability and tranquility! It was not until the *late* 1960s, when the baby boomers reached youthful maturity, that everything seemed to break loose, and change really accelerated.

In today's hyperchange society, individuals have little stability in their lives: Jobs are increasingly temporary, and so are marriages. People who remain for years in the same residence discover that the neighborhood has changed and their friends have moved elsewhere. Change brings new demands, conflicts, and stress as people cope with new jobs, new residences, new spouses and children, and new colleagues.

Furthermore, there seems to be a general consensus today that change will continue to accelerate in the years ahead, and the anticipations of some observers are mind-boggling. The noted inventor Ray Kurzweil says:

> The whole twentieth century was actually not one hundred years of progress at today's rate of progress. It was twenty years of progress at today's rate of progress. And we'll make another twenty years of progress at today's rate of progress, equivalent to the whole twentieth century, which was no slouch for change, in another fourteen years. And then we'll do it again in seven years. That pace will continue to accelerate, and because of the explosive nature of exponential growth, the twenty-first century will be equivalent to twenty thousand years of progress at today's rate of progress; about one thousand times greater than the twentieth century.

The acceleration of change has inspired a lively debate about the possibility of a technological "singularity" occurring at some time in the twenty-first century. The technological singularity would be such a massive amount of change we cannot even begin to predict its consequences.

Opinions differ on just what this event would be, but the idea is that at a certain point in the future—perhaps even in the decades just ahead—technological progress will become so rapid that really weird things happen. Technology will have escaped human ability to control it or to forecast it, so it's anybody's guess what might happen. Kurzweil says that the singularity could "rupture the very fabric of human history."

Other observers generally agree that change will be extremely rapid but are doubtful that it will reach the extraordinary speed anticipated by Kurzweil and others. Theodore Modis, a scientist and strategic analyst, says that complexity and change have grown at accelerating rates throughout history, and he agrees that they may soon reach a turning point. Unlike most other scholars, Modis is a specialist in the study of growth and cycles in widely different contexts, and what he predicts is the opposite of a singularity. The rule, he says, is that growth—wherever it occurs—eventually slows. On the other hand, it can be very difficult to know when the slowing will occur.

Where does this leave us? It seems that we must anticipate an extremely high rate of change in the years ahead. However, we should also recognize that there are braking forces on technological progress. One of the most effective is people's refusal to pay for it: For instance, people dashed the hopes of many Internet entrepreneurs by just not buying the services they offered. Governments also often restrict or forbid new technologies, such as pharmaceuticals and genetically modified foods.

Exploring the Transformation

Now let's explore the causes of this increasingly rapid change, using the concept of culture. Anthropologists define culture as the socially transmitted knowledge and practices of a group of people, and it is all-important in human life. We learn our cultures as we grow up, from our families, playmates, and teachers. And, almost immediately, we begin to pass on what we have learned to others.

Putting the Great Transformation in the context of our cultural evolution is useful for understanding what is happening now. Over thousands and thousands of years, the culturally transmitted knowledge possessed by humans has accumulated and been refined. New and improved ways were found to do things and old ways discarded. The result was an increasing ability to achieve human purposes.

As humans, we are so completely immersed in our culture that we hardly notice it; yet it is the great tool we use in dealing with the world. It is what has separated us from other animals. A few other animals such as our close relatives, the chimpanzees, develop very primitive cultures, but according to anthropologist C. Loring Brace man is the only animal that is completely dependent on culture for survival. Through the eons of human evolution, culture evolved in tandem with anatomy as our ancestors responded to new challenges and made new discoveries.

As genetic changes occurred, cultural evolution became less and less limited by human anatomy: Our brains enlarged; hands became more adapted to using tools, and legs became adapted to walking long distances over the African territories that humans inhabited. By about 200,000 years ago, humans were essentially the same *genetically* as they are today.

But their *cultures* were still incredibly primitive. All of our ancestors then lacked almost everything that we today take for granted as a necessity for ordinary life, and their ignorance concerning everything beyond the little African territory that they inhabited was nearly total. Everybody everywhere was illiterate, since writing had not yet been invented; to make matters worse, people spoke languages that were unintelligible except within their small bands.

So, despite having bodies and brains like ours today, our distant ancestors probably lived in a manner closer to that of their chimpanzee neighbors than to the way we do now. Nonetheless, our ancestors slowly enlarged and improved their cultures until their descendants—ourselves—were able to enjoy the benefits of complex and secure civilizations.

At the beginning, the path of cultural development was extremely difficult and slow. Humans in the Old Stone Age (or Paleolithic period) spent hundreds of thousands of years to progress beyond the hand axe—simply a stone with a sharpened edge—to the wide variety of stone awls and scrapers that characterize New Stone Age cultures. With the New Stone Age (Neolithic period), progress speeded up, with each advance enabling further advances. Yet humans were still in the Stone Age when many moved out of Africa into Asia, Europe, and the Americas. As they migrated, they encountered new environments that enabled them to make more discoveries such as grain cultivation in the Mideast.

From an overall perspective, cultural progress has accelerated to our own times. Now seemingly it is reaching warp speed. We can think of this as a kind of compound interest for the tens of thousands of years our ancestors invested in the cultures we have inherited from them.

Three Technological Revolutions

Technological progress is perhaps the most useful avenue for us to travel in analyzing the Great Transformation. Other factors, such as environmental changes, can be important, but the main driving force in recent cultural evolution seems to have been the accumulation of technological knowledge. Technology, in this context, does not just mean machines or material objects but knowing how to achieve practical purposes. Here, we will focus on material technologies because they are easier to observe and analyze than social or intellectual "technologies" (laws, institutions, theories, etc.).

To understand how technology progresses and changes society, it is useful to employ technological revolutions as models for what happens. These great events are not only important and much studied, but their impacts are clearer. So let's focus now on three great technological revolutions, each of which began with a key discovery that acted as a catalyst for massive technological, economic, and social change: the Agricultural Revolution, the Industrial Revolution, and the recent Cybernetic Revolution.

Historians have long recognized the importance of the Agricultural and the Industrial Revolutions. We are now postulating that the revolution stimulated by the computer is worthy of being compared with the two earlier revolutions. Later, we will consider the possibility that a fourth revolution—the Biotech Revolution—may already have started, though we cannot yet feel sure.

The Agricultural Revolution began with the early cultivation of grains, notably the ancestors of wheat, in the Middle East about 11,000 years ago. Grain cultivation greatly boosted the amount of food that could be produced in a given territory. (A natural environment produces relatively little food suited to humans.)

As grain cultivation was perfected, farmers displaced hunters and gatherers, and population soared. Rising population encouraged the development of towns and cities, which provided markets for goods and services of all kinds. Specialized occupations and trading developed, which led to the development of accounting, mathematics, and writing. Human culture flowered with such wonders as the pyramids of Egypt, the Bible, the Homeric epics, Confucius, Aristotle, the Roman Empire, and, eventually, the Renaissance.

The Industrial Revolution, the second great technological revolution, began in the 1700s when steam-powered engines began to replace horses in pumping water out of British coal mines. A single one of Thomas Newcomen's steam engines could do the work of fifty horses. But the early steam engines were very inefficient, and it required a generation before they were good enough to be applied in factory production and transportation.

Three Technological Revolutions

	Agricultural	Industrial	Cybernetic
Origin	Near East, 11,000 years ago	Britain, 1750	United States, 1944
Catalytic Technology	Grain cultivation (wheat)	Steam engine	Computer
Benefits	More food per unit of land; grain storable and tradable	Inexpensive, dependable source of power	Fast, cheap decision making for problems soluble by algorithms
Uses	Feeding people, safeguarding food supply, trading goods (functions like money)	Mechanized pumps, machine powered vehicles, power machinery in factories	Mathematical calculations, processing records, word processing, database management, telephone exchanges, etc.
Effects	Population increase, early cities, roads, shipping, accounting, metal-working, wheeled vehicles, writing, scholarship, science	Factory towns, urbanization, railroads, automobiles, rising living standards, airplanes, surging demand for natural resources—metal ores, coal, petroleum	Faster, cheaper information handling; better management of communications; tighter inventory controls; better distribution of goods; higher standard of living
Workers Displaced	Hunters, gatherers	Farmers, weavers, craftsmen, home workers	Clerks, typists, telephone operators, typesetters, small grocers, middle managers
New Jobs	Early: Farmers, construction workers, carters, brewers, specialized crafts. Later: scribes, scholars	Miners, factory workers, ironworkers, steamship builders, railroaders, steel workers	Computer operators, programmers, repairers, systems analysts, Webmasters, electronic game designers

Railroad trains powered by steam engines became the great marvel of the early nineteenth century. Steam power also could be used to generate electricity with great efficiency, thus providing factories, homes, and cities an inexpensive and highly convenient new source of power. Inexpensive electric power led, in the 1880s and 1890s, to an extraordinary wave of innovation, pioneered by inventors like Thomas A. Edison, who used electricity to power his new inventions—electric light bulbs, phonographs, motion pictures, and more.

The Industrial Revolution spread gradually around the world, causing innumerable changes in the societies affected. However, many areas remain relatively untouched even today, and a few have yet to experience the Agricultural Revolution.

The Cybernetic Revolution

The computer's influence on today's society has been so broad and powerful that this new technology can reasonably be compared with grain cultivation and the steam engine as the catalyst of a new technological revolution.

This third revolution originated with Harvard professor Howard Aiken's conception, in 1937, of a large-scale automatic digital calculator that could perform very quickly an enormous number of mathematical calculations. At the time, nobody was ready to fund the development of this machine, but after World War II broke out the U.S. military wanted such a device for ballistic calculations. Aiken got the money he needed. (This was perhaps the first of a number of key assists that the U.S. government would give to the development of computers.) IBM built this computer according to Aiken's specifications in a laboratory in Cambridge, Massachusetts, and it was ready for duty in 1944. The first computer had more than 750,000 parts and filled a room, but it could do arithmetic at the rate of three additions per second, far faster than a human being. Speed was its key virtue in wartime America.

The basic advantage of the computer was that it could do what humans had always had to do in the past: It could make decisions, and it could make them faster and cheaper than could humans. Once a computer had been given a suitable set of algorithms—precise instructions on how to make a series of decisions—the computer could accomplish in seconds a task that might occupy humans for days.

Computers got more support from the U.S. government after World War II, because U.S. military leaders knew that the Soviets were hard at work developing both atomic bombs and rockets. Alarmed, Congress appropriated almost any amount of money the military claimed it needed for defense, and much of the money went into the development of computers as well as other areas of science and technology.

Electronics in general became a top Defense Department priority because military leaders had been deeply impressed with the effectiveness of communications and detection systems in winning wars: Without radar the British would likely have lost the battle against German aircraft, and without sonar most of the ships carrying essential supplies to Britain would have been sunk. After sonar appeared, German Admiral Karl Doenitz, who commanded his nation's submarines, lamented: "The enemy has rendered the U-boat ineffective.... He has achieved this objective, not through superior tactics or strategy, but through his superiority in the field of science; this finds its expression in the modern battle weapon: detection. By this means, he has torn from our hands our sole offensive weapon in the war against the Anglo-Saxons."

The drive to maintain military superiority over the Soviets stimulated a broad demand for innovative technologies, and since new technologies depend critically on scientific advances the arms race morphed into a knowledge race. In 1950, Congress passed legislation creating the National Science Foundation, a special government agency, to spend taxpayers' money for basic scientific research. Since scientists were eager to use computers, NSF money also nourished computer development.

The 1950s and 1960s were a halcyon period for science and technology. Almost any U.S. physical scientist with a reasonable research proposal could get funding for it. Never in history had scientists had it so good, and they responded with a wealth of new discoveries that had significant applications to technology. Computers became a hot area for both business and government. Companies could see enormous possibilities for using computers not only to process records but also to take on numerous other tasks.

The computer initiated a major transformation in the production, financing, marketing, and distribution of goods and services in the U.S. economy. With the advent of microcomputers in the 1970s, the economic transformation intensified, since individuals and very small businesses were able to have computers. In the 1980s, as personal computers proliferated, the Internet developed into a convenient vehicle for ordinary people to communicate instantaneously with each other.

By the beginning of the twenty-first century, cell phones were being linked into the global network of interconnected computers and telecommunications systems, which communications scholar Joseph Pelton describes as "the world's largest machine." If people opt to have Internet links implanted in their bodies, which seems likely in the future, a new type of being will emerge—a huge cyberorganism with a body that is part protoplasm, part electronics or photonics, and part cyberspace.

Future Revolutions

Technology seems nearly certain to advance even faster during the twenty-first century than it did during the twentieth. Business firms are investing far more now in technology than they were at the start of the last century, and new technologies such as computers are dramatically boosting the productivity of scientists and technologists. The computer has increased the effective intelligence of humans just as the steam engine increased their physical power, and the future amplification of human intellectual power promises to be mind-boggling. Computers may surpass humans in intelligence very soon: Already, they are able to beat the best human players at chess.

As a result of the computer's enormous boost to science and technology, a fourth technological revolution may already have started in biotechnology, notably in genetics. We cannot be sure of this, because it will take more time for biotechnology to restructure the economy in a manner that can be compared to the steam engine and the computer.

Biotechnology promises revolutionary changes that could be even more extraordinary than those wrought by the computer. Genetic engineering has already started to redesign plants and animals so they can be more productive and satisfactory to human purposes, and there are numerous applications in industrial production. However, the most important applications are likely to lie in biotechnology's potential for enhancing the physical, mental, and emotional capabilities of humans themselves.

Genetic knowledge is already being used to reduce defects in newborn babies, but that is only a start in the improvement of our bodies and brains. In the years ahead, parents will use whatever new technologies become available to try to make sure that theirs is no ordinary son or daughter, but one that is superior in one or more ways. They may try to give their children the musical capabilities of a Mozart or the mental abilities of an Einstein. Of course, other parents will be doing the same for their children. We can only speculate on what might happen if the world has millions upon millions of babies designed according to their parents' wishes. We might hope for millions of Einsteins, but get millions of Elvis Presleys.

Human capabilities could also be enhanced if biotechnologists find a way to reduce our fatigue and sleepiness. At present we have to sleep about seven or eight hours a day and take occasional rests during waking hours. Being forced into oblivious idleness fifty-six hours every week represents an extraordinary loss of time. Imagine what we might accomplish with an extra eight hours every day to do our work, care for our families, and have fun! A really effective cure for fatigue might trigger another techno-economic revolution all by itself.

Another potential benefit of biotech would be a cure for aging. The aging process (senescence) progressively robs us of much of the vigor and capacity that we enjoyed in our youth. If we could retain the full youthful vigor of our brains and bodies for an extra thirty years, we might be able to accomplish twice as much in a lifetime as we do today and enjoy life more fully. A cure for aging also suggests the possibility of quasi-immortality: Death might not come for many centuries. If certain trees, such as the bristlecone pine of the American West, can live for several thousand years, why can't we learn their secret and find a way to apply it for our own benefit?

By the year 2100, teachers may be telling their students: "Before the Biotech Revolution people suffered terribly from enormous disabilities, and most died prematurely. Now, thanks to genetics and other biotechnologies, we are all able to be healthy, strong, and intelligent, and we can look forward to many centuries of life." On the other hand, we must assume that biotech advances pose many risks and that there will be difficult choices for both individuals and society.

But Where Are We Going?

Our investigation of the Great Transformation suggests that it can be seen as the latest stage of humanity's cultural evolution. This evolution has speeded up enormously in recent centuries due to rapid technological progress, which leads to massive change in the economy, government, and institutions of society. So we now have a partial explanation for the Great Transformation that we are experiencing. Though we do not know what we are being transformed into, this metamorphosis seems to be proceeding faster than ever. In the next chapter, we will examine some of the most important trends of this Great Transformation and attempt to anticipate what might happen in the next few years.

3

Six Supertrends Shaping the Future

To understand the Great Transformation, we must simplify it. Otherwise, we become lost in the sheer complexity of the phenomenon.

Simplification means that we must decide which are the very most important trends—or currents of change—in the Great Transformation, and then focus our attention on them, at least until we get a little better understanding of what's happening.

In the last chapter, we identified technological progress as the main engine driving the rapid cultural evolution that we are now experiencing. In past times, environmental changes or something else may have played a more important role in driving cultural evolution, but today, technological progress seems to be the primary force for change. *Technological progress* is the first supertrend we will consider. It encompasses many lesser trends, such as incremental improvements in computers, materials, biotechnology, nanotechnology, and hundreds of other technological specialties.

But technological progress is more than a supertrend; it is also a *superforce*, in that it creates massive change, including other supertrends, which are powerful instruments of change in their own right. The most obvious supertrend produced by technological progress is *economic growth*. Better technologies make it possible to produce cheaper and better goods and services. Since people want these goods and services and are willing to devote their time and energy to getting them, technological progress becomes an engine for economic progress, which has been so massive over the past two centuries that it qualifies as a second supertrend.

In combination, these two supertrends—technological progress and economic growth—have driven an astounding amount of change in human society. Today, techno-economic growth is producing change even faster than in the past, and the resulting changes come in many different forms. However, four shifts wrought by techno-economic growth merit special attention because they exert such a powerful influence that we can think of them, too, as both supertrends and superforces. They are trends because they are currents of change and forces because they cause so many other changes.

These four supertrends are: *improving human health, increasing mobility, environmental decline,* and *increasing deculturation.* In identifying these shifts as critically important, we are viewing the world from a global, long-term perspective. At various places in various times, these global supertrends may actually reverse their course, and today they may be operating faster or slower depending on the region one considers. For example, health has declined in recent years in both Africa and Eastern Europe, though on a global basis it continues to improve.

We now have a total of six supertrends to use as tools for understanding the Great Transformation. Each qualifies as a supertrend because it summarizes a key category of change and acts as a key force in human life today. Improving health, for example, has led to rapid population growth and an increasing number of elderly in the population, and both of these changes are having enormous consequences.

Each of these supertrends can be analyzed by their component trends when desired, but our purpose here is to get a macroscopic or "big picture" view of the Great Transformation now shaping our future.

Now let's take a look at each of the six supertrends. Then, we will use them as tools for developing a rough picture of what the world may be like in the year 2040.

The Six Supertrends

Supertrend One: Technological Progress

Technological progress includes all the improvements being made in computers, medicine, transportation, and other technologies, as well as all the other useful knowledge that enables humans to achieve their purposes more effectively. We can think of technological progress as the growing capability of humans to achieve their purposes.

Technological progress has been the supremely important trend in human evolution for millions of years: When it weakened or even reversed in one area, it flourished elsewhere, such as in China during Europe's Dark Ages. The power, persistence, and current acceleration of this trend suggests that it will continue through the twenty-first century and perhaps much longer. We can speculate that technological progress *might* come to a halt in the years ahead, but, if that were to happen, the most likely explanation would probably be that some massive calamity had occurred. Scientific research continues to provide massive amounts of new knowledge that technologists can exploit. The Cybernetic Revolution is still racing ahead. Biotechnology promises a fourth technological revolution, and there could be a fifth through nanotechnology or some other area of technology. So there seems more reason to think of progress racing ahead even faster than to anticipate that it will slow down soon.

Supertrend Two: Economic Growth

Technological progress promotes *economic growth*—our second supertrend—because people are eager to use their know-how to produce goods and services, both for their own use and to sell to others.

Economic growth is also a self-sustaining process. The accumulation of capital goods (factories, highways, office buildings, railroads, bridges, etc.) as well as consumer goods and social capital (institutions, knowledge, etc.) means that each new generation starts with more capital goods and wealth, making it ever easier to produce still more.

World economic growth has been prodigious since the Industrial Revolution, according to economist Angus Maddison. In his book *Monitoring the World Economy, 1820-1992,* Maddison reports that world GDP skyrocketed from a mere $695 billion in the early nineteenth century to nearly $28 trillion in 1992. Growth continues in the twenty-first century, though the *rate* of growth is often viewed as unsatisfactory because it remains inadequate for the world's needs, let alone its greeds.

Maddison reports that world GDP, measured in 1990 U.S. dollars, rose from $565 per person in 1500 to $651 per person in 1820—an increase in wealth per person of only 27¢ per year. By contrast, output per person increased $26 per year from 1820 to 1994—ninety-six times as much per year as in the earlier period.

If this trend continues, the *average* person in the developed countries may be wealthy (by the standards of today) by about the middle of the twenty-first century. The problem will be that everyone will still know people who are wealthier than they are.

Supertrend Three: Improving Health

Technological progress and economic growth have led to improving human health because they have produced more food, more effective sanitation, better health services, and so on.

Improving health leads to increasing longevity, which has two very important consequences: population growth and a rise in the average age of the population.

Population soared in the 1820-1992 period from just over 1 billion to nearly 5.5 billion, Maddison notes. Today, population is over 6 billion and still climbing. Population is growing because more people are living long enough to produce children, yet birthrates have not declined enough to forestall a rise in the population. In the past, periodic famines, violence, diseases, and other factors controlled population growth. Now, population swells, largely in poor countries, adding to their poverty.

Increasing longevity also means that the average age of populations is rising. In America, centenarians are the fastest-growing age group. In France, a woman named Jeanne Calment reached the age of 122 before dying in 1997. She was the oldest person known to history.

The rapid growth of the elderly in the population is now raising numerous issues for society, partly because they tend to be retired and dependent on government assistance programs, thus imposing heavy costs on younger people, who are required to pay for their support. To make matters worse, Social Security and pension plans were devised when relatively few people reached the age of sixty-five; but now more and more people reach sixty-five and then live on and on. And more and more people retire at sixty-five in the industrialized countries. The countertrend is that many take on new "post-retirement" work, either contributing as volunteers or earning money. More baby boomers could mean more retirees, but not necessarily the total dependency that's been predicted.

Supertrend Four: Increasing Mobility

Technological progress, economic growth, and population increase combine to cause a fourth supertrend: *increasing mobility*.

Increasing mobility gets less attention from scholars than the first three supertrends, but its importance should not be underrated. People, goods, and information move from place to place faster and in greater quantity than ever before. Jet aircraft and superhighways move goods and people at speeds that would have seemed incredible in the past. Containerization, super-tankers, and mechanized port facilities now convey petroleum, automobiles, and other goods around the world at relatively low cost. When speed is important, goods increasingly travel by air. Now transportation experts are considering the use of pilotless aircraft, or drones, for commercial purposes; the U.S. military whetted interest in drones by using them to fight terrorists in the Middle East.

Meanwhile, people are increasingly traveling for pleasure and education, and some futurists believe that the tourist industry may become the world's biggest industry during the twenty-first century—if terrorism and other violence are controlled.

Increasing mobility seems to be the principal cause of globalization—the increasing worldwide integration of human activities. Regional, national, and transnational organizations and networks are linking governments, business firms, and individuals. Meanwhile, local institutions are often declining, due to competitors that offer goods and services unavailable locally at acceptable cost. A single Wal-Mart can make scores of local businesses uncompetitive economically unless they can change their product line.

Despite its advantages, mobility also creates many problems. Terrorists and criminals can more easily move around the world, eluding capture. Diseases now move around the world on jet aircraft; in 2003, air passengers swiftly spread the SARS (Severe Acute Respiratory Syndrome) virus from China to countries around the world.

Mobility can also cause social and cultural disruption. When people move from one city or country to another, they sever or weaken their ties to their families and communities. A wife, a husband, children may be left behind, sometimes permanently. Mobility encourages a short-term perspective: People may see little point in improving their local community if they expect to move elsewhere. Mobility also weakens social institutions: Churches lose their parishioners; service groups like the Scouts cannot find volunteers; local merchants that depend on long-time customers may have to close their doors.

Supertrend Five: Environmental Decline

Environmental decline is continuing for the world as a whole because of continuing high population growth and economic development. Certain nations have made major efforts to reduce pollution and other environmental abuse, and these efforts have often been remarkably successful: Pittsburgh is no longer enveloped in factory smoke, and the fish have returned to the River Thames. Nonetheless, Mother Earth remains sick and is still getting sicker.

Among the trends making up this much-lamented supertrend are:

- Petroleum, a nonrenewable natural resource, is being rapidly burned up. Just how long the supplies will last is much debated, but serious problems may arise as petroleum stocks dwindle.
- Freshwater supplies are declining everywhere around the world, with lakes drying up and water tables falling, causing wells to run dry.
- The supply of arable land available for farming is also dropping steadily even as population increases. Farmers desperate for land are laying waste to large swathes of the rain forests of Brazil and Africa. Overgrazed scrubland is turning into desert.
- The oceans are already overfished. Fishing in many areas has had to be outlawed to allow fisheries to recover.
- Numerous species of animals and plants are becoming extinct even before they can be identified, studied, and evaluated for potential medical benefits.
- Global warming is melting the polar ice caps, causing the oceans to rise and threatening coastal areas around the world.

Supertrend Six: Increasing Deculturation (Loss of Traditional Culture)

Deculturation occurs when people lose their culture or cannot use it because of changed circumstances. Due to high mobility, rapid change, economic growth, and other factors, *increasing deculturation* on a global scale qualifies as a sixth supertrend.

We experience deculturation when we go to a country where people speak a language we do not understand or do things differently from what we are used to. In this situation, we have suddenly lost the ability to use key elements of our culture—our native language or ingrained habits and expectations—to get things we need. So we are likely to get a feeling of helplessness, and, in fact, we may actually be rather helpless unless we have someone to translate for us. This phenomenon is often called "culture shock."

Many people today experience culture shock without ever moving to a foreign country; instead, a new culture takes over much of their homeland, with the result that the original inhabitants become surrounded by people who do not share their culture. Their native language no longer works so well for them, because the newcomers do not understand it. In some cases, the newcomers may even force the natives to learn a new language. Today, the world is estimated to have 6,000 languages, but the number is expected to dwindle to about 3,000 by the end of the twenty-first century due to high mobility, globalization of economic activities, and other factors.

Urbanization also contributes to deculturation. It is happening on a massive scale in the developing nations, largely because people in rural areas cannot make a living. By moving to cities, people leave behind the social and cultural support systems of their native communities, and they must function in an alien environment where people do not speak or act as they did back home. In such a situation, the newcomers often turn to crime, making cities increasingly dangerous.

Travel writer Paul Theroux has described the cancerlike growth of African cities, many of which have become "miserably improvised anthills, attracting the poor and desperate from the bush and turning them into thieves and devisers of cruel scams." He explains that "scamming is the survival mode in a city where tribal niceties do not apply and there are no sanctions except for those of the police." Many cities around the world, including those in the developed nations, have similar problems.

Another form of deculturation occurs when your native culture changes rapidly, so that your accustomed ways of speaking, behaving, and doing things no longer fit with your environment. Alvin Toffler described this phenomenon as "future shock" and made it the title of a 1970 book that sold millions of copies to people who recognized that they were experiencing this phenomenon because of the rapid changes in the world around them.

Will the Supertrends Reverse?

We have been thinking of supertrends as ongoing currents of change that flow in the same direction and cause massive changes in many aspects of our lives. However, we must recognize that a trend—even a supertrend—is likely to change course or speed, and often unexpectedly. We can imagine circumstances that would cause technological progress, for example, to slow drastically or even reverse, so that it becomes technological regress. An all-out nuclear war might have such a result and cause widespread technological decline; some scholars have foreseen increasing environmental problems that could disrupt technological progress.

At least two of the supertrends—environmental decline and deculturation—are probably regarded by most people as problems. However, for the purpose of understanding the Great Transformation and where it is taking us, it is good to first defer thinking in terms of problems and how to solve them. Instead, we need to keep sharply focused on trying to understand what is happening and where it is likely to lead us in the future.

The World in 2040: What It *Might* Be Like

By projecting our supertrends forward in time, we can create a new *scenario* or picture of what the world *might* be like at a specific point in the future, say, the year 2040. This scenario assumes that the supertrends will continue much as they are now and that there will be no big surprises to invalidate our expectations. It can be described as a "continuation scenario."

We must definitely not think of our scenario as a forecast, but rather as simply one way to think about what may happen in the future. In fact, we ourselves might want to make every effort to prevent certain aspects of our scenario from ever coming to pass. The special virtue of scenarios is that they can get us psychologically into the future, so we can begin to think more realistically and freely about what life might be like for us in 2040 and what we might do to make it better.

We can begin our scenario by assuming that, by 2040, the world's stock of scientific and technological knowledge will be far larger than today. There are already millions of scientists, technologists, and scholars working on innovative ideas, and there are likely to be more in the years ahead. Furthermore, they will have increasing assistance from computers, telecommunications, and networks. We *might* guess that we will have twice as much knowledge in 2040 as in 2000, but making a precise estimate would depend heavily on alternative assumptions about how we measure such knowledge: What value might we place on Charles Darwin's theory of evolution or Nicolaus Copernicus's idea that the earth revolved around the sun instead of vice versa?

Most of today's familiar technologies will have made enormous advances, and progress will be most impressive in newer fields, such as genetic engineering and nanotechnology. Genetic engineering will have established its usefulness, and the world will be enjoying much better health as a result. In 2040, plants will grow bigger, mature quicker, need less fertilizer, and resist insects and diseases. Consumers will be able to buy better food at very low cost—if they are willing to settle for quality no better than that found at the beginning of the century. Public fears about genetic foods will be forgotten, as normally happens when a new technology has had a chance to show that it isn't really as dangerous as people first feared.

New materials will have made possible innumerable new products that are greatly superior to those back in 2000. The products will meet customers' wishes for goods that are longer lasting, lighter, stronger, sharper, or cheaper. New materials will give architects the ability to design amazing structures that would have been impossible a generation earlier.

Computers, cellular telephones, and the World Wide Web will have enabled people around the world to collaborate more closely and efficiently than ever before. This long-distance cooperation will allow expertise to flow easily and cheaply to places where it is needed: Surgeons will routinely operate on patients thousands of miles away. Faster computers, better portable telephones, more sophisticated networks, and other electronic advances will be able to boost human productivity, both on and off the job, but many people will prefer to use them for entertainment rather than work.

Higher Living Standards

Humans will be better off economically 2040 than they have ever been in history. Wealth will have increased due to rapidly improving technology and increased efficiencies achieved through the globalization of production and distribution, and other factors.

The Problems of Progress

In general, what we call "progress" can lead to abuse of the natural environment, the burden of learning new jobs, and general disorientation due to change itself. Examples of other negative consequences of "progress":

Better machines ⟶	Displaced workers, loss of status
Growing wealth ⟶	Increase in rich/poor disparity, fewer workers for less-desired tasks
New products ⟶	Difficulty of making choices
More, better food ⟶	Obesity, clogged arteries
Better health care ⟶	Rising costs, higher expectations
Longer lives ⟶	Cost of supporting idle elderly, increase in disability, stress on natural resources
Saving newborn ⟶	More birth defects
Better transport ⟶	Decline of local communities
More TV programs ⟶	Inactivity, desocialization
Increasing comfort ⟶	Boredom, apathy
Portable telephones ⟶	Forced exposure to noxious chatter
Easy bill paying ⟶	Credit-card fraud, identity theft
Quick information ⟶	Internet hoaxes, scams, viruses
Cheap, easy messaging ⟶	Junk e-mail, insensitive comments

Hundreds of millions of people whose parents were dirt-poor peasants will live in homes that are like mansions compared to the places inhabited by their parents and grandparents. An extraordinary number of people will be superrich—multibillionaires in today's dollars. There will still be many millions of poor people in 2040, but real destitution—the lack of even the bare essentials of life—should be much rarer than it is now.

On the other hand, *relative* poverty—feeling poor because you know someone else who has more than you do—may be just as prevalent in 2040 as it is today—or even more so! In the 1960s, psychologist Abraham Maslow claimed that as people's material wants were satisfied they would naturally turn to nonmaterial or spiritual goals. But economist Richard Easterlin's investigations revealed that steady improvements in the economy have not been accompanied by a decline of interest in material goods.

"Despite a general level of affluence never before realized in the history of the world," Easterlin writes, "material concerns in the wealthiest nations today are as pressing as ever and the pursuit of material needs as intense. The evidence suggests there is no evolution toward higher order goals. Rather, each step upward on the ladder of economic development merely stimulates new economic desires that lead the chase ever onward.... While it would be pleasant to envision a world free from the pressure of material want, a more realistic projection, based on the evidence, is of a world in which generation after generation thinks it needs only another 10 to 20 percent more income to be perfectly happy."

The perception of needing more money even as one's income rises has become worldwide. People whose living standards are rising often become less happy if other people are doing better—or seem to be. We can blame this on television, which flaunts the lifestyles of the rich and famous in the homes of the humblest people. A Chinese-American journalist, Suein L. Hwang, reports that her father's family eked out a meager existence on a rural China commune in the 1970s, but being isolated from the rest of the world they believed they lived in the greatest country on earth.

"Now, the same relatives are living there in spotless, heated homes, thanks to an economic boom," she reported. "Yet, they bemoan their privations. What has changed? The appearance of television sets, with endless images of other people who have it better."

In short, the people of 2040 will likely be, on average, richer than people today, but they may not be happier.

Work and Education

Due to rapid technological change, globalization, and other factors, workers will need to change jobs with increasing frequency to stay employed in 2040. There may be few jobs that assure lifetime employment. Most workers will have to reinvent their careers to keep up with the fast-changing workplace. To cope with the complexities of the job market and find positions suited to their talents and interests, workers will be more dependent than ever on career counselors, coaches, and mentors.

Even when not actively searching for employment, more workers will probably maintain contact with employment agencies. Many ordinary workers will have agents to represent their interests in securing and negotiating a new position.

To meet changing job requirements, workers will be forced to constantly update their education and skills. Education will no longer be viewed as an activity for young people but as a continuing necessity throughout life. The world of 2040 may even have laws requiring adults to continue their education so they can remain economically productive and play a constructive role in civic affairs. (Already, welfare recipients in the United States may be required to attend training courses as a condition of receiving benefits, and judges may make a convict's early release from jail contingent on his learning to read.)

A More-Crowded World

Life expectancy will have risen due to improved drugs and medical devices, new information about preserving health through better nutrition, and other factors. There may be millions of centenarians in the developed nations, and a tiny but growing minority of people will be over 120 years old.

By 2040, scientists will likely have found ways to slow or reverse the aging process (senescence), and people should already be benefiting. Babies born in 2040 may live for *centuries.*

Longevity has a serious downside, however, because people develop increasing disabilities as they age. On the other hand, much more sophisticated medical treatments and prosthetic devices will be available to assist the disabled. Researchers will likely have found effective ways not only to prevent but often to cure blindness, deafness, muscular deterioration, and other frailties of age. This means that more people will be quite able to work and support themselves for years, or even decades, beyond the typical retirement age of sixty-five. By 2040, governments will have updated their social-security systems to remove the incentives for people to retire as early in life as they do now.

Due to increased longevity as well as a continued high rate of births, the world's population will be both larger and older in 2040 than in 2000. UN projections suggest that the population that year may be about 8 billion, compared with 6 billion in 2000. Certain Third World countries will have sprawling megacities teeming with 30 or 40 million people, largely migrants from rural areas. Feeding and housing this huge population will strain the environment as well as the ability of governments to cope with runaway human needs.

A Devastated Environment

Due to the demands of soaring population and an economy ravenous for resources, the environment in the year 2040 will be in a desperate condition. The strenuous efforts of environmentalists to preserve the world's forests and wildlife and keep the oceans free of human garbage will have slowed but not halted the damage.

The world's forests will have shrunk substantially, and thousands more species of animals and plants will have become extinct. Freshwater supplies will be disastrously short through much of the world; pumps in most areas will have run dry as water tables dropped. Water will be more costly all around the world, making food more expensive and making agriculture as we know it economically impossible in many more areas. Globally, the oceans will be more polluted and the air more poisonous than they are today.

Aware of the impacts of the deteriorating global environment on their health, well-off people will pay to have their personal air and water purified. New buildings and apartment houses will have systems for cleaning the air supplied to tenants. Much of the concern about air pollution will focus on allergies and lung damage due to house dust and other contaminants.

An Expanded Human Habitat

By 2040, humans will have pushed out the frontiers of human settlement in every direction. The moon may have its first year-round inhabitants, and the first Lunarian may have been born.

On Earth, underground construction will have made major advances due to the need to develop more habitable space for human activities in urban areas. Building *down* may be viewed as more desirable than building *up*, partly because skyscrapers are viewed as more vulnerable to attack by terrorists.

Advancing technology will have solved many of the problems of living and working in unfriendly environments, such as outer space, Antarctica, under the oceans, or in the polar regions. Antarctica will have thousands of residents, and newlyweds may see it as a "cool" place for a June honeymoon. Similarly, the Himalayan Mountains may have become highly developed, thanks to their wondrous scenery. Mount Everest may be dotted with luxury hotels as well as honky-tonk amusements for visitors bored with the scenery. People living on the new frontiers of the human habitat will be able to work for employers around the world because they will have all the equipment needed to communicate easily with anyone anywhere.

The oceans will have become far more developed than they are now, and the development will be particularly apparent along coasts. Ocean farming may have become a serious rival to land farming, and a considerable portion of the oceans will become, in effect, marine farmland. Using techniques analogous to those of land farmers, ocean farmers will increase the production of selected marine plants and animals by means of fertilizers, defenses against predators, and selective breeding.

Politically, economically, socially, and culturally, the world's nations in 2040 will be linked together more tightly than ever before. Spreading telecommunications and transportation systems will have intensified the globalization of the economy, and a global international culture will have emerged due to the increasing contact of peoples with each other. The global elite will lead the way as they travel and pick up foods, clothing styles, drinks, games, sports, and customs from other countries.

A network of superhighways will tightly link Asia, Europe, and Africa. Residents of Shanghai, Calcutta, and Bangkok will be able to drive comfortably and rapidly across the Eurasian land mass to Edinburgh, Paris, and Madrid. Prime tourist destinations such as Venice will have instituted extraordinary measures to protect their unique art works and monuments from the hordes of visitors.

Despite faster trains and better highways, most travelers will still prefer to fly to more distant destinations. Space-planes may reduce the Tokyo–New York flight time to a couple of hours. On arrival by plane, travelers may board a high-speed train to complete their journeys.

Shaping Our Future

Our scenario is emphatically not a forecast for the actual world of 2040, but rather a way to determine where we may be at a future date *if* we keep going the way we are now. Many other scenarios could be prepared on the basis of different assumptions. We might decide, for instance, that population will not grow as large as projected because of certain identifiable factors, such as AIDS or a new birth control method, or that the world economy will have declined by 2040 due to environmental devastation and political incompetence. But whatever we decide about where we are headed, we humans do not have to accept our fate passively. We can act to create a different future for ourselves—to avert specific problems or create new benefits that are not now on the horizon. Scenarios help us to understand our options for the future.

Trends are not forces of destiny; they can and do change, and they may do so in response to deliberate human action to alter them. We are not, for example, forced to accept environmental decline, though we may have to make some hard choices if we want to stop it.

Summary

In the previous chapter, we identified the Great Transformation as the process in which the human future is being created. We considered a model that can help us to explain what is happening in the Great Transformation and perhaps anticipate future changes.

In this chapter we identified six supertrends that can be used as tools for anticipating future changes. We then attempted to project these great trends forward to try to anticipate what the world will be like in 2040 if the supertrends continue.

Our next task will be to look more carefully at how our world is changing in some ways but not in others. As we shall see, the continuities of our world are at least as important as the changes.

4

Understanding Change

The six supertrends discussed in the last chapter have given us a way to begin thinking about the global changes now occurring, and they have also introduced the concept of trends as a way to think about change.

A special value of trends is that they give us a bridge from the past to the future. By using trends we can convert knowledge of what has happened in the past into knowledge about what might happen in the future. Our knowledge of the future is, of course, a very weak and spotty kind of knowledge, but it can be used to create some crude maps of what may lie ahead. Like the great explorers, we must make use of whatever maps we can find, because any knowledge about what is really important is worth more than piles of knowledge about what is quite trivial. Trends give us important information about what may lie ahead, so they are a valuable asset in making practical decisions in our work and other activities.

The longer a trend has lasted, the more certain we can generally feel that it will last at least a little longer, though we must be on our guard because even long-term trends are likely to reverse directions, sometimes quite unexpectedly. Let's look at two trends—the increasing longevity and height of people in the Western world.

Historical data show that the average man in the industrial nations in 1800 was five feet seven inches tall and lived to be thirty-five years old. By 1900, the average man was five feet eight inches and lived to be fifty. By 2000, the average man reached five feet ten inches and had a life expectancy of seventy-six.

If we project these trends into the future, says forecaster Graham T.T. Molitor, men in the industrial nations will average six feet in height and live to be eighty-one by the year 2050. Whether or not these projections are realized in 2050, they enable us to think more realistically about the future of human height and longevity. At least we have a place to start.

Many people will wonder what longevity and height will *really* be like in 2050, but we cannot make a firm, precise forecast; these trends, like most others, are likely to deviate from our projections for a wide variety of reasons.

We can point to factors that seem likely to keep both these long-term trends continuing—and even accelerating. Medical advances can be expected to help people grow taller and improve their chances of living a long life. Given the continuing promise of better technology, and considering many people's desire to live longer and be taller, there could be major advances that would allow people to live for centuries and, perhaps, grow to seven or eight feet tall.

On the other hand, we can imagine reasons why males in 2050 *might* be shorter and die sooner. For instance, the world economy might collapse, causing a global Dark Age, with increasing hunger and disease that cause people to grow up shorter and die younger. An abrupt change in our priorities might also reduce our stature: The human race should be shrunk for ecological and health reasons, management consultant Thomas T. Samaras has argued in scholarly journals. Shorter people tend to consume fewer resources and live longer. Nonetheless, most parents today would rather see their children become basketball stars than dwarfs, and some are already using human growth hormone to increase their children's size.

By projecting trends, we come up with concepts of what conditions *may* be like in the unknown future. These concepts raise the question, Do we want the future we are headed toward, or should we try to change it? Trends are not forces of destiny, and trends in human activities result largely from people's decisions. Since these choices are voluntary and can shift greatly over time, the resulting trends are also likely to shift, sometimes radically.

The uncertainty of forecasts based on trends is not something to be deplored but rather celebrated, since it results from the increasing ability of humans to choose their futures. But to choose our futures we need to understand the possibilities of the future. Trends give us an excellent way to begin this very important task; they can enable us to make better decisions about what we should do.

Watching Trends

Some of the most useful trends are actually indexes; that is, they combine a number of different trends into a single overall measure that tells us something useful. The Consumer Price Index (CPI) is one of the most-watched statistics in the United States because of people's interest in the prices of the things they buy. Their interest is further whetted by the fact that their salaries or benefits may be decided on the basis of the CPI. To prepare this index, the U.S. Bureau of Labor Statistics sends data collectors into thousands of stores and offices around the country to determine the actual prices consumers pay for goods and services. The Bureau compiles and analyzes this price information to create the Index.

The Bureau provides an inflation calculator on its Web site (www.bls.gov) so visitors can see precisely how much the purchasing power of the dollar has declined over the past ten years. Based on what has happened during the previous decade, we have a clue as to what is likely to happen in the next. It's hardly certain that our anticipations will be on the mark, but the trend in the CPI may enable us to make better practical judgments about our finances.

The index of leading economic indicators also gets much attention because people are concerned about whether business activity will grow or shrink in the coming months. To prepare this index, The Conference Board, a business-research group in New York City (www.conference-board.org), uses ten indicators—that is, things such as stock prices and new orders to manufacturers—that can indicate whether a change is occurring. By watching the indicator over time, we can see whether there is an upward or downward trend in what interests us. Most of us aren't interested in how many building permits are issued each month, but that number says something about economic activity: A rise in permits indicates that builders want to do more building, which suggests that they will be spending more money for goods and services. So the number of building permits issued is a good indicator of future business activity. But, in a large and highly diverse economy, that indicator could be misleading, so The Conference Board uses ten different indicators for its leading index. We may not care about building permits, but we do want to know whether business will be growing or shrinking because that gives us clues about whether we can find a new job easily or get a salary increase.

By watching trends in the tension between nations, observers can judge whether a war is likely in the future. International indicators include such actions as one nation warning another nation or breaking diplomatic relations. Government agencies make extensive use of such indicators, but very little of their research is made public, due to possible reactions by the governments involved. However, if we wanted to know how likely a people is to become violent, one of the best indicators is unemployment among young men, according to forecaster Marvin Cetron, who often consults with U.S. agencies. Young men are the demographic group most responsible for political violence and terrorism, and their inability to find work produces great frustration.

On a more personal level, a knowledge of trends can help us to spend our money wisely. Consumers Union (www.consumersunion.org) tracks the performance of certain goods over a period of years. By collecting data about the actual experience of consumers using certain products, Consumers Union can tell us, for example, whether people who bought a certain model of car have had to make a lot of repairs on it or very few repairs. If a model we are interested in has had a favorable rating over a few years, we can reasonably hope that the trend will continue in the future, and we can save a lot of headaches if we buy that car rather than one with a poor record for repairs.

Overall, automobile manufacturers have gone a long way toward making vehicles more reliable, safer, and more comfortable since cars first appeared in the late nineteenth century. If we wished, we could use automobile quality as one indicator of the quality of life. If that indicator is combined with a number of others to create an index of the overall quality of life, we would have a way to start keeping statistics that would allow us to judge whether we are really making progress in improving human life or not. Furthermore, we also would have a way to judge whether we are on the right track or not.

Governments and businesses increasingly use indicators to measure their progress. The government of India, for example, is trying to find accurate ways to measure the country's level of poverty; this would allow the nation to know whether its economic programs were really working to help the poor. However, indicators of quality or performance often lead to controversies because nobody wants to receive an unfavorable rating.

But if we are serious about improving the future, we have to monitor our progress toward the goals we have set for ourselves. Monitoring key indicators so we can know whether the trend is up or down is likely to be highly important for our success.

There are now enormous new opportunities to learn more about how human life is changing. One reason is that we now have computerized systems for collecting basic data and then sorting and analyzing it very efficiently. Retail store chains such as Wal-Mart now use sophisticated systems to collect detailed data on sales of hundreds of different items at thousands of stores. This represents massive amounts of potentially useful information, and this knowledge can have immediate benefits. For instance, accurate real-time data on sales of prescription and over-the-counter drugs might serve as an early-warning system for disease epidemics or terrorist activities.

The practice of anticipating the future by means of trends is becoming increasingly important because we can't know even the present world simply by being in it. We need information, and we also need to make sure that our information is up to date. It seldom is. We don't really know the world as it exists *right now*, but only an outdated image of the past world.

Our Unknown World

In a fast-changing world, knowledge quickly goes out of date, so very quickly that each day we become ignorant of things we once were familiar with. As a result, we all live psychologically in the world of the past. The actual world is quite different from what we think.

For an insight into this problem, just imagine that we stayed home for twenty years without ever leaving or talking to anyone or receiving any news from the outside world. If we then emerge from isolation, we must expect to face a huge series of surprises and shocks due to all the changes that have occurred in the intervening years.

Today, most of us are in a position much like that. We live highly hermetic lives, shut off from the world around us by our own concentration on our personal affairs and our limited contact with what is happening beyond our immediate sphere of interest. As a result, what we think we know about the world around us is mostly out of date.

The extent of this problem was demonstrated to novelist Tom Wolfe after he published *The Bonfire of the Vanities*. Critics surprised Wolfe by describing his book as "prophetic." But they were wrong, Wolfe said; he had not described New York as it might be in the future but simply as it was while he was writing. "The book only showed what was obvious to anyone ... who had gone out and looked at the new face of the city." Many readers, however, had apparently not done so, and they had mental images of New York based on what it had been like in the past. So they decided that Wolfe must be talking about the New York of the future!

To stay current in our knowledge of the world, we cannot simply learn about the world in school and then assume that what we learned remains correct. If we want to live psychologically in the real world of today, we must learn to think in terms of trends, so that we can anticipate how the world must have changed while we weren't looking, and how it will continue to change in the years ahead.

Here's an example of how a study of current trends taught managers of a large corporation what the world around them was *really* like rather than what they *thought* it was like. In the 1960s, the General Electric Company produced a report describing current social trends and projecting them into the future. Some time later, an admirer asked the report's author, Ian H. Wilson, how the company was making use of his report: "Just what is the company doing differently now?" Wilson responded that the biggest impact of the report on the company was the finding that white-collar workers were increasing very rapidly as a percentage of the U.S. workforce and might eventually become the majority. Struck by this forecast, GE managers looked at the company's current workforce and found, to their surprise, that white-collar workers had *already* become the majority, yet the company was still structured as if blue-collar workers were dominant. This experience at GE illustrates how an effort to see the future can reveal the present, enabling people to correct their out-of-date beliefs and practices.

Our thinking suffers greatly from antiquated beliefs about the world around us. We may continue to think of the Soviet Union as a great power long after the Soviet Union has ceased to exist. Or we may think there is no cure for a physical problem we suffer from because we are unaware of what physicians can now do for us.

How can we realistically overcome our outdated thinking about the world?

First, we must recognize that it is quite impossible to keep up with everything that is going on in our fast-changing world. However, we *can* learn a lot of very useful things about it, and the question is, How can we best go about this task? How can we equip ourselves with the *most essential* knowledge about the world around us? That's where trends come in. Trends help us to *organize* our thinking about the changes, giving us a clearer picture of the really important things that are going on. From this awareness often emerges key insights to aid in solving practical problems.

Besides helping us to know where we are right now, trends can suggest where we are likely to be in the years ahead. For instance, if our city has been growing steadily of late, it may well continue to grow. As a consequence, property values may increase, because more and more people will be trying to buy land in the city and its surrounding area. This recognition gives us a time-tested formula for making money in real estate: Buy in the path of growth. However, following such trends blindly can be risky. Population growth might induce some people to move elsewhere, either to take advantage of rising land prices or to avoid increasing traffic congestion, crowded schools, and soaring taxes. This, too, will affect the value of the land you might consider buying.

No trend continues forever. Eventually it will slow, halt, or reverse. The once-mushrooming city may suddenly start losing business and population, causing property values to collapse. But if a trend is used cautiously, it gives us a good starting point for thinking about the future.

Cycles: Trends That Reverse

We think of trends as continuing indefinitely in the same direction, but a trend may reverse course. If a trend swings back and forth between positive and negative phases, we call it a cycle.

The daily increase and decrease of sunlight is probably the first cycle that people become aware of. Since sunlight is so important, people in the past felt they had to worship the sun to make sure it would not abandon them. We now know the cycle results from the rotation of the earth, and we don't worry about it. But we do worry a lot about the cycles that affect business.

The upswings and downswings in economic activity are far less regular than sunlight cycles, but they greatly impact on the ability of companies to sell their products. Certain goods, such as luxury items, are especially sensitive to changing phases of the business cycle. Home builders have to be very wary about building just before demand for housing starts to decline. If the builders can detect early signs that prices are likely to plunge, they can stop building and sell off their inventory as quickly as possible.

People in business listen carefully to economists, hoping for guidance about what is to come in the level of business activity and other economic cycles. But the cycles are irregular, and even if we knew just what they are, it might be difficult to judge where in the cycle the economy is now. So economic predictions are often wide of the mark. This has led to a cynical joke: "Economists have predicted nine of the past five recessions."

The long-term cycle in the economy has attracted much attention but remains quite uncertain and controversial. This so-called Kondratieff wave gets its name from Russian economist Nikolai Kondratieff. In the 1920s, Kondratieff studied the economic history of Britain, France, Germany, and the United States over a period going back nearly two centuries. He found that, over a period of about fifty or so years, wholesale prices in those nations would rise to a peak and then decline; after bottoming out, the prices would again rise and fall, creating a new cycle. Kondratieff was later arrested and executed by Joseph Stalin's government, which disapproved of evidence that there might be forces beyond its control. However, his theory survived, though it has remained controversial.

The Kondratieff wave theory has great theoretical importance because severe economic downturns, exemplified by the Great Depression of the 1930s, can lead to political instability, revolutions, dictatorships, and military aggression. Unfortunately, it seems quite possible that the long-term cycle is irregular and unpredictable due to the operation of chance factors and the operations of chaos, subjects that we will be discussing in the next chapter.

We may not be able to do much about the Kondratieff wave, let alone the phases of the tide, but other cycles—such as the upswings and downswings of animal and plant populations—may be controllable to some extent. The population of deer in a certain area may increase steadily as fawns are born, find adequate food, and reproduce. Eventually, however, there are so many deer that they can't find enough food and begin to starve, eat the bark off trees, uproot the vegetation, and generally destroy their environment. The population may then plunge due to starvation and disease. After most of the deer have died off, the survivors can again find enough food to meet their needs, so population growth resumes, starting a new positive phase of the cycle.

Understanding the mechanism of the population cycle permits humans to intervene, if they wish, to prevent the adverse impacts of the cycle. In the case of deer, the herds may be culled and the excess animals sold for venison; alternatively, contraceptives can be given to the animals to keep too many fawns from being born.

Patterns of Change

Some changes are part of a sequenced pattern of changes, so once we know the pattern we can anticipate what is likely to come later. The most familiar of these patterns of change is the growth cycle in animals and plants. A moth egg develops into a larva, which forms a cocoon and pupates into a moth that will lay more eggs, restarting the cycle.

A knowledge of stages of development can help us to anticipate future changes. A veterinarian examining a dachshund or greyhound puppy can forecast its adult size by knowing the normal size attained by the breed. Similarly, arborists can forecast (within limits) the eventual height of a sapling by knowing the tree species to which it belongs.

Because human growth cycles, controlled by our genes, are highly dependable, we can confidently forecast that an infant human will develop into a toddler, child, adolescent, and adult. Since these sequences of changes recur so reliably, we can use them to make detailed forecasts of the changes an individual is likely to undergo as time passes. Our forecasts may occasionally prove erroneous, but they are reasonably accurate and useful. Certainly we should not assume that the infant we see today will still be the same helpless little person twenty years from now.

The growth cycle helps demographers to make useful population forecasts. For example, if we know about how many three-year-olds there are in a population, we can estimate how many children will be starting first grade in two years, so the authorities can take steps to minimize overcrowding in class-rooms.

Forecasts of the U.S. population over the next five years can be reasonably accurate, because all the adults and most of the people who will be counted five years from now are already alive. But like other forecasts, estimates of future population become less reliable as we attempt to look farther and farther into the future. Over a period of decades, birthrates may change greatly due to such factors as new contraceptive technologies, government policies, and cultural attitudes. The U.S. birthrate plunged in the 1930s due to the Great Depression, then soared in the late 1940s with the end of the Great Depression and World War II. In the late 1960s, the U.S. baby boom came to an end, causing a "birth dearth" that also affected many other industrialized nations.

Current demographic forecasts for the long-term future may be upset if scientists discover a way to reverse the aging process. But an antiaging drug might be countered by new plagues such as AIDS and SARS or a resurgence of other diseases. The Black Death, a plague that ravaged Europe between 1347 and 1351, claimed about a third of the continent's population; it was the greatest catastrophe the Western world had experienced up to that time.

Due to the many uncertainties, demographers now create a number of scenarios for future population growth. These scenarios often reflect varying assumptions of the birthrate, which is highly subject to fluctuation due to many causes: In November 1965, an electrical blackout of the northeastern United States caused a surge of births nine months later.

Stages in Technology and Society

New technologies do not evolve in as formulaic a manner as anatomical growth, but they do go through recognized "stages of innovation," with each successful technical advance representing an advance in the practicality or use of the technology. Technological forecaster Joseph P. Martino lists the following stages:

- *Scientific findings:* Basic scientific understanding of some phenomenon has been developed.
- *Laboratory feasibility:* A technical solution to a specific problem has been identified and a laboratory model has been created.

- *Operating prototype:* A device intended for a particular operational environment has been built.
- *Commercial introduction or operational use:* The innovation is not only technologically successful but also economically feasible.
- *Widespread adoption:* The innovation has shown itself to be superior in some way to whatever was used previously to perform its function and begins to replace previous methods.
- *Diffusion to other areas:* The innovation becomes adopted for purposes other than those originally intended.
- *Social and economic impact:* The innovation has changed the behavior of society or has somehow involved a substantial portion of the economy.

Knowing these stages means that if we can recognize a certain stage in the development or diffusion of a new technology we may be able to anticipate future changes. If we recognize that a potential change could be important, we can watch for confirmation and, when we get it, take whatever action we think is appropriate.

Social or political issues also evolve by identifiable stages, according to Graham T.T. Molitor, who has studied the issue-attention cycle while working for business and political clients. Initially, a few articles on an emerging issue may appear in scholarly journals; later come articles in the general press and bills introduced into local legislatures; eventually laws are passed and implemented. Knowledge of these stages allows us to monitor issues that may eventually generate new laws and governmental actions.

Nations go through a series of stages as their economies develop, and some economies have followed a pattern similar to that of the Western economies in the eighteenth and nineteenth centuries. Just as the advanced nations did earlier, a developing nation today is likely to shift its focus from agriculture to "first-stage" industries like cloth production. Later it may move into heavy industries like steel mills, and eventually develop very high-tech laboratories. However, the stages-of-development model, based largely on what happened during Britain's Industrial Revolution, may not prove a reliable guide to the future.

Now, due to the globalization of the world economy, multi-national companies can set up factories to manufacture high-tech products in developing countries. Meanwhile, heavy industries are more difficult to develop in the Third World because of a global surplus of certain industrial products, such as steel and automobiles. To make matters worse for developing nations, industrialized countries set up barriers to prevent them from selling to local consumers. Theories of economic development thus may need refining, but they do help us to think about the sort of things we may anticipate as a country's economy develops.

Change and Stability

Change is the star on the stage of world events. Change gets the applause and hisses, because people notice change and respond quite emotionally, both positively and negatively. But change has a twin—continuity—which is just as important but gets little notice.

In futuring, however, continuity gets a chance to star, at least at times, because continuity is what enables our enterprise. If everything constantly changed, we could not possibly know anything about the future—or anything else, for that matter. We are able to anticipate future changes because of the continuity of the past with the future through the medium of time. Though change is normally our focus, we have to recognize that much remains constant, and it is this continuity that allows us to anticipate future events and plan what we should do.

In this chapter, we looked at types of change in which continuity plays a prominent role. This continuous sort of change is sometimes described as *linear* because it seems to move ahead in a straightforward manner. We can identify patterns in this type of change, and it is often not too difficult to use them to anticipate something that will happen in the future.

But there is another kind of change, which may be described as discontinuous, nonlinear, or even quirky. Nonlinear change seems to work like a Rube Goldberg invention: An impulse of change jumps from one situation to another in a wildly erratic manner. This less-predictable sort of change arises from the fact that we live in a world of interacting systems subject to the forces of chance and chaos. Discontinuous change is extremely difficult to anticipate, but it is very important, so we will look at it in the next chapter.

5

Systems, Chance, and Chaos

A system may be defined as any group of things that are connected together so that they act in some ways as a whole. Our universe can be described as a stupendous megasystem, composed of an infinitude of systems and subsystems. These systems are as large as galaxies or smaller than atoms, and they are constantly in flux: Connections are being established and broken within and among systems, keeping the universe in a state of constant change.

The systems concept helps us to think in very broad terms about how events occur. It adds a useful bit of structure to broad-gauge thinking, helping us to understand highly complex and largely unknown situations. The systems approach can suggest the sort of things to expect, so it gives us a useful way to understand what is happening in the world around us.

One reason the systems approach is so useful is that it focuses our attention on relationships rather than on things. It is relationships among things, more than the things themselves, that shape events. Yet our thinking normally focuses on things, because things are visible but relationships are not. For example, if we see two people standing a few feet apart, we tend to focus on the people themselves rather than on the relationships that may connect them. We can see the people's faces and clothing, but we cannot see the relationships between them. Are they man and wife, bound together in the system known as marriage? Or are they bitter rivals, bound to each other by mutual dislike and suspicion? These relationships are critically important in understanding what happens between them and what may result from their interaction.

The role of a system in giving importance to its constituent elements is apparent in the human body: The body is a marvel of systems engineering. It is composed of myriad intricately connected and interacting systems of enormous subtlety and elegance. This system of systems has an incredible record of ingenious achievements, but its importance lies in the power given to it by the relationships of the various parts to each other and to its external environment. A human body reduced to its component parts is merely water, gas, and dirt.

The Importance of the Systems Approach

The systems approach helps us to understand relationships that exist across space, time, and domains. Therefore it is particularly relevant to thinking about multidimensional events, trends, and complex relationships. The systems approach does not replace analytical, historical, and other approaches, but it offers a useful way to begin thinking about the complex situations in which important changes occur; it also can offer hints about significant things to look for.

The systems perspective helps us to move from a static picture of reality to a dynamic view—a world in which things are constantly changing into other things. Furthermore, it helps us to think about very different kinds of things—particularly those in the area of human systems, such as language or foreign policy. This can be important because one system can shape another system of an entirely different type. Religious systems, for example, can affect technological systems: In the twenty-first century, Amish farmers in Pennsylvania are still using horse-drawn buggies.

Living systems may be divided between biological systems (e.g., a tree or a dog) and social systems (e.g., the Roman Catholic Church, the U.S. economy, or a pack of hyenas). James G. Miller, in his monumental work *Living Systems*, describes seven levels of living system:

1. The cell (examples: the amoebae, a muscle cell)
2. The organ (artery, liver)
3. The organism (plant, woman, whale)
4. The group (family, jury, gaggle of geese)
5. The organization (school, factory, county, government)
6. The society (Argentina, Vatican City, Russia)
7. The supranational system (NATO, European Community, UN)

Living systems, even if they consist of only one cell, contain a large number of subsystems, including systems for making decisions. Just to survive, a living system must determine whether something in the environment should be absorbed into its body or kept out.

Social systems have a Promethean ability to change quickly and pervasively, often in totally unexpected ways. A business corporation may begin as nothing more than someone with an idea for a business. Then it can expand to include thousands of employees and millions of customers. Later, it may completely change its personnel, owners, customers, suppliers, and products. Investor Warren Buffett converted a corporation that made shirts into an investment firm, focused largely on insurance companies (Berkshire Hathaway).

A World of Interacting Systems

Newton's third law of motion tells us that for every action there is an equal and opposite reaction. In our world of complex systems, the first law is that for every action there are many reactions, and they may be quite different in character from the original action. Furthermore, the effects of our actions move through time, space, and domains, changing their nature as they proceed.

If you throw a stone into a small pond, ripples spread out across the water, causing whatever is floating at the surface to bob up and down. What is unusual and engaging about the stone-tossed-in-the-pond situation is that it allows us to observe the effects of an action moving away from the touchdown point, through time and space, in beautiful waves. Systems theory tells us that every action has many effects, but few are as obvious and beautiful as the ripples on a pond.

Pond ripples disappear quickly, but part of the energy of each moving ripple is transferred to the air above: The air is repeatedly pushed slightly, affecting the atmosphere and therefore the weather. In addition, some molecules of water have been transferred from the pond to the air, and all the living things in the pond have been subjected to various sounds, shocks, and other effects. The stone itself sinks to the bottom of the pond, creating a new feature of the bottom's topography.

All of these effects of our tossed stone may seem trivial, and so they may be in this particular instance. The effects of the tossed stone quickly escape our power to follow them as they pass from one domain to another. There is reason to think, however, that the effects are not necessarily trivial; they could be highly consequential, at least in some instances. This perspective comes to us from research in two other fields of inquiry: chance and chaos.

Although the longer-term consequences of an action rarely become known, historians and other researchers seek to know the precise causes of certain highly important events. What they generally find is that such events would probably not have happened except for some trivial or chance circumstances that ordinarily would be viewed as having no importance. So when we do things, we must assume that we are necessarily creating thousands of invisible effects that will move out through time and space like the ripples on a pond. They could, under certain circumstances, shape the course of history.

Here's how a young man from Savannah, Georgia, unwittingly caused a ripple of change that became a political tidal wave.

The young man, Frank Wills, visited Washington, D.C., in 1971 and decided that he would like to live there. He got a job as an $80-a-week security guard. The following year he was assigned to work from midnight to 7 a.m. at the Watergate office complex. On the night of June 17, 1972, Wills was making his rounds when he noticed a piece of adhesive tape covering part of the lock mechanism on a door between the parking garage and the basement stairwell.

Wills removed the tape, thinking it had been left by the cleaning crew that had just gone off duty. But when he came back, about an hour later, he found the lock had been retaped, so he called the District of Columbia police. It was one of history's most important telephone calls.

Rushing to the scene, the police arrested five men wearing surgical gloves and carrying bugging equipment inside the Democratic National Committee headquarters, which was located in a Watergate suite. The resulting scandal led to the resignation of President Richard Nixon—the first time in history that an American president had resigned from office—and to Gerald Ford becoming the next president. But none of it might have happened if Frank Wills had not visited Washington and decided to stay.

In a world of interlaced systems, where everything is connected to everything else, we cause many ripples of change as we go through our daily lives. Our every action leads to changes, which lead to more changes, then still more changes, ad infinitum. As environmentalist John Muir said, "When we try to pick out anything by itself, we find it is hitched to everything else in the universe." We can never do just one thing. We cannot even scratch our noses without sending out ripples of change through the universe. This perception does not require us to hire a think tank to develop a report on the consequences of scratching our noses, because we know that such an action is unlikely to produce a serious change that can be traced to it. Yet this does alert us to the fact that every action we take can have many effects that we do not expect and never considered beforehand. And we have a duty to consider these potential results when we have reason to think they might be consequential.

Tracing a causal link across interacting systems from one event to other events is critical to knowing what is happening in our complex world, but it is not easy; for example, the causes of the disappearance of frogs and salamanders around the world are still unclear after years of painstaking research. Chemicals are suspected, but which chemicals, and who is responsible for them? Suspicion also attaches to the growing human population, which is destroying the animals' environment by building roads and houses and by clearing land for grazing. If these suspicions are confirmed by scientific studies, ways may be found to halt population growth or limit its impact, but uncertainty stymies action. Meanwhile, reports indicate that reptiles are also disappearing. Will birds be next?

Ripple effects are multiple, widespread, and continuing. Over time, they spread across the world. They can assume semipermanent forms and thus last for years or even millennia. We can see this in language: We today are still creating words based on Latin and Greek roots that were already ancient in classical times.

But these are exceptions. Just as physical energy disintegrates into heat, the energy of a change is gradually dissipated as it comes into contact with competing forces that hold it in check and neutralize it. Here and there, a few bits of things that the change has created remain as semipermanent realities until they, too, become swallowed up in other changes.

Still, even a transient system can have a profound and long-lasting influence on the world. Think of a human system such as a group of men conversing at a table in a restaurant: The scene occurs every day all over the world. But after one such encounter in Munich in 1919, one of the participants, an ex-soldier and unsuccessful artist named Adolf Hitler, decided despite grave doubts to join the tiny political party the men had just formed. If the meeting had gone just a tiny bit differently, he probably would have chosen to go his own way. As it was, he quickly became the newborn party's leader, and from this humble beginning the tiny party morphed into the dominant force in Germany. Later, it plunged Europe into World War II.

Somehow, the little system in the Munich restaurant had the power to alter the global system, showing the tremendous leverage that a small event resulting from a brief-lived system can exercise over the entire human enterprise. For more insights into this phenomenon, let us look more closely at how chance and chaos affect our lives.

The Enormous Potential of Chance Events

Humans have only limited control over the world, so chance events occur constantly. Most of the time we pay little or no attention to them because they are trivial or ordinary. But chance events include some that we can recognize as having been crucial turning points in our lives.

Chance concerns us here because it continues to shape the future, including our own personal lives. Our activities are embedded in numerous complex systems (biological, social, political, etc.), and these systems are extremely susceptible to chance events. Complex systems can be influenced by tiny details because they consist of multiple subsystems plus connections to numerous other systems, all interacting with each other in complex and bizarre ways. In such a complicated situation, the presence or absence of some trifling object, the precise location of a particular person at a particular time, a few micrograms more or less of a certain chemical in one individual's brain, or even a minor environmental disturbance, such as a noisy truck going down a street and interrupting a discussion, can redirect the flow of events, leading to a dramatic shift away from what otherwise would have resulted.

Extremely important events can turn on the presence or absence of a few atoms: The difference between a harmless virus and a killer may be as little as three atoms in five million. No one can identify, measure, forecast, or control all such details, yet these "trifles" can have huge consequences. This fact reminds us of the nursery fable that explains the downfall of a kingdom as being due to a missing nail in a horseshoe: "For lack of a nail, the shoe was lost; for lack of a shoe, the horse was lost;

for lack of a horse, the rider was lost; for lack of a rider, the kingdom was lost, and all because of a three-penny nail."

The sensitivity of political systems to seemingly trivial contingencies can be extraordinary. A famous example is the assassination of the archduke of Austria in the Balkan city of Sarajevo in 1914. The assassination would not have occurred if any number of possible circumstances had kept Archduke Ferdinand from visiting Sarajevo. Once he was there, only the perversity of chance led his chauffeur to drive up to the very café where a Serb student was consoling himself after failing in an earlier assassination attempt. Though astounded by this totally unexpected opportunity, the student, Gavrilo Princip, had the presence of mind to leap to his feet and fire his weapon, killing the archduke and starting the chain of events that led directly to World War I. That war, in turn, produced the Russian revolution, which brought the rise of communism and provoked the Germans to embrace Nazism. This further led to World War II, whose consequences include atomic bombs, rockets, computers, and the landing of men on the moon.

Similar events might have occurred without the assassination of the archduke, but not necessarily, and history would certainly have been quite different. If the archduke had not been assassinated, there probably still would have been wars and technological advances, because that would have been a continuation of well-established trends. Yet the two world wars might have been avoided, and in a different climate Hitler and Stalin might have been little more than harmless cranks. Atomic bombs might still exist only in science fiction.

How Chance Influences Our Lives

Chance events constantly shape our personal and organizational lives. In business, a chance meeting in an airport lounge may lead to a multibillion-dollar merger. A future married couple will first meet unintentionally: "We happened to be on the same plane, and she spilled coffee on me." The event could more easily have not happened than happened; the fact is that it did happen despite its improbability.

In Frank Capra's classic motion picture *It's a Wonderful Life* (1946), the hero (played by James Stewart) becomes so depressed that he is on the point of suicide, but is miraculously given an opportunity to see what would have happened if he had never lived. After he recognizes how important his life has been to the town and the people he cares about, he forgets about suicide and returns to his normal self. Though the film is a fantasy, one of its premises is valid: An ordinary individual—no matter how humble—produces an enormous amount of change during his or her life. The changes wrought by an individual are not necessarily good, but for better or worse, they significantly influence the future.

The role of chance in scientific discoveries is well known: A telephone engineer, Karl Jansky, trying to determine the source of static on telephone lines found that it was coming from the Milky Way: This quite unexpected discovery initiated the science of radio astronomy. Even within a scientific laboratory, chance often gives researchers the clue they need to solve problems. Researchers trying to find a way to preserve human sperm through deep freezing had no luck until a sample accidentally mixed with glycerol produced an unexpected success. Perhaps the best-known chance discovery occurred at London's St. Mary's Hospital, where researcher Alexander Fleming noticed that the Staphylococcus bacteria he was cultivating did not grow near the Pencillium mold that happened to fall into his cultures. This observation led to penicillin and spurred the development of many other antibiotics.

Chance is important in scientific research because scientists often do not know exactly where to find what they are looking for. The trick is to look in places that logic or experience suggest but to be ready to pounce if the desired answer, or some other interesting result, turns up in a very unexpected way.

Nature's secrets remain secrets until they are discovered. Scientists typically focus their attention on the areas where discoveries are likely, but they can't look everywhere, so discoveries often occur by chance, though they still require a discoverer. Quite a few people may have seen cultures where Penicillium mold was killing germs but had no idea that what they were seeing was important. A chance discovery requires a person capable of discovery.

But being an expert on what is being discovered is not always essential: Nonscientists and amateur scientists have made many important discoveries after getting curious about something. Though Louis Pasteur became famous because of his research on microorganisms, the creatures were first discovered by a Dutch janitor with a great deal of curiosity, Antonie van Leeuwenhoek.

Chance may be a scientist's friend at times, but it is often the deadly enemy of people charged with safety. A safety officer must spot and eliminate vulnerabilities, that is, situations where chance has an opportunity to cause major damage. In safety, the guiding principle is Murphy's law, "Whatever can go wrong will go wrong." So nothing must be left to chance. Safeguards must be introduced so the harmful events cannot occur. If there is any risk that can't be eliminated, then there should be a fail-safe plan or second-line of defense so that no real harm is done.

Every major accident or dramatic incident is embedded in a tangled web of chance, and chance circumstances determine who lives and who dies. The terrorist attacks on the World Trade Center and Pentagon on September 11, 2001, produced thousands of such cases, such as the mother whose ticketing problems for an earlier flight forced her onto the doomed American Airlines Flight 77. Emilio Ortiz, who worked at the World Trade Center, went to work early because he had to fill in for a fired co-worker.

Jimmy Walsh, a computer programmer at the Center, almost listened to his wife and took the day off for his daughter's second birthday.

All three were missing and presumed dead after the attacks, but other people survived because of an unusual circumstance: Monica O'Leary had been fired the day before from her job at the World Trade Center.

Greer Epstein had slipped out of the Center for a cigarette.

Joe Andrew made a last-minute switch in his flight from Boston.

The event also reverberated around the world, causing countless odd effects. For example, in Texas a convicted murderer got a brief reprieve from execution because the U.S. Supreme Court had closed, delaying a last-minute appeal.

Confronting tragedies, we want to know why chance spares one person while dooming another. Human reason and sensibility crave explanations that satisfy the demands of justice as well as logic, but often there is none. The victims were killed without regard to their merits or faults.

After such a disaster, we need to determine, as best we can, exactly why it occurred. Careful investigations into the causes of automobile and plane accidents have led to cars and planes that are safer than ever. Though we cannot know exactly when a combination of circumstances will result in a specific accident, we can identify the types of circumstances that create risks of disaster. By reducing the risks, we reduce the likelihood of future disasters and prevent innumerable future disasters even though we still cannot eliminate all possible ways for an accident to occur.

Now let's turn to the phenomenon known as chaos to see more clearly how a big change can occur due to seemingly trivial circumstance.

The Influence of Chaos

In the early 1960s, meteorologist Edward Lorenz at MIT was using a computer to simulate changing weather conditions so that better forecasts could be made. Lorenz would type into his computer various equations to simulate weather conditions, then he would see what happened as the conditions interacted with each other.

On one occasion, Lorenz wanted to examine a portion of a graph in more detail, so he repeated the run, but the second run was different from the first even though it should have been identical. Lorenz thought the computer had malfunctioned, but after ruling out that possibility, he discovered that the deviation had occurred because, to save time, he had rounded off some of the data he put into the computer for the repeat run. Lorenz soon confirmed that a trivial change in the specified initial weather conditions could result in huge differences in the weather sometime later. This discovery proved a bombshell in the world of meteorology. It meant that long-range weather forecasting—the holy grail of meteorologists—might actually be a will o' the wisp, because it would never be practical to make all the necessary observations in sufficient detail for a forecast that would be good for longer than about two weeks. Furthermore, seemingly trivial nonmeteorological events could cause big problems; a serious perturbation might arise from a bonfire, the exhaust of a truck, or even the flight of a butterfly.

The possibility that a butterfly flapping its wings in Brazil could cause a tornado in Texas stirred the interest of scientists and others outside meteorology in the early 1970s, and some began looking more closely at chaotic systems. These include not only weather, but such phenomena as water coming out of a faucet and swarms of locusts. In chaotic systems, individual units (such as molecules of air or water or individual locusts) seem to move about randomly, yet the whole exhibits a definite structure. The chaoticians confirmed Lorenz's observation that very small differences in the initial conditions of these systems can grow into very large differences as time passes. Furthermore, the apparently random activity in a chaotic system is not wholly random but produces patterns shaped by what are called "strange attractors."

By the 1990s, the language of chaotics had spread widely in business and academia. Investors, for example, now worry about the "butterfly effect" in financial markets. The sharp sell-off of Thailand's currency in 1997 did not cause a tornado in Texas, but it did cause a hurricane of financial and political disorder, including riots in neighboring Malaysia and Indonesia, a storm in the emerging markets in general, and a nasty rain on Wall Street's bull market parade. It is now an article of faith among investment theoreticians that chaos theory explains much of the activity they see in stock, futures, and currency markets.

The chaos scientists have demonstrated in laboratory experiments using computers that what may seem like an utterly negligible difference in the input into a system can have huge long-term effects on the system. A nanoscopic change in a system can grow, as time passes, into a metamorphosis of the entire system. The minute alteration may be likened to a seed of change that grows overnight into a monstrous plant. On the other hand, a seemingly major event or factor may do relatively little to alter the system.

In a few instances, such as the assassination of the Austrian archduke that triggered World War I, a chain of cause and effects can be traced, giving us a partial explanation for a significant event. More typically, the causal chain that can be traced is very short, because there is no means today of recording all the minor events happening around the globe, much less identifying and recording all the connections among them. Thus it is doubtful that meteorologists will ever be able to get a Brazilian butterfly indicted for causing a tornado in Texas. It may even be that scientific determination of such a link is fundamentally impossible, due to basic limitations in the precision with which science can identify, measure, and record events. In 1927, German physicist Werner Heisenberg established that it was impossible to specify or determine both the position and velocity of an atomic particle with full accuracy. Heisenberg's principle makes little difference ordinarily because the amount of indeterminacy is inconsequential. However, chaoticians have shown that trivial details in the initial conditions of a system can, over time, lead to huge differences in later conditions. Thus it may never be even theoretically possible to track down the ultimate causes for many significant events, or to predict all the results that our actions may produce.

The Implications of Chaos Research

The butterfly effect probably operates even more decisively in human systems than it does in weather systems, because a human has a much broader scope of activity and because social systems are probably more sensitive than weather systems. In the past, people believed that only certain exceptional individuals had power over great events. Now, chaos theory provides something close to scientific proof that all humans have that power, at least to some degree.

Another empowering implication of chaos theory is that any complex system can produce a multiplicity of results. A system can evolve in numerous different ways; it does not have a single future toward which it inevitably moves, but rather thousands or billions of distinguishably different futures, any one of which may be realized as the system evolves. Due to the limitations of time and space, the events that achieve actuality must be only an infinitesimally small percentage of all potential events. There are countless choice-points, where only one possibility among two or more is realized, and that choice changes the situation permanently. Actual events represent a minuscule selection by chance or by choice among a stupendous number of potential events.

Consider two well-known blunders made by brilliant military commanders: Napoleon's decision to invade Russia in 1812 and Robert E. Lee's decision to order General George Pickett to charge the Union forces at Gettysburg in 1863. If either blunder had been avoided, much subsequent history would have been different. We can only speculate on just what the differences might have been. However, we can say with near certainty that, if Napoleon had not invaded Russia, Pickett's charge would never have occurred, even though there is no direct connection between the two events.

Why?

Napoleon's invasion caused so much change in the world that it would almost certainly have disrupted at least one of the fragile gossamers of events that, in combination, produced Pickett's charge. There were numerous potential weak points in the web of circumstances causing the event:

- Abraham Lincoln's election as U.S. president in 1860, pre-cipitating the Southern states' secession from the Union in 1861.
- Lee's assuming command of the Southern forces.
- The accidental shooting of General Stonewall Jackson by one of his own men, which crippled Lee's command struc-ture at a critical juncture.
- Lee's invasion of Pennsylvania. The circumstances that led to the two sides taking up the precise positions they did at Gettysburg.
- Lee's uncharacteristically poor judgment in allowing Pickett's charge.

Eliminate any of these contributing circumstances, and Pickett's charge would never have occurred; it took place despite the stupendous odds against it. Even a very slight change in the events leading up to the Civil War, the previous conduct of the war, or the circumstances of the battle would have sufficed to keep Pickett's charge from happening.

Napoleon's invasion of Russia produced change on a colos-sal scale, any detail of which could have taken other directions and altered all of subsequent history. So we are justified in saying that without the invasion of Russia Pickett's charge would almost certainly never have occurred, even though the two events had no obvious connection with each other.

This leads us to recognition that the people on earth today represent a completely different set of people from those who would exist now if Pickett had not made his charge. This thesis is supported by the same logic as that which led to the state-ments above. As it turned out, Pickett's disastrous charge gave the North a complete victory over the Southern forces at Get-tysburg and ended the hope that the South would achieve independence. The North's victory led to freedom for the Southern slaves and to innumerable other changes in the United States. With so much change flowing from Pickett's charge, it can be viewed as certain that life all over America and other nations was affected. Countless events would have been shaped a little differently, and, as we know from chaos theory, each little change can be fairly quickly magnified into substantial change.

One further implication is also clear: If Pickett had not charged, we would not exist. Presumably there would be people on earth, but not us. So we can be grateful for Pickett's charge. It was one of the many circumstances essential to our being born!

The Infinitude of Our Possible Futures

Systems, chance, and chaos give us ample reason for being discouraged about our ability to make accurate forecasts or to know the full consequences of our actions. But we can find comfort in their other implications.

The first important implication is that perfectly ordinary people like you and I can produce miracles. If a butterfly can touch off a tornado, could not an ordinary human make a desert bloom? Or save the lives of a thousand future children? We ordinary folks do make a real difference in what happens in the future. Our dilemma is that we don't know exactly how to be sure our influence is for the better and not for the worse. But once we recognize our power over the future, we have the responsibility to exercise that power as well as we can. This means that we must seek to understand the possibilities of the future and how to work toward influencing events in a way that will be beneficial to our futures.

The second implication is that our future is not singular; it is multitudinous. Myriad potential futures lie before us. This does not, of course, mean that absolutely anything can happen, since we are still limited by the laws of nature, but those laws do allow us fantastic freedom.

History records events that actually occurred; it does not record events that might have occurred but did not. We can think of the world around us as a colossal mass of potential events constantly shedding a relatively tiny number of actual events. The historian focuses on the actualities of the past; the futurist must deal with the infinitely more numerous potentialities of the future.

Since potential events have never had any actuality, we can only imagine them, and many lie beyond the reach of our wildest imagining. However, we can get a few hints of how incredible must be those things that we cannot imagine. For instance, historians and ethnographers have abundantly documented the astonishing variety of ways in which different groups of people have obtained food, built homes, expressed themselves in language and music and art, and devised objects of worship. Each cultural pattern represents a series of choices that a given people has made during its social and cultural evolution. In a sense, each people has carved out a different destiny for itself.

Any visit to an art gallery demonstrates that painters can create an astonishing variety of unique pictures on a few square feet of flat surface. If so much can be done with so little, we can only wonder how many things billions of humans can do and create in the future with all the media and environments of an entire world at their disposal.

Michelangelo, who sculpted the famous *David* and many other statues, fancied that when he worked on a block of marble the statue already existed and was waiting for him to liberate it from the block in which it was encased. Yet no sculptor other than Michelangelo would have "liberated" the David we know from that block of marble. On the other hand, other sculptors could have "liberated" other masterpieces from the same block. Perhaps it would have been possible to create from the same block thousands or more of entirely different masterpieces.

The same multiplicity of possibilities within a small compass may be seen when kindergartners are given a lump of clay to work with. People who supervise children soon get used to seeing clay turned into balls and snakes, but, examined closely, each ball and snake or whatever a child molds is likely to have a bit of individuality. The hands of the great artists could turn the same lump into many entirely different works of wonder.

As humans, we add conscious choice to the influence of chance and chaos on our lives. Just as we can choose to shape clay into many very different things, we have enormous freedom to shape and reshape our lives. Our futures are not rigidly fixed but plastic: We can be Michelangelos creating something wondrous out of our futures if we can master the art of learning how to do it.

Summary

In Chapter 4, we saw how certain types of change follow fairly regular patterns, enabling us often to anticipate certain future events. In this chapter, however, we have recognized that the complex interactions of systems over time can cause events to take quite unexpected turns. Seemingly trivial details often have enormous consequences due to chance circumstances. To deal with these uncertainties, we must abandon the notion that we must have absolutely certain knowledge before we can act. Instead, we must base our actions on probabilities and highly uncertain knowledge.

We need to train ourselves to think both *realistically* and *creatively* about the future. Thinking realistically about the future means that we must simplify—even oversimplify—very complex realities so that we can bring them into our thinking, and not allow complexity to defeat us. We also need to become comfortable dealing with *potential* realities, which sometimes represent either major opportunities or risks for us. Thinking *creatively* about the future means freeing our thought processes to imagine a much wider range of possibilities than we are in the habit of doing. As we shall see, there are many ways to do this.

The next chapter will introduce four futuring methods that demonstrate the diversity of techniques that can be used as we explore the future.

6

Futuring Methods

The goal of futuring is not to predict the future but to improve it. We want to anticipate possible or likely future conditions so that we can prepare for them. We especially want to know about opportunities and risks that we should be ready for.

To help us in this endeavor we have a number of useful methods. They are not arcane or esoteric techniques like astrology or crystal-ball gazing, but rather the more ordinary procedures that most of us use occasionally in ordinary life. What has happened over the past half century is that a number of the common methods have been refined, because both government and business now face more challenges than ever from the rapid changes in our modern age, and some money has been invested in finding better ways to think about the future.

Later on we will see how some of these tools were developed by government and business researchers (Chapter 14), but in this chapter and those that follow we will focus mainly on the methods themselves and how they can be used. Many of these approaches will already be familiar, because most of us have already used some primitive version of them to a limited extent. However, we are not likely to be familiar with sophisticated versions of the techniques. Knowing what these methods are and how they can be used is very useful for thinking about the future of our organizations and of our own careers and other concerns.

In this chapter, we will introduce futuring methods by looking at four different approaches—polling, gaming, modeling and simulation, and visioning. These techniques are not as commonly used as some that we will look at in separate chapters, such as trend scanning and scenarios, but the methods discussed in this chapter will serve to show the wide range of ways in which we can think about and prepare for the future.

Each method has strengths and weaknesses, and purposes for which it is well suited, so each can make important contributions to our understanding and preparation for the risks and opportunities that the future will bring.

Consulting Experts

If we are in a quandary about what to do, we often ask other people for their views. This simple, time-honored approach has received the blessings of modern science. Experiments have shown that, yes, two heads are better than one: A group can bring more knowledge to the solution of a problem than can a lone individual. On the other hand, an individual who has relevant expertise can offer better advice than a group of people who do not. So the ideal way to make a good decision is to have it made by a group of people with relevant expertise.

Consulting a group of knowledgeable people has been popular through history and is still used at the highest levels of business and government. Yet there are problems with it. During the Cuban missile crisis of 1962, the Soviet Union and the United States were on the verge of nuclear war. The Soviet Union had started shipping nuclear missiles to Cuba, and President John F. Kennedy had ordered a blockade to keep the missiles from reaching Cuba. What would the Soviets do next, and how should the United States respond? Since both the Soviet Union and the United States had nuclear missiles ready for launching against each other, fear of an all-out nuclear war became palpable in Washington. This crisis was perhaps the most dangerous episode in the history of mankind.

To decide what to do, Kennedy summoned his key advisers to long, tense meetings in the White House. He would go around the room asking selected advisers for their views, but time was short; and despite the gravity of the situation, he never called on everyone, so some advisers never got a chance to express their views.

The crisis was resolved peacefully—the Soviets withdrew their missiles—but the incident revealed the shocking mismatch between the sophisticated technology of mass destruction and the primitive state of national decision making. At the highest level of government, decisions affecting the fate of the planet were made by a method no more advanced than that of a tribal council in prehistoric times.

Social psychologists and others have identified various problems with group decision making: It is difficult to identify and assemble appropriate experts and when they are together they interact in ways that create problems. One or two individuals may dominate the process by virtue of their talkativeness rather than their knowledge and wisdom; high-status participants may inhibit subordinates from speaking frankly; a charming manner or a clever phrase may be more persuasive than a sound judgment based on long experience.

To improve the process of getting expert judgments, two RAND Corporation scientists, Olaf Helmer and Norman Dalkey, developed a polling process that they called the Delphi method in 1953. A Delphi pollster typically gets each member of a group of experts to answer questions, keeping their answers separate and anonymous to minimize social influences.

Questions are posed in a series of rounds, and the responses are reported to participants in a carefully structured way so that nobody but the pollster knows who has said what. The result is a package of judgments that may reveal consensus on certain issues but not on others. Additional questions can further clarify the collective judgment so that a decision maker knows clearly what the experts agree on and what they don't, and why. This procedure may also identify important issues that had not previously been recognized. Developed under military auspices, the Delphi method was first used secretly to answer military questions such as, How many Soviet atomic bombs would be needed to destroy the U.S. munitions industry?

Studies have shown that the Delphi method is effective in improving and clarifying the collective judgment of experts. By using computers and telecommunications, a Delphi exercise can involve experts around the world, not just those who can be assembled in a room. On the down side, a Delphi is generally time-consuming, often expensive, and easily misused. All told, the Delphi method has stood the test of time as a useful way to get input for important decisions requiring human judgments.

Very Serious Games

Military leaders have long used war games to test tactics and equipment and to train personnel. In North Carolina, U.S. Special Forces troops at Fort Bragg play war games four times a year, enlisting local civilians to assume the roles of resistance fighters and enemy soldiers. A local librarian has played the role of a partisan fighter, smuggling coded messages in Dr. Seuss books. Meanwhile, in Louisiana, the Army's Joint Readiness Training Center at Fort Polk uses a mock town with twenty-nine buildings of cinder block and plywood, where snipers, civilians, irregulars, and terrorists can hide in simulations of Third World conditions. The mock town even includes goats and geese.

War games can also be played on an abstract level by military experts using computers. The games can be exceedingly elaborate, involving teams located at think tanks, military installations, and government agencies at great distances from each other.

Games played by RAND Corporation analysts are credited with having had a major influence on the development of U.S. military policy. For example, a series of games begun during the 1950s examined the possible role of the Air Force in a war in the Middle East, while another series of games initiated during that period dealt with the role of the military in limited wars. Together these games cast doubt on the then-prevalent doctrine of "massive retaliation," and suggested that the United States must also prepare for limited warfare.

War games are more popular than ever with the military. Colonel Sam Gardiner, a professor at the National Defense University, has fought more than twenty "wars" between India and Pakistan. The India–Pakistan mock wars began when the United States began worrying about a clash between the two nations.

"These are not fanciful intellectual exercises, but serious, two-week-long simulations used to educate American officers, choose weapons systems they will need for the future, and prepare the U.S. to respond to complex international conflicts," Gardiner said. "In the past, these 'games' have been extraordinarily good prognosticators of events. In the case of India and Pakistan, the outcome was nearly always catastrophic. And even after the carnage, the fundamental problems dividing the two nations remained unresolved."

Gardiner said the leaders of India and Pakistan would do well to play these games, which indicate that both sides would suffer huge losses. For example, a relatively primitive 20-kiloton atomic bomb dropped on New Delhi would instantly kill half of the people within a one-mile radius of the blast. Buildings would be damaged up to three miles away, and radiation would extend for hundreds of miles depending on the weather.

If decision makers can use war games to anticipate accurately what is likely to happen, they might very well refrain from many actions that would prove disastrous for themselves and countless others. It's not unreasonable to think that if Napoleon and Hitler had known from war games that they would lose their campaigns against Russia, the battles of Borodino and Stalingrad would never have occurred. War games—along with Herman Kahn's scenarios of thermonuclear conflicts—probably did play a substantial role in preventing nuclear war between the United States and the Soviet Union by helping both sides to see more clearly the frightening likely cost of a real nuclear war.

Top civilian leaders now join military personnel in U.S. national security war games. "The secretary of state plays, the joint chiefs play, the director of the Central Intelligence Agency plays, only the president does not," reports Michael Schrage in his book *Serious Play* (1999). "The U.S. national-security establishment has decreed that no one should know how the president might react to speculative scenarios. Presidential advisers in real national-security emergencies should not be influenced by prior knowledge of how the president responded to a simulated crisis. Nor should the potential enemies of the United States."

Games can also be used to simulate international political affairs, because the military planners must be alert to circumstances in which political leaders may require military support. In some games, players assume the roles of individual leaders (e.g., the president of France or the secretary-general of the United Nations) or of entities such as Russia or NATO.

Gaming can also be used to simulate the functioning of a business or a city. For a business, one player might take the part of a key supplier, while another plays the CEO and still another the CEO of a rival company. For a city simulation, players might assume the roles of the mayor, city council, taxpayers, labor unions, etc. (A group or class can be represented by a single player in a game.) Once the group is constituted, the game master can give the players a problem to solve, such as how to dispose of the city's garbage when the local landfill is closed. The players try to respond to the problem in the way they believe their role model would respond.

The reactions of the role-players to the problem—and the interactions of players during the game—can help policy makers understand whether various proposed solutions to a problem will be acceptable to the community.

Models and Simulations

A model is something that we use to represent something else; a simulation is an action that represents some other action. Children use models of airplanes, ships, rockets, animals, and people (dolls) to simulate the flight of aircraft, the driving of automobiles, and the care of babies. Architects use models of buildings to help people visualize a future structure and make informed comments. Clothing stores use models (mannequins) to show how suits and dresses will look when worn.

A very different type of model, the mental model, consists of the various images and perceptions that we have in our minds about something. We may have a mental model of a city or a horse or a criminal. Mental models tend to be vague and ill-formed, but they are essential in our thinking. When we think, we are playing with our mental models—examining and testing them, putting them together in new ways, etc. In this process, we sort through our memories for information and ideas that we can use in solving our current problems. We normally use this method to develop mental models of what we want to achieve in the future and to test the means we have for reaching the goals we set for ourselves.

Sometimes we try to impose discipline on our mental simulations by trying to force a rapid solution to a current problem; at other times, we let our thoughts go where they will, and often this free fantasizing produces remarkable results. Patrick Brown, a Stanford University professor who loves to fantasize, was engaging in this activity a few years ago when he got the idea of embedding thousands of genes in a tiny glass wafer. The result was the gene chip, one of the hottest tools in biotechnology. Fantasizing plays a major role in new scientific breakthroughs, inventions, and scenario development, because it permits what Einstein called "thought experiments," imagining what would happen under a chosen set of circumstances.

Computer modeling has been used to study industrial processes, cities, and many other things. World models got much attention in the 1970s when MIT professor Jay W. Forrester and his colleagues developed a world model that dealt with such global variables as population, pollution, economic growth, and natural resources. The model indicated that the growth of the world's population and economy would bring about a global catastrophe in the twenty-first century due to environmental destruction. The pioneering MIT world modeling, publicized in a controversial book, *The Limits to Growth,* led other researchers to develop world models that produced less pessimistic results. The study highlighted the fact that computers may produce precise but not necessarily accurate results, and success in modeling is critically dependent on the construction of the model and the data that are used.

A computer model of a modern economy might consist of hundreds of equations showing how different variables affect each other. Once the model is set up in the computer, it is possible to ask such questions as, "What would happen if the real estate tax were raised 10 percent or the sales tax abolished?" If the model is properly designed and operated, it can allow decision makers to anticipate the effects of a decision before it is actually implemented.

A special virtue of computers is the speed with which they can process vast amounts of data. Speed is critical in weather forecasting because conditions change rapidly and forecasts must be constantly updated. In February 2003, the National Weather Service predicted a heavy snowstorm for the Washington, D.C., area with a snowfall of twenty to thirty inches. The forecast gave residents adequate time to prepare for heavy snow, which turned out to be one of the heaviest in Washington's history.

Speed of forecasting can be a matter of life or death in the case of disease epidemics. So public health officials are now using mathematical models of epidemics to forecast what may happen as an infectious disease spreads. Health officials need to know what symptoms are serious enough to warrant having a person taken to a hospital or placed under mandatory quarantine.

Fortunately, computers and telecommunications now make it possible for the international community to collect and analyze data quickly and send it instantaneously to people and organizations that need to respond to emergencies.

Computer models can help us to anticipate how very complex systems may respond. Often their responses are quite different from what we expect intuitively. Here are examples of how a system can behave in frustrating ways if we are not careful:

- To cure a patient, the physician administers a new drug, but the drug fails to do what it is supposed to do or actually causes the patient to get worse.
- To reduce congestion on a highway, government officials decide to widen it. However, congestion actually worsens because more cars are attracted to the road, and new businesses are established to benefit from the increased traffic.
- To relieve poverty in cities, governments build subsidized housing projects and make them available at low rent to poor people. The effect is to concentrate poor people in areas where there are few business enterprises or wealthy people to provide jobs. So the poor may find themselves trapped: They cannot afford to move closer to the jobs, nor can they travel every day the long distances to where they can find work.

Ideally, computer simulations will enable planners to anticipate such feedback problems before people have to suffer the real-world consequences of a misguided decision.

Visioning

Robert Jungk a German-born writer, futurist, and social inventor, spent his life protesting what he saw as great social wrongs. As a young man in Germany in the 1930s, he wrote newspaper articles trying to rally opposition to Nazi party leader Adolf Hitler. After Germany was defeated in World War II, Jungk found something new he considered a terrible evil—atomic bombs. He went around the world protesting nuclear weapons.

Then something happened that changed his thinking completely. While in Japan in 1960, he interviewed a man dying of leukemia as a result of the atomic bomb dropped on Hiroshima. The man said, sadly, "Now you protest against the bomb, but it's too late. You always begin too late."

Jungk suddenly realized that he had spent his life protesting against things that had already happened, such as the Nazi takeover in Germany and the development of nuclear weapons. These things had happened because people failed to stop them earlier. So Jungk thought to himself, "We must do something to prevent the crises of tomorrow so that we can avoid disasters. We must mobilize people ahead of time."

The key to preventing future disasters, Jungk decided, was changing people's ideas about the future. These ideas should not come from a charismatic leader like Hitler but from the people themselves. So Jungk developed a democratic process whereby groups of people would create their own vision of the future.

Starting in 1962, Jungk organized and conducted "future workshops," in which he encouraged people to review and revise their ideas about the future and then try to create a vision of what they wanted the future to be like.

As Jungk described it, "The workshop itself begins with the critique phase, during which all the grievances and negative experiences related to the chosen topic are brought into the open. There then follows the fantasy phase, in which the participants come up with ideas in response to the problems, and with their desires, fantasies and alternative views. A selection is made of the most interesting notions and small working groups develop them into solutions and outline projects. The workshop concludes with the implementation phase, coming back down into the present with its power structures and constraints. It is at this stage that participants critically assess the chances of getting their projects implemented, identifying the obstacles, and imaginatively seeking ways round them so as to draw up a plan of action."

While Jungk was organizing future workshops in Europe, Edward Lindaman in America was working for Rockwell Corporation as a director of program planning for the Apollo Spacecraft Project, which the U.S. government launched to fulfill President Kennedy's 1962 vision of putting a man on the moon by 1969. Lindaman saw how Kennedy's awe-inspiring vision mobilized people so powerfully that they achieved an historic "miracle"—a feat so remarkable that the world was agog with the sheer wonder of it. This experience caused Lindaman to become committed to what he called "thinking in the future tense."

After retiring from NASA, he became president of Whitworth College in Spokane, Washington, where he began to organize meetings that involved ordinary citizens in creating visions of desirable futures for their communities. If we can put a man on the moon, Lindaman argued, why can't we envision and build an ideal community?

Lindaman introduced his future-oriented thinking to Ronald Lippitt, a behavioral scientist interested in group dynamics and organizational development. Together, Lindaman and Lippitt created a new method called Preferred Futuring, which has since been used by tens of thousands of organizations and groups.

A Preferred Futuring program can take a variety of forms, but the participants generally have these eight tasks:

1. Review the organization's common history to create a shared appreciation.
2. Identify what's working and what's not. Brainstorm and list "prouds" and "sorries."
3. Identify underlying values and beliefs, and discuss which ones to keep and which to abandon.
4. Identify relevant events, developments, and trends that may have an impact on moving to a preferred future.
5. Create a preferred future vision that is clear, detailed, and commonly understood. All participants, or at least a critical mass, should feel a sense of investment or ownership in the vision.
6. Translate future visions into action goals.
7. Plan for action: Build in specific planned steps with accountabilities identified.
8. Create a structure for implementing the plan, with midcourse corrections, celebrations, and publicizing of successes.

Today, there are hundreds of futurists and other consultants who facilitate "visioning" programs for companies, communities, and other groups. These programs differ widely in the terms they use and in procedural details, but the general approach tends to be much the same. Clement Bezold, president of the Institute for Alternative Futures in Alexandria, Virginia, with many years of visioning experience, outlines five stages in building a vision: (1) identification of problems, (2) identification of past successes, (3) identification of desires for the future, (4) identification of measurable goals, and (5) identification of resources to achieve those goals.

Bezold says that a scenario addresses the head, but a vision addresses the heart.

"A vision is a compelling statement of the preferred future that an organization or community wants to create. Visions move and inspire us by stating why we are working together, what higher contribution flows from our efforts, and what we are striving to become. Vision development is the most powerful way to clarify where you would like change to go."

The continuing popularity of visioning suggests that it has genuine value as a technique for generating ideas, encouraging interaction in a group, and focusing the group on a common set of goals. "There is no more powerful engine driving an organization toward excellence and long-range success than an attractive, worthwhile, and achievable vision of the future, widely shared," says Burt Nanus, author of *Visionary Leadership* (1992).

But a few caveats must be added. One warning comes from Peter Senge, senior lecturer and chair of the nonprofit Society for Organizational Learning at MIT's Sloan School of Management. Senge says that, for a vision to effect positive change in an organization, two conditions must be met. First, the vision must be *shared:* The members of the organization must be committed to it, because they need to stretch themselves to make it happen. Second, the group's members must believe that they *can* make it happen. The people in the organization must really believe that they can shape their future and commit themselves to doing it.

A shared vision, Senge explains, is "a force in people's hearts, a force of impressive power. It may be inspired by an idea, but once it goes further—if it is compelling enough to acquire the support of more than one person—then it is no longer an abstraction. It is palpable. People begin to see it as if it exists. Few, if any, forces are as powerful as a shared vision."

Visioning has become widely popular among business managers, and it does seem to work despite some skepticism about it. The Center for the Study of American Business at Washington University in St. Louis included visioning in a critical assessment of techniques recently popular in business, and judged it "a useful tool" for empowering employees and motivating the organization. However, the authors of the study cautioned that "moving from vision to *work* is the real trick."

Easy Ways to Use the Methods

We can apply simple versions of these methods, without getting special training, in a variety of situations. Here are a few examples of what can be done.

Polling one's associates for their opinions is something most of us do already, because we recognize that other people have knowledge and ideas that we do not possess ourselves. However, it is helpful to know about the Delphi technique and why it was developed, so we can be aware of the problems that occur in group meetings. We also are forewarned about the risks of getting people's views only in a group situation. On the other hand, as we shall see later in discussing brainstorming, there can be real value in using a group at times.

The bottom line is that if you are serious about your career or your business, it can be useful to get other people's views while bearing in mind that knowledgeable people are more likely to offer useful advice than those lacking the background for judging the issue. Furthermore, people may speak more freely when they are outside a group situation, and people who are quiet in a group may have much wiser counsels than those who dominate it.

Gaming normally requires two or more people and generally they are competing in some way to win some kind of reward, though possibly just the joy of victory. Gaming produces the excitement of a competition so it can be useful in getting people emotionally involved in thinking about problems and how to solve them. Attorneys in a law firm can stage mock trials that can reveal how a judge or an opposing attorney may behave at the actual trial. A teacher can use gaming to stimulate students to think about community problems and how they might be solved. At Pace University in New York City, Professor Chris Malone teaches politics by means of a three-day mock Democratic Convention. An employer might use gaming to get workers more excited about winning against the competition. A group of students can use gaming to try to anticipate and practice for future situations they will face (getting a new job, dealing with an unpleasant employer, etc.).

Computer programs now are available so that we can simulate alternative ways for doing things, such as preparing a household budget or figuring out how we can best save money on our taxes. Many electronic games such as SimCity have become widely popular and may help many young people to think about the complexities of human interactions.

We can often use a model when we are dealing with physical objects. We might, for instance, create a model of our home and models of furniture that we have or are thinking of buying. Again, computer programs are available to help with this kind of project.

We can apply visioning within our homes and at our workplace to get people thinking how they might do better in the future. With a little thought and imagination, we may be able to follow the steps listed for Preferred Futuring in the Visioning section of this chapter.

Our emphasis on do-it-yourself futuring does not mean, of course, that we cannot get great benefit from having a professional futurist to help us with this process. Professionals definitely can help and should be used when a situation warrants. However, we all should recognize that we could do a lot of futuring by ourselves, and probably with great benefit to our personal goals.

Now let's move on to scanning and trend analysis, perhaps the most popular of all ways to begin thinking about the future in a serious way.

(For an overview of futuring methods refer to pages 78-79.)

An Overview of Futuring Methods

Here are a few of the most common techniques for anticipating, forecasting, and assessing future events. These methods are rational, empirical, and scientific. They are mostly refinements of the common-sense techniques that people use in everyday life. But they are completely different in character from arcane, other-worldly, supernatural practices such as crystal-ball gazing and astrology.

Scanning: An ongoing effort to identify significant changes in the world beyond the organization or group doing the scanning. Typically, scanning is based on a systematic survey of current newspapers, magazines, Web sites, and other media for indications of changes likely to have future importance. Scanning focuses mainly on *trends*—changes that occur through time—rather than *events*, changes that occur very quickly and *generally* are less significant for understanding the future. (Chapter 7)

Trend Analysis: The examination of a trend to identify its nature, causes, speed of development, and potential impacts. Careful analysis may be needed because a trend can have many different impacts on different aspects of human life, and many of these may not be apparent at first. Longer life spans, for example, increase the number of people for whom resources must be provided but also increase the number of people who can contribute to the economy and society through paid and unpaid labor. (Chapter 7)

Trend Monitoring: Trends viewed as particularly important may be carefully monitored—watched and reported regularly to key decision makers. For example, a rapidly rising unemployment rate or the appearance of a deadly new disease may have significant impacts on many different organizations and communities. (Chapter 7)

Trend Projection: When numerical data are available, a trend can be plotted on graph paper to show changes through time. If desired, the trend line can then be extended or "projected" into the future on the basis of the recent rate of change. Such a projection shows where the trend should be at some point in the future *assuming there is no shift in the rate of change*. Example: A population with a steady 2 percent rate of annual growth will double in about thirty-five years. (Chapter 7)

Scenarios: The future development of a trend, a strategy, or a wild-card event may be described in story or outline form. Typically, several scenarios will be developed so that decision makers are aware that future events may invalidate whatever scenario they use for planning purposes. (Chapters 8 and 9)

Polling: Collecting people's views on the future and other topics. Data may be collected through face-to-face conversation, telephone interviews, and questionnaires sent by electronic or ordinary mail. Delphi polling, popular among futurists, uses a carefully structured procedure to generate more-accurate forecasts. (Chapter 6)

Brainstorming: The generation of new ideas by means of a small group assembled to think creatively about a topic. Group members are encouraged to build on each other's ideas and withhold criticism. Brainstorming is useful in identifying possibilities, opportunities, and risks. Other idea-generating or problem-solving methods are also common, such as idea mapping, impact analysis, and the systematic identification of all possible variables. (Chapter 10)

Modeling: The use of one thing (the model) in place of something else that is more difficult or impossible to experiment with. In addition to real-world models, such as miniature airplanes and houses, a set of mathematical equations can be used to represent a complex system. The model can then be put into a computer and used to simulate the behavior of the system under a variety of conditions. For example, a model of the U.S. economy might show the possible effects of a 10 percent increase in taxes. (Chapter 6)

Gaming: The simulation of a real-world situation by means of humans playing different roles. In war games, real soldiers may become actors in a mock battle, which helps them to understand what actual combat is like and helps generals to test out alternative strategies and tactics they may later use. (Chapter 6)

Historical Analysis: The use of historical events to anticipate the outcome of current developments. Often a current situation can be compared to one or more situations in history that seem to be similar. The U.S. invasion of Iraq in 2003 was compared by some commentators to the Vietnam War, with the implication that the Iraq War would also prove disastrous. (Chapter 11)

Visioning: The systematic creation of visions of a desirable future for an organization or an individual. Typically, this procedure starts with a review of past events and the current situation, moves on to envision desirable futures, and concludes with the identification of specific ways to move toward the desired future. A visioning procedure often prepares the way for more-formal goal setting and planning. (Chapter 6)

7

Knowing the World Around Us

If we could first know where we are and whither we are tending, we could better judge what to do and how to do it.
—Abraham Lincoln

To think seriously about the future, we must first find out what is happening *now* that has lasting importance. This is not easy if we depend on television and newspapers to keep us informed, because the media see their job more as entertainment than as enlightenment.

The media focus on current *events* that provide vivid drama or other interest, but most really important changes are *trends*, long-term shifts that may affect us in innumerable ways—even if we are totally unaware of them. Compared with some trends, such as the supertrends discussed earlier, even a major war may be relatively unimportant.

Trends provide a path for us to follow from the present world into the future world, because they indicate conditions that we will probably have to deal with in the years ahead. This information gives us our starting point for exploring our future in a realistic manner.

One Baby vs. 100 Million

A baby's birth is a joyous event to be celebrated by the family, but a hundred million births is just a statistic. At least, that's the way most people think. Yet we all must recognize that a hundred million births will have far more impact on the world than a single baby.

With so many babies being produced, and fewer people dying, the world's population is swelling. This growth in population has enormous consequences. Consider what might happen if our local community suddenly acquired an additional million people. Where would they sleep? Where would they find food? Obviously, the community would become radically different from what it is now. If it happened overnight, there would probably be masses of people everywhere you looked.

A baby is an important consumer even before birth because the mother will be buying extra food and perhaps visiting an obstetrician. Relatives and friends may start buying gifts, and the parents may buy or rent extra furniture and other equipment. These purchases, in turn, lead to further consequences, such as the manufacturers increasing production and hiring more workers. So the total number of births is an important statistic that many businesses and governments monitor closely.

A company making baby formula can readily see the connection between the birthrate and possible sales of baby formula over the next few years. If births are going up, it may be time to buy stock in a company making baby formula or nursery toys. Babies also can have a political impact long before they vote, at least in the United States, where the Constitution apportions seats in the House of Representatives according to a state's population. (A new baby adds immediately to the population.)

Scanning the World Around Us

The process of identifying significant changes in the external environment—that is, in the world beyond our immediate area of operations—is now generally known as scanning. It can be thought of as the effort to identify and understand those phenomena or aspects of the world that are most relevant to the people or groups who need this information for important decisions.

A business scanner systematically reads magazines, newspapers, government reports, and other publications and monitors selected Web sites, searching for relevant information using key words. The techniques for collecting, reviewing, and analyzing current literature were originally developed by military intelligence officers, who would scan publications for clues to what was happening in enemy countries. The resulting analyses would then be submitted to military chiefs, who could use them in planning strategies. The so-called "scan, clip, and review" approach was used extensively during World War II and continues to be used in business and government.

In the 1970s, the Institute of Life Insurance in New York developed a Trend Analysis Program to alert insurance people to developments outside their industry that might be relevant to their business. The program used volunteers to scan publications for items that indicated a possibly significant change. Two criteria were used in selecting items:

- The item treats an idea or event that is indicative of a trend or a departure from a previous trend.
- The implications to be drawn from the item have some relation to the long-range concerns of society and to the life insurance business.

The program's staff analyzed the material provided by the volunteers and published reports for the life insurance industry. This scanning group explicitly recognized that changes develop over time and that it is important to recognize them at an early stage to ensure adequate lead time for responding to emerging risks and opportunities. When the insurance institute moved away from New York, the leaders of its scanning operation formed an independent consulting firm, Weiner, Edrich, Brown, Inc., which now provides scanning services for many clients. The president of the group, Edie Weiner, and the chairman, Arnold Brown, say that constant scanning updates our knowledge of the world and acts as a radar system for business and government.

"An environmental scanner looks primarily for developments or trends that are likely to have major impacts on human life, particularly in areas likely to be important to the scanner's organization," they write in their book *Supermanaging*. "Generally speaking, these developments do not consist of a single isolated event but are elements in a major trend—such as the rapid improvement in global communications—that causes many changes as it proceeds."

Weiner and Brown recognize the importance of *ideas* in initiating change. "Ideas give birth to change in society and therefore it [is] necessary to determine as a first step where influential ideas arise and how they circulate through society to ultimate emergence as change factors," explained Edie Weiner. A system is needed to "spot, identify, evaluate, and track ideas that might shape our future world."

Classifying Trends

Classifying trends enables us to think about them more systematically and use them more effectively, so researchers have developed various ways to classify them.

A system developed by Philip Kotler, a professor of marketing at Northwestern University, has become widely used in business thanks to his popular textbook *Marketing Management* (now in its eleventh edition).

Kotler decided that the trends significant to business today could be most naturally classified into six broad categories: Demography, Economy, Government, Environment (the natural environment), Society/culture, and Technology. The first letter of each category forms the acronym DEGEST, by which it can be easily remembered. This system is also used by the World Future Society, whose magazine, *The Futurist*, publishes in each issue a selection of current trends arranged according to this system. (Other systems in current use are likely to omit Environment or Demography as a separate category, but the editors felt both merit category status.)

This simple classification scheme provides us with a surprisingly powerful tool for improving our understanding of the world around us. Without such a system, we face a chaotic assemblage of trends, and it is much harder to see how they fit together. With the DEGEST system, we can think sequentially about demographic trends, then economic trends, then governmental trends, and so on. In doing so, we may find it makes sense to combine a number of trends into a single major trend that includes them all. After that, we may be ready for the more difficult task of making connections across the categories. For example, how might the number of baby births affect communications technologies? Here is why each of the six DEGEST categories is important:

- *Demography:* The world's population has soared past 6 billion people—the highest number that ever lived simultaneously on our planet. Yet each person is an individual with a unique set of abilities, needs, and aspirations. Knowing about people's changing characteristics—residence, age, sex, health, education, language, etc.—has become increasingly important in our globalizing multicultural world.

- *Economy:* The economy provides jobs, income, and products essential to our lives. But the world's economies are changing furiously: This means there will be many more opportunities for new businesses and new jobs—but also big challenges for individuals and communities.

- *Government:* Laws and regulations change constantly, affecting all aspects of our lives. Governments levy taxes, make war, enforce laws, administer schools, and administer the social-security system. The government is the biggest employer in most nations.

- *Environment:* Our physical environment consists of what nature provides, plus the buildings, roads, and other things added by humans. The environment provides the air we breathe, the water we drink, and the food we eat. Traditionally we thought of the environment as largely unchanging; now we know it is changing, and we need to pay attention.
- *Society:* Education, science, religion, the media, arts, sports, amusements, and other social or cultural activities absorb much of our waking moments, fill our thoughts, and shape our knowledge and values. Trends in this area not only shape our private lives, but also have major impacts on the economy, government, and other sectors.
- *Technology.* New technology is revolutionizing human life everywhere. To stay current, we need a general understanding of what's happening in computers, telecommunications, biotechnology, the Internet, etc. New technologies raise living standards and save lives, but they also pose a wide variety of disturbing problems, which we ignore at our peril (new weaponry, privacy challenges, etc.).

Many trends and developments could be classified in two or more categories, so choosing a particular category is sometimes difficult. If desired, a list of trends in a given category can include cross-references to selected trends in other categories.

For particular purposes, a trend analyst is, of course, free to add new categories or modify the DEGEST system as desired. However, there is considerable advantage to having a single set of categories that is normally used, because people can learn to use it effectively. Constantly shifting categories add more confusion to the already difficult process of analyzing trends.

Many organizations now engage in the search for trends and other developments that might be important. Scanning does not necessarily require a large staff and budget. Useful scanning can be done quite simply and inexpensively, and a modest project can be quite enlightening.

SELECTED U.S. TRENDS: 1900-2000

This chart shows the six standard DEGEST categories, with sample trends.

Demography. Increase of women in workforce: In 1900, few married women worked outside their homes. Men worked as long as they were physically able. Social security did not exist. By 2000, the majority of married women worked outside the home, and millions of physically fit adults were retired.

Economy. Growing wealth: In 1900, the U.S. economy was only a fraction of its present size; the average person was dirt poor, at least by today's standards. People spent most of their money to buy poor-quality food that most people wouldn't eat today. In 2000, the U.S. economy was producing more goods and services than ever before in history, and Americans were enjoying a standard of living beyond the dreams of people a century earlier.

Government. Growing government regulation of business: In 1900, U.S. business leaders did pretty much whatever they liked with little interference from federal and state governments; by the year 2000, businesses faced a thicket of government regulations. To cope with regulations as well as lawsuits, businesses now must hire phalanxes of lawyers and lobbyists.

Environment. Antipollution efforts have been producing significant results in areas. In 1900, U.S. industries and communities freely used rivers as sewers for their sewage and other waste products; factories belched so much smoke into the air that cities were wrapped in smog. By 2000, thanks to tight environmental regulations, Pittsburgh and other cities had emerged from smog, and factory owners were taking enormous precautions not to pollute waterways. However, these victories must be viewed in the context of deterioration in other aspects of the U.S. environment.

Society/Culture. Rising divorce, fewer children: In 1900, most people remained married for life; divorce was rare and scandalous when it occurred. Homes were generally crowded, since people had more children and more relatives but were less able to afford housing. In 2000, fewer adults were married and those who were had fewer children. People now have more living space in their homes than ever. Singles are buying about as many houses as married couples. More people now live alone.

Technology. Increasing technological knowledge: In 1900, people were impressed with some recent innovations such as electric lights and automobiles, but, for most Americans, it was still the age of the horse and buggy, oil or gas lamp, icebox, and chamber pot. By 2000, a flood of innovations had completely altered how people live and work—radios, televisions, airplanes, computers, etc. New technology was arriving at an ever-faster rate, radically restructuring almost every occupation and activity.

Trend Extrapolation

If statistics are available for a trend, it is generally possible to graph them to show how the trend has evolved over time, and the trend line can be projected into the future according to its current direction and speed. This technique, called extrapolation, allows us to anticipate a future condition. But that does not necessarily mean that our anticipation will prove on target; quite likely, it will be off to some degree, and it may be off enormously. The farther out in time we try to project the trend, the more likely it is that our anticipation will prove very wide of the mark.

By extrapolating trends, it is possible to make forecasts for a wide variety of things, such as the future population of nations or the likelihood of war between certain nations. A forecast for possible war might be based on an extrapolation of rising hostility between two nations, with the degree of hostility being gauged by means of various indicators, such as newspaper editorials critical of the other nation or the recall of ambassadors.

There are mathematical formulas for projecting a trend line, and a variety of curves can be plotted on the basis of different assumptions about how the trend may develop. Trend extrapolation often assumes that the same change will continue according to the past pattern of change. For instance, if the population of a city is known to be increasing at the rate of 2 percent a year, we may assume that it will continue to do so in the future, and we can use this to calculate what the population should be in five years.

Current trends offer an excellent way to begin exploring the future of almost anything. To think about the future of our community, for example, we might begin by getting information about how the community's population is changing. If our town seems likely to have about 15 percent more people in five years, we can begin to ask what some of the consequences would be. Assuming the perimeter of the community remains the same, we begin to envision more automobile traffic, bigger buildings, less green space, more businesses and cultural activities, more pollution, more crime, and so on. These visions would not necessarily be realized, but they give us a conceptual structure within which we can think about the future of our community in realistic terms. We can also start asking ourselves questions about what we want for our community and what we must do to get it. Too often, people talk about what to do and how to do it before they understand the situation they are in and how it is shifting.

Trend extrapolation is most useful over the short term, and even then it must be used cautiously. At some point, an upward or downward trend in some indicator will slow, halt, or later reverse because of various constraints. An extrapolation of the recent growth in the number of lawyers in the United States might suggest that the country would soon have more lawyers than people! That seems unlikely, and we may want to consider what could happen instead.

Sometimes just when we expect growth to slow—or even when it has actually started to slow—it suddenly picks up again. Such situations have occurred in the history of technology, and when we consider the nature of technological development, we can understand why. In most technologies, many technical approaches are tried. Each approach encounters limitations, but just when the technology itself might seem to be encountering an insurmountable obstacle, something new arrives to keep the technology improving.

Joseph P. Martino, author of *Technological Forecasting for Decision Making,* offers this example:

The top speed of aircraft increased quite steadily during the twentieth century despite the fact that aircraft engineers kept encountering factors that seemed to make higher speed impossible. Almost as soon as a barrier was identified, a way around it was found, and airplanes continued to get faster. Fabric-and-wood airplanes gave way to all-metal craft; the open cockpit gave way to the enclosed cockpit; and reciprocating engines gave way to jets.

A similar pattern applies to a number of trends in computers. For instance, the minimum size of a computer has steadily declined since the 1940s, when a computer consisted of a whole roomful of gear. Then came smaller mainframe computers, minicomputers, laptops, notebooks, and PDAs (personal digital assistants). Now there is talk of nanocomputers. Each round of miniaturization in computers has followed the development of new electronics technologies to replace vacuum tubes, first with transistors and then with ever smaller varieties of integrated circuit.

Causes and Impacts

The identification of a trend puts us on notice that it exists, but we also want to know the causes and impacts of a trend. In *causal analysis,* we seek to identify the forces that are creating and shaping the trend. Often, these forces are themselves trends, so we may have to probe further to identify the causes of the contributory trends. This analysis is especially important if we want to slow or halt the trends.

India is an overpopulated nation in the view of most observers, yet the population continues to grow at a rapid rate, frustrating the efforts of the government to raise living standards, particularly those of its poorest people. The Indian population's growth results from a great excess of births over deaths. The birthrate was always high, but a high death rate once served to check population growth. Indians now are living longer, and the birthrate has not declined enough to prevent population from surging.

The problem might theoretically be eased by raising the death rate, but that solution would be unacceptable. We can look for alternatives by studying the various factors that support the high birthrate. How could those factors be influenced? The Indian government has made some efforts to reduce the birthrate, but clearly they have been insufficient up to the present. Further study might identify more effective ways to solve the problem.

Impact analysis aims at identifying the effects that the trend is having on other things. All too often, important consequences escape notice. A trend can have many surprising consequences, and these can often be hard to anticipate; trend analysts learn to identify more of these consequences than an untrained person.

An impact analysis might begin with, say, a Census Bureau report that the number of U.S. women remaining single at age forty is reaching new highs. This demographic change might offer growing opportunities for companies with products that might interest single women in their forties and fifties; at the same time, products designed for married women over forty might suffer. Using our imaginations, we might think of many other possible consequences of this trend.

Here is an example of a simple trend analysis, which identifies both causes and impacts:

Trend: **Life expectancy is rising.**

Causes:

- Rising living standards—more abundant food, shelter, clothing, etc. Better sanitation and other health measures. More effective responses to illnesses.
- Women are bearing fewer babies, thereby reducing the number of young people in the population and permitting each baby to enjoy more food, better medical treatment, etc.
- Social security and other programs ensure basic support for the elderly.
- A steady flow of new medical knowledge produces more effective drugs.
- Governments protect people against physical abuse or injury due to workplace dangers and poisonous air.

Consequences:

- People will spend more of their lives in retirement.
- A higher percentage of the population will suffer from disabilities and will need personal or technological assistance.
- With a growing percentage of adults older, retired, and disabled, there will be a greater burden on younger people to pay the cost of supporting them.
- Growing need for housing, consumer goods, services, etc., to meet the needs of the elderly.
- Social security and other programs to assist elderly and disabled people may become strained. At the same time, the elderly will be a growing political force agitating for their interests.
- Families will have more elderly to care for. Parents' attention and resources may be diverted from children to elderly.
- Declining percentage of children in the population.

How Might a Trend Affect Us?

A knowledge of current trends and their possible implications can be highly relevant to the practical decisions we make. Let's take the trend of increasing longevity among most of the world's countries and see how it might relate to specific sorts of people. We can begin by stating the trend as follows: People in our nation (like those in most nations) are living longer. As a result, the percentage of elderly people in the population is increasing rapidly.

Here is how different sorts of people might relate the growth of the elderly population to their personal concerns:

A *college student* thinking of his or her future career might begin to think about the growth of jobs in services for the elderly. The elderly will need more medical attention, so that means more jobs for doctors, nurses, administrators, physical therapists, etc. The elderly also have more time to travel, and they are often free to live wherever they choose. Most of them are in good physical shape and enjoy sports and other recreational activities. What might I do to help them in some way?

A *government official* thinking about serving the public may see the need to intensify efforts to make government and business workplaces more accommodating to elderly people so they can rejoin the workforce and help in areas where workers are in short supply. With good planning, the elderly might be able to take on more tasks in hospitals, education, and elsewhere. They could provide important help for the community and also, perhaps, earn money to meet their needs.

An *investor* might note the increase in elderly and combine that trend with another—the rapid improvement of medical technologies. With more exciting products and more potential customers, there should be a strong demand for medical technologies useful to the elderly. Thinking along these lines, the investor might be led to invest in corporations manufacturing such technologies.

Trend information can be extremely valuable in making wise decisions, but it should never be the *only* consideration. Career choice for a student also depends on the student's abilities and interests. Investors must beware that other investors may have also noted the elderly trend and bid up the prices of stocks expected to benefit.

The value of understanding trends is increasingly recognized in business because executives know that a firm that fails to adapt to current trends is soon left behind. Knowledge of significant world, national, and regional trends provides an invaluable background for making practical judgments about one's goals and strategies. Not knowing the trends means keeping one's head buried in the sand and facing the possibility of having a business, career, or investment crushed by a wave of unrecognized change. By using trends, individuals and organizations can hope to ride the waves of change toward their goals.

A "Surprise-Free" Future

If we project a number of trends into the future, we create what futurists call a "surprise-free future"—a summary of what conditions may be like at some future date. By creating a surprise-free future, we take a serious, albeit modest, step toward determining "whither we are tending."

Here are some points that might be covered in a surprise-free future prepared for the United States ten years from today:

- *Economy:* Estimates of the U.S. gross domestic product (GDP) can be generated based on the current GDP and its rate of growth. We can also develop projections for different sectors of the GDP, such as computers and peripherals, banking and financial institutions, etc.
- *Technology:* Estimates for the future capabilities of computers, telecommunications, drugs and medical treatment, transportation equipment, etc.
- *Government:* Estimates can be made for the future size of the various levels of government based on current growth.
- *Demography:* Projections for the overall population can be made on the basis of the current rate of population growth. This general forecast could be broken down to include projections for specific categories—age, sex, race, education level, religion, marital status, health or disability, etc.
- *Environment:* Future air and water pollution, areas in wilderness, cropland, size of metropolitan regions, etc., can be projected based on statistics generally available from government agencies.

Historical data for many U.S. trends may be found in the yearly editions of the *Statistical Abstract of the United States,* prepared by the U.S. Department of Commerce and distributed by the Government Printing Office. Despite its enlightening data and other virtues, however, it illustrates a few of the problems encountered in working with trends. For example, there are frequently no data on the trend one is seeking, despite the fact that the volume contains more than a thousand compactly printed pages.

Besides giving us a rough idea of what our future *might* be like, a surprise-free future offers a basis for creating numerous alternative scenarios, because each of the indicators can easily be shifted up or down from the surprise-free point. Instead of anticipating that our company's revenues two years hence will be 20 percent higher, we might project that they will be only 10 percent higher, or that they will be 10 percent lower. We can also use scenarios to deal with almost any type of surprise event that occurs, such as a fire that destroys our home office.

With scenarios, we can explore many probing questions: What might cause this trend to shift direction? If a shift occurs, what might be the consequences? We may also want to pose value questions, such as, Are we happy with where we seem likely to be two years from now? If not, how can we change that outcome? Trend scanning and analysis also is an important way for us to anticipate possible surprise events—which we deliberately excluded from our surprise-free scenario. For instance, if we started with the longevity trend, we might ask, What may happen if a treatment for the aging process (senescence) is discovered? What would that do to social security or politics or whatever?

The scenario technique opens up so many exciting possibilities that we will devote our next chapter to examining this method and what it offers. Like trends, scenarios enable us to "better judge what to do and how to do it," but they do it in a different way. Trends enable us to get a glimpse of where we seem to be going. We can think of it as a beachhead in the future. Scenarios allow us to fan out beyond our beachhead and explore many new possibilities.

8

Using Scenarios

Understanding what's happening in the world today by means of current trends gets us to the threshold of the future but does not quite get us over it. For that purpose we must use scenarios—conjectures about what *might* happen in the future.

One way to develop a scenario is simply to project a current trend into the future, but that gives us only one kind of scenario. Developing others is important because most if not all trends eventually change direction and speed as time passes. Furthermore, the accelerating changes in today's world make it ever more likely that any given trend will not proceed as we might anticipate. So we need to use our imagination and special idea-generating techniques to develop concepts for what might happen to make the future different from what the current trend suggests.

In this chapter, we will look at selected ways to develop and use different types of scenarios. But before we begin to explore the development of the modern scenario method, let's recognize that humans have probably always had the ability to develop and use scenarios *intuitively*.

Prehistoric humans could not match the teeth and claws of Africa's lions, nor could they outrun the gazelles, but they evolved the ability to think creatively about ways to kill a gazelle for food and defend themselves against marauding lions. Using effective strategies for these purposes permitted human survival, so we have inherited a natural ability to think creatively using simple scenarios. But now our problems are far more complex than in the past, so scenarios for business and government may be quite complex and created through group efforts.

The Development of the Scenario Method

The current recognition of scenarios by top-level decision makers may be traced to physicist-turned-futurist Herman Kahn and his colleagues at the RAND Corporation in Santa Monica, California, who worked for the U.S. military in the 1950s. Kahn and his RAND colleagues became writers of very,

very serious fiction, because their fiction would be used by U.S. military planners thinking about the most terrible weapons ever devised. The military was responsible for being ready for every contingency, so the planners demanded to know things like: What would happen if ten U.S. cities were hit by thermonuclear bombs? How might New York City be evacuated on short notice? Under what circumstances might a thermonuclear war be won? So the RAND group developed chains of events that might lead to a thermonuclear war, as well as what might happen during such a war.

Kahn needed a term for the fictions he was preparing. They clearly weren't forecasts, and they weren't simply science-fiction fantasies. What to call them? Santa Monica, where Kahn was working, was not far from Hollywood, so it was not too surprising that he should find himself discussing the problem with a screenwriter, Leo Rosten, who suggested using the term *scenario*. This word was once used in Hollywood for what is now called a screenplay. Kahn readily accepted *scenario* and began popularizing it through his books and lectures.

One of the prime virtues of scenarios is that they provide a way to deal more effectively with almost any situation that is important but uncertain. We begin by admitting that we do not know what will happen, but instead of simply giving up and saying that we can do nothing but accept our ignorance, we try to identify things that *might* happen. As we identify these possibilities and create scenarios describing how they might actually happen and what their consequences might be, we are, in the most literal sense, analyzing our problem—that is, breaking it down into components and looking carefully at each. This analysis helps us to evaluate something in terms of its likelihood of occurrence and its desirability. Scenarios are invaluable in situations where uncertainties might otherwise lead us to think that because we cannot have knowledge that is certain we should proceed in total ignorance.

Kahn's scenarios were born at a time of extreme tension between the United States and the Soviet Union. The U.S. Strategic Air Command was constantly on trigger alert. At the first sign of a Soviet attack, the Command was ready to dispatch a strike force loaded with nuclear bombs destined for Soviet targets. But there was a problem: How could they be sure that the

Soviets had launched an attack? Being wrong about this could be absolutely catastrophic.

In 1958, a United Press article revealed to the world by means of a vivid scenario how catastrophically dangerous the situation had become. The writer, Frank H. Bartholomew, reported that the U.S. counteroffensive striking force had been repeatedly sped on its way by alerts created by flights of meteors registering on the DEW (Distant Early Warning or DEW Line) radar scopes, by interference from high frequency transmitters, or by "the appearance of foreign objects, flying in seeming formation, that simply never have been explained."

Fortunately, the United States had a fail-safe system in place: The pilots flying toward Soviet targets with nuclear bombs were under orders to turn back automatically once they reach their fail-safe point if they did not later receive an order by radio confirming that they were to stay on course for their targets. Bartholomew explained how easily the system could fail and offered scenarios showing the horrendous results.

Publication of Bartholomew's article in the *New York Times* alarmed the Soviet Union and many Americans because it made clear how close the world was to an accidental Armageddon. Peace movements became strong in many nations, and there was strong public interest in Kahn's 1960 book *On Thermonuclear War*. But the book also produced severe critics who blamed the messenger for delivering the horrifying news.

"Is there really a Herman Kahn?" demanded one outraged reviewer of *On Thermonuclear War*. "This is a moral tract on mass murder: how to plan it, how to commit it, how to get away with it, how to justify it." The reviewer declared that "the evil and tenebrous book ... is permeated with a bloodthirsty irrationality such as I have not seen in all my years of reading."

Kahn, along with Henry Kissinger and Wernher von Braun, served as a model for the deranged scientist whose name provided the title for Stanley Kubrick's 1964 film *Dr. Strangelove*. Preferring to live in a world without nuclear weapons, many people sought to make the nuclear problem disappear by hushing up talk of things like megadeaths and doomsday machines.

But people seriously interested in public-policy issues began paying attention to Kahn and became familiar with his scenario technique, popularized particularly in such books as *Thinking about the Unthinkable: Scenarios and Metaphors* (1962). During the

1960s, the method became widely accepted by military thinkers and increasingly by other people in government and business. Today, scenarios are in widespread use in the Western nations.

Scenarios for Population and Economics

Demographers now use scenarios when decision makers in government and business want to know how population will grow in the future. Previously, demographers simply projected population on the basis of recent trends, but they found this was a risky practice. Back in the 1940s, for example, they assumed that the low birthrates of the 1930s would continue; instead, birthrates jumped in 1946 as the baby boom began, and population grew rapidly, embarrassing the forecasters. Properly chastened, demographers began to offer scenarios, especially for longer-term forecasts. The scenarios are based on various assumptions regarding birthrates, death rates, immigration, etc. Such scenarios now are regularly published by the United Nations Population Division and the U.S. Bureau of the Census.

The multiple-scenario approach sensitizes us to the uncertainties, while giving us plausible possibilities that can be used in formulating strategies. In the case of demographic projections, the scenarios diverge increasingly as they reach further into the future. If we require a single figure to plug into our planning for the future, we are free to take the median projection, but we do so in full knowledge that it is likely to be wide of the mark. As time passes, we can review the scenarios along with other information to see which scenario most closely approximates the actual course of events.

Economists also think increasingly in terms of scenarios because of the great uncertainties in forecasting business activity and other dimensions of an economy. Knowing when to expect a recession is very important to company leaders, because a business initiative can easily fail if it is launched at the wrong moment in the business cycle. If the company knew when a recession would start, it could postpone untimely actions that otherwise would be disastrous. Unfortunately, economists cannot accurately predict when a recession will start or even whether there will be a recession in the next twelve months. However, economists are generally willing to offer an opinion, which might be expressed as a range for the presumed growth of the economy—e.g., 2 percent to 3 percent growth—or a couple of scenarios, such as slow-growth or recession.

Making Choices and Forecasts

The first rule in anticipating future events is this: We must do it as best we can and keep trying even though we cannot do it very well. This rule follows the general principle that it's important to *do* many things even if we cannot do them well.

Well-thought-out scenarios make us aware of the costs and benefits of an action that we may take and of the various consequences that may ensue. We can use scenarios to help us decide almost anything—where to spend our vacation, whether to accept a new job, how to succeed in our school work, whether to invite someone on a date, etc.

Scenarios to Forecast Future Events

First, we imagine possible future events in a given situation and then we try to develop plausible scenarios to show how these events might occur. If we wanted to decide how likely it is that Canada as now constituted will break up by the year 2030, we could prepare a series of scenarios to explain various ways in which a breakup might occur. If we found it easy to write plausible scenarios for a breakup, we would view this as evidence that a breakup is likely. We might give it a probability of, say 30 to 60 percent. However, if we could not write plausible scenarios, we would have an indication that a breakup is unlikely.

A technique that can be applied to many situations is to create not one, but three alternative scenarios. The first assumes that current trends will continue without much change. This can be called the Surprise-Free or Continuation Scenario. A second scenario can be based on an assumption that things will go better in the future than in the past: Call it the Optimistic Scenario. A third scenario could envision things getting worse: Call it the Pessimistic Scenario.

Developing these two additional scenarios forces us to think about the future in terms of *alternative* possibilities rather than as a single pre-set future. We might even add two more—a Disaster Scenario, anticipating that something awful might happen, and a Transformation or Miracle Scenario, in which something absolutely marvelous happens. That gives us five scenarios, and we may want to stop there because it takes time and effort to develop each of them.

We now have a set of five scenarios:

1. *A Surprise-Free Scenario:* Things will continue much as they are now. They won't become substantially better or worse.
2. *An Optimistic Scenario:* Things will go considerably better than in the recent past.
3. *A Pessimistic Scenario:* Something will go considerably worse than in the past.
4. *A Disaster Scenario:* Things will go terribly wrong, and our situation will be far worse than anything we have previously experienced.
5. *A Transformation Scenario:* Something spectacularly marvelous happens—something we never dared to expect.

Here is how we might use scenarios depending on whether we are a business owner, a worker, or a student:

Scenarios for a business (two-year projection):
- *Surprise-Free:* Profits will grow by between 2 percent and 5 percent.
- *Optimistic:* Profits will grow by between 6 percent and 30 percent.
- *Pessimistic:* Profits will grow by less than 2 percent or drop to a loss of up to 10 percent.
- *Disaster:* The company will suffer a loss of more than 10 percent.
- *Transformation:* Profits will increase by more than 30 percent.

Scenarios for a worker (two-year projection):
- *Surprise-Free:* My salary goes up by about 6 percent over the next two years.
- *Optimistic:* My salary will rise by more than 6 percent over the next two years.
- *Pessimistic:* I will receive no increase in salary.
- *Disaster:* I will be laid off or be unable to work due to an accident.
- *Transformation:* I will be promoted to a higher-level job and receive a huge salary boost.

Scenarios for a student (two-year projection):
- *Surprise-Free:* I will do *about as well* in my exams as I did last year.
- *Optimistic:* I will do *better* than last year.
- *Pessimistic:* I will do *worse* than last year.

- *Disaster:* I will flunk my exams and have to leave school.
- *Transformation:* I will do so well in my exams that I win an award for a scholarship.

For each scenario, we can try to identify reasons why it might or might not come to pass. As these factors are identified and assessed, we can try to decide the likelihood that each scenario will be realized based on how the current situation is trending. We can give each scenario a probability expressed as a percent of the total for all the scenarios. For instance, the continuation scenario might be given a 50 percent probability, optimistic scenario 20 percent, pessimistic scenario 20 percent, disaster scenario 5 percent, and transformation scenario 5 percent. Requiring that the total add up to 100 percent forces us to judge the likelihood of each. We can keep readjusting the figures if we think there is reason to believe that any of our scenarios has become more or less likely.

We can also evaluate the scenarios in terms of desirability by giving each a score on a scale ranging from -10 to +10. When we do so, we should be asking ourselves how much of a sacrifice we are willing to make to bring this scenario to reality or keep it from being realized. In many cases, the people running a business are not really interested in making huge profits: They may really be more interested in having the modest income that comes with an undemanding job. Similarly, a student may not want to succeed brilliantly in his schoolwork, because such success might alienate him from his friends.

Thus, the scenario technique can pose thought-provoking questions about our values. It does not provide precise knowledge about things that will happen in the future or what we should strive for. Instead, it enables us to clarify our thinking about various issues, so that we can make better decisions. If we wish, we can submit our scenarios to other people and see whether their judgments differ from our own—and why.

Scenarios can encourage desirable action by showing people that they may be headed for an undesirable future unless they mend their ways. As fiction writers have made clear, a vision of an undesirable future can lead to reform. In Charles Dickens's *A Christmas Carol*, the crusty miser Scrooge reforms his behavior after he sees a vision of the future that would result if he did not.

A disaster scenario—if it seems plausible—can encourage an individual or an organization to reform current practices or a general mode of operation. A student might decide to party less in order to avoid flunking out. An employee might decide to repair a frayed relationship with his employer. A business might decide to cut back costs or take other precautionary measures. Scenarios cannot dictate actions, but they can promote desirable change since they influence decisions in a way that generally should be positive.

Forecasting and "Backcasting"

Up to now, we have anchored our scenarios in the present. That is, we have started with our current situation and tried to decide how it might develop, based on current trends. This approach, known as extrapolation, is a natural outgrowth of trend analysis and is one useful way to begin thinking about the future. But there is another approach that does not begin with where we are, but rather with where we want to be or might be at some future date. Since it involves a norm or goal, it is known as normative forecasting. More popularly, however, it is known as "backcasting," because we are, in a sense, forecasting backwards from a possible future, rather than forward from the present.

To backcast, we first postulate a future goal, event, or circumstance and then try to develop a sequence of steps or stages to explain how the imagined future goal or event came to pass. Backcasting can be used both to decide what is likely to happen in the future and to determine how to achieve one's chosen goal.

Let's suppose the president of the United States becomes concerned about cancer and wonders if it could be eliminated by the year 2050. If so, the nation might decide to make that a national goal.

So the president's advisers are asked to study this possibility, and futurists are brought in to help him decide how the goal might best be reached and what would be involved in doing so. The futurists might use backcasting as a way to think back from the goal (eliminating cancer) to the specific stages whereby the goal might be achieved. In working back from the goal, the futurists quickly decide that three preconditions must be satisfied for the goal to be achieved. These are:

- Scientists would need a more precise understanding of how cancers form in the body. This necessary knowledge might come from ongoing research in genetics and cellular biology, but progress is slow because the research is underfunded. The pace of scientific discoveries might be speeded up by providing more funds for research. The money would go to university, government, and industry laboratories. They constantly complain about their lack of money to hire researchers, but would Congress agree to appropriate the required funds?

- Elimination of environmental factors known to cause cancer, such as tobacco smoke, air pollution, and some chemicals, would reduce the risk of disease. How soon can they be eliminated?
- People would need to adopt healthy lifestyles. How soon can they be induced to do so?

The backcasting exercise might indicate that it would probably not be possible to eliminate cancer completely by 2050, but a serious effort might cut the morbidity rate for cancer by 90 percent; fatalities might be lowered to less than 5 percent of the current rate.

Maybe, just maybe, the president would decide to go for it. Back in 1960s, President Kennedy set forth an even more breathtaking goal for the United States—putting a man on the moon by 1969—and thus initiated an astonishing feat of backcasting, planning, and accomplishment. The leaders of the Apollo space program, created to carry out Kennedy's mandate, had to determine exactly what must be done in order for the program to reach the goal the president had stipulated. Kennedy had stated what he wanted, but he had not explained how it could be actually achieved. Success with rocketry had encouraged experts to believe that such an astounding feat was possible, but very careful backcasting was required to translate the grand vision into a sequence of achievable stages. With available know-how, backcasting, careful planning, and substantial funding the Apollo was launched and eventually achieved the goal.

Once we develop almost any goal, we can use backcasting to figure out how best to reach it. A business executive, for example, might tell his team, "In two years, the company expects our department's revenues to be $2 billion a year. Currently, our revenues are only $1 billion. Can we create a scenario showing how we can reasonably reach the goal if we put our minds to it?" A variety of alternative scenarios may be developed; then a decision can be made as to which scenario to follow. Based on the scenario, alternative strategies can be proposed and discussed. Eventually, specific tasks can be assigned to the members of the team.

How do you climb a mountain? Many people might say that you start at the bottom and work your way up—a bottom-up approach. But visionary executives, says management Professor Stephen C. Harper, will respond, "From the top down."

They know that by mentally envisioning what it would be like to stand on the summit, they can see the best path for climbing the mountain. If they were to climb the mountain from where they currently stand, it would limit them to the path immediately in front of them.

Visionary executives realize that there may be many paths to the summit, and that the best path may not be the easiest, shortest, or the one they are currently on. With the long-term backwards approach, executives identify where they want the company to be in five to seven years. Then they work backwards from that date by asking, "If we want to be there in the year 20XY, where will we need to be in the year prior to 20XY?"

Other Uses of Backcasting

Backcasting may be a new word, but the basic procedure is one that scholars have long used to solve historical mysteries. In the case of the disappearance of the dinosaurs, paleontologists knew what had happened: Studies of rock strata containing the fossilized remains of dinosaurs showed that the animals suddenly disappeared from the fossil record about 350 million years ago, but there was no obvious explanation for it. The scientists were left to speculations. They reasoned that the sudden disappearance must have been caused by some big event that affected the whole world. But what could it have been? They developed three plausible scenarios: (1) a devastating epidemic, (2) a catastrophic change of climate, and (3) an asteroid colliding with the earth. Scientists around the world looked for evidence that might show which of the scenarios might be the best explanation. Today they feel they have enough evidence to reject the first two scenarios, but the asteroid scenario fits all the known evidence and today is the generally accepted theory.

So far, we have looked at two uses of backcasting: first, to help explain a past event, such as in the dinosaur disappearance, and, second, to devise a strategy and procedures for achieving a goal. A third use is to assess whether some imagined future event is likely. Herman Kahn would discount the possibility of certain suggested future events on the grounds that it was hard to write a plausible scenario explaining how they *might* happen.

Suppose, for example, someone claimed there will be a manned colony on Mars five years from now. To assess such a projected future, we might try to prepare scenarios outlining how a colony could be established within that time frame. Backcasting, we decide that it might be possible to use robots to construct the base and conduct tests to make sure it was safe for humans. Conceivably, a human expeditionary force would not be needed to establish the base. However, having robots construct the base would be incredibly challenging; almost certainly there would be many setbacks along the way. Then it would require more years for the first human colonists to make the perilous journey. The bottom line is clear: It seems virtually certain that no Martian colony will be in operation within five years. Going through this exercise will, of course, help us to start estimating how many years it might take to actually accomplish the goal.

Will world peace be achieved in the next fifty years? To make a judgment on that question, we can postulate the existence of world peace fifty years from now and then try to construct plausible scenarios for how it might have come about. We might start by fantasizing an armada of spaceships filled with extraterrestrials landing here and imposing peace on us quarrelsome earthlings. However, most people would feel that this scenario lacks realism.

We might next develop a scenario based on strengthening the United Nations' peacekeeping ability. If we could also show how this could realistically be accomplished and why the national governments would accept it, we might be able to fashion a credible scenario. This would be evidence that peace might indeed be achieved in fifty years; moreover, it might indicate a path to peace that the nations could follow. On the other hand, if we cannot devise a plausible scenario to explain how peace could come about in fifty years, we might decide that this suggestion is not very realistic—that there's hardly any possibility that it could happen within half a century—and we would have to come up with a better scenario if we want to forecast world peace in fifty years.

Personal Backcasting

Backcasting can also be used to save your life. Imagine being killed in an automobile accident. (Since auto accidents are a common cause of death, this is no idle fantasy.) Now start developing scenarios to explain how that might happen: e.g., the driver was drunk; the weather was bad; the driver coming in another car had a heart attack and ran into your car, etc. You can then assess the likelihood of your getting killed under the different scenarios and devise ways to avoid danger. For this purpose, it is helpful to have some knowledge of the influence of such factors as drunkenness and seat belts in car fatalities.

Choosing a place for your vacation? After identifying a possible destination, you can use backcasting to help identify its potential costs. If you wish, you can evaluate a number of destinations and make lists of their costs and benefits, so it is easy to compare them and make a final choice.

Backcasting can also help you decide whether you yourself can reasonably achieve some goal. You might, for instance, fantasize about being a famous movie star ten years from now. To decide whether to go for it, you outline the steps by which you would reach that status. In this case, the steps seem to pose problems. You need to be able to act, and you have no acting experience except for walk-on roles in a few school plays; and, come to think of it, you really didn't enjoy acting, and nobody raved about your performance except your mother. Furthermore, you have no contacts with theater professionals, or even any knowledge of the entertainment business. So your scenario should explain how you could reach your goals despite all these handicaps. If your backcast scenarios all seem unrealistic, you might decide that it would require a miracle for you to become a movie star, and miracles rarely happen. On the other hand, if you can show how you can reasonably overcome the obstacles through certain actions, you may be able to create a plausible scenario for becoming a star. You might, for instance, try out for parts in amateur theatricals or go to a drama school to see whether your enjoyment increases and your "reviews" improve. This scenario might later serve as the start of more-detailed plans for reaching your goal. However, your research should also inform you that Hollywood is crowded with would-be movie stars, and very, very few will ever reach their goal.

Scenarios for Careers

A high-school student who gets the idea of becoming a lawyer can take a first step toward realizing this goal by thinking back from the goal (being a practicing lawyer) to where he or she is now. A first step is to find out what is required to become a lawyer. One requirement nowadays is a law degree, which means graduating from a law school. That, in turn, requires acceptance by the law school and then years of study before graduation. Acceptance by a law school requires graduation from a college, which means being accepted by a college, which means graduating from high school or otherwise demonstrating the ability to perform college work.

So the high-schooler might prepare the following scenario:

Scenario for a high-school student

To realize my goal of becoming a lawyer, I choose high-school courses likely to be useful in legal work. I learn more about what lawyers do. As soon as possible, I apply to several colleges, and am accepted by two.

In college I take courses in political science and history. In my senior year, I am accepted by a law school.

Over the summer before my last year, I intern at a law firm.

I receive my law degree. I become an associate in the law firm where I interned.

Having backcasted that scenario, the student must decide whether he or she is ready to commit to following the steps indicated by the scenario. A final decision is unnecessary, but if the student wants to retain the option of becoming a lawyer, he or she should commit to graduating from high school and thus preparing for college.

Scenario for an aspiring entrepreneur

Year One: I decide to go into business selling toy automobiles to collectors. I set up a Web site on the Internet. Business is very slow. I need to advertise and have a larger variety of toy automobiles to sell. I prepare a business plan and show it to potential investors.

Year Two: Two investors (my cousin Louis and my sister Helen) provide a little capital. I start advertising. Business improves.

Year Three: I am now getting many customers and am actually making money. I have reached my goal.

Though this scenario leads to success, most people who set out to run a profitable business fail. So if we are really thinking of going into business, we should develop other scenarios to guard against the possibility that the dream may not work out well. Since the ways to fail in business are numerous and the chances of long-term success are low, a would-be entrepreneur needs be careful about borrowing money from relatives and friends.

Scenarios can identify both potential obstacles and, often, ways to overcome them. It is, unfortunately, only too easy to create scenarios for failure for both the high-school student and the aspiring entrepreneur. Most people are not well-suited to being lawyers or entrepreneurs. Would-be lawyers may neglect their schoolwork for sports and partying, or even become involved in drugs, which will make it much more difficult to succeed in their chosen field. In the case of entrepreneurship, most people lack the required judgment, dedication, and people skills to create and run a successful business. Even if they do possess those assets, they may not be sensitive to market forces so that they can have the right product at the right time for the market. Even with the right skills and product, easy-to-make mistakes can still drive a business under—borrow too much money, get into a lawsuit, fail to find suitable employees; the list is nearly endless. Some people thrive on entrepreneurship, but not everyone.

If it proves difficult to construct a realistic scenario for achieving success in one type of career, it is wise to reconsider one's options: There are plenty of other routes to occupational success. The same is true of almost any other goal. Figuring out which goals are worth pursuing, and which strategies are most likely to lead to them, is a purpose for which scenarios can be very useful.

Scenarios give us an excellent way to think in an orderly manner about future possibilities, assess their probability and likelihood, and evaluate strategies that we might employ to achieve a chosen goal. But imagining scenarios is a challenge to our creativity: We need to come up with lots of ideas about what might happen in the future, since we cannot expect the future to be simply a replay of the past. The current pace of social and technological change makes it virtually certain that our future will be radically different from our past.

Scenarios are particularly useful in dealing with "wild cards," events that we do not expect to happen—at least in the near term—but could have enormous consequences if they did. We will consider wild cards in the next chapter.

9

The Wild Cards in Our Future

The most surprising thing that could happen in the future would be if there were no surprises, because the future has surprised us so often in the past. Many of the surprises to come will be fleeting, with little lasting impact. Others will be really startling and will have very important consequences. These big, important surprises are often called *wild cards*.

Wild cards merit special consideration because they can dramatically alter subsequent events and people's outlook on the future. The terrorist attacks of September 11, 2001, disrupted people's lives all over the world, even if they were not personally involved in the attacks. Stock market prices plunged. Workers in hotel, airline, and other industries lost their jobs. Thousands of people saw loved ones and friends sent off to fight. The media stopped covering other events in order to focus on terrorism.

Wild cards demonstrate that we all carry around in our heads unconscious forecasts or expectations about what will happen in the future. This set of expectations—a kind of "map of the future"—is what causes us to experience surprise when something unexpected happens.

Once faced with a surprise, we have to deal with it, at least psychologically. Most unexpected events are so trivial that we hardly think of them as surprises, and they cause little change in our attitudes or behavior. But wild cards have the power to upset almost everything.

Personal Experiences with Wild Cards

Two millennia ago, a devout Jew named Saul set off from Jerusalem to put down the troublesome Jesus-cultists in Damascus. Along the journey, Saul saw a great light and fell to the ground. He heard a voice he believed to be that of Jesus saying, "Saul, why do you persecute me?" Totally unprepared for this overpowering personal experience, Saul completely reversed his previous thinking. Adopting a new name, Paul, he turned into a dedicated missionary for the sect he had once reviled and eventually became the most influential figure in Christian history aside from Jesus himself.

Saul's great surprise can be viewed as a wild card in an individual's life, and it illustrates two key points about this type of event:

First, he was totally surprised. He certainly did not expect to have a personal encounter with Jesus when he set out on the road to Damascus. The more extraordinary the surprise event—that is, the more it upsets our expectations—the more it qualifies as a wild card. However, we may discover when we look back at previous events that we should not have been as surprised as we were. In Saul's case, scholars have identified certain experiences that had readied him for conversion: For example, he had become familiar with the Christians that he was persecuting; he also had been rather disillusioned with his mentors' rigid interpretation of Jewish law and their insistence that every rule be rigorously obeyed.

Second, a wild card has important consequences for a particular individual or group, and sometimes for the larger community. Saul's life changed completely, and his conversion led to major developments in the new religion and subsequent human history. What was a wild card for Saul became a wild card for the world.

A more common type of wild card in an individual's life is the unexpected death of a close relative, spouse, or lover. Such a loss makes one reconsider one's outlook and options, because the structure upon which one's life is based is shaken, and sometimes collapses. Being unexpectedly dismissed by one's employer or one's lover can also be a wild card, especially when the relationship has been long and extensive, shaping one's lifestyle and demanding emotional investment.

For most people, an earthquake that wrecks one's home is most definitely a wild card—so wild, in fact, that few people spend any time considering the possibility. Yet, mild earthquakes are fairly common in most parts of the world, and severe ones occur somewhere every year. The year 2001 may be best remembered for the terrorist attacks of September 11, but the death toll of about 3,000 was surpassed by the 20,000 to 50,000 people killed by an earthquake in India earlier that year.

New York City experienced a modest earthquake on October 27, 2001, only a few weeks after the terrorist attacks on the city's

World Trade Center. Many jittery New Yorkers panicked after feeling their beds shake and hearing pictures fall from walls and glass and crockery break. Yet most calmed quickly when they learned it was not due to a terrorist bomb, but was "only" an earthquake!

When New Yorkers move to San Francisco, however, they may discover that an event they consider unlikely is viewed by their neighbors as a serious danger. San Francisco experienced a devastating earthquake in 1906; 667 people were killed, and thousands more in the ensuing fires. Buildings were leveled throughout much of the city. In 1989, an earthquake in nearby Loma Prieta again caused major destruction in San Francisco.

John Rockfellow, co-author of a report on wild cards for the Copenhagen Institute for Futures Studies, says that when he was growing up in San Francisco, his father kept their basement filled with bottled water and canned foods in preparation for the next "Big One." Many San Franciscans continue to make such preparations. Even if they never have to contend with a Big One, they can probably sleep better knowing they have planned for the worst.

Wild cards are not always bad; in fact, they can be extremely beneficial, such as unexpectedly inheriting a large amount of money. Winning big in a lottery is, for millions of people, a wild card that they devoutly pray for. On November 7, 2001, a Pakistani-born taxi driver named Ihsan Khan won $55 million in the Washington, D.C., "Powerball" D.C. Lottery—the largest win in the lottery's history. Almost immediately, his lifestyle began to change: He moved out of his modest apartment and took up residence at an undisclosed location. Asked whether he would continue to drive a taxi, he replied, "What do you think?"

Any sudden success in one's occupation may also function as a wild card, because it opens extraordinary new opportunities and changes one's relationship to other people: The lucky person starts attracting new offers of employment as well as new companions; old companions and colleagues drift away.

Future Wild Cards

Futurist John L. Petersen discusses eighty wild cards of the future in his book *Out of the Blue: How to Anticipate Big Future Surprises.* Petersen's highly diverse assortment includes:

- A Western state secedes from the United States.

- The United Nations collapses.
- The United States takes over Mexico after its economy collapses.
- Nuclear terrorists attack the United States.

Another list of wild cards was assembled in the early 1990s for the report co-authored by John Rockfellow and his colleagues from the Copenhagen Institute for Futures Studies, BIPE Conseil in Paris, and the Institute for the Future in Menlo Park, California. This report discussed sixteen wild cards, including:

- Hong Kong dominates the Chinese economy.
- Europe dismantles the nation-state: It is replaced by strong regional representation in the European Community.
- Life expectancy approaches 100.
- Women leave the workforce.

Co-author Rockfellow said the main purpose of having business managers think about wild cards is to free up their thinking. Wild cards, he said, act as "jackhammers" for chipping away at the rigidities of business managers' ideas about the future. Few want to admit that there will be any change in their market niche or the goals of their corporate department. As Rockfellow explained:

> Most organizations do not include in their planning the possibility of the organization's market coming to a sudden end. For example, suggesting to the world's largest toy manufacturer that the children of the future may not play with toys is likely to try the executives' patience at the outset. However, once they begin to see the benefits of deconstructing their perception of reality, a new level of creative thinking opens up.
>
> The most-successful products throughout history could only have been anticipated through wild-card thinking. The leap from horse to car, from pen to typewriters, and from typewriter to computer were wild-card events.

Rockfellow believes the U.S. Department of Defense could have benefited from wild-card thinking during the Cold War. Little attention appears to have been given to the possibility that the Soviet system would collapse, bringing to an end the conflict that had shaped global strategy since the end of World War II. When it actually happened, Defense Department planning offices had to make radical changes everywhere. Bases had to be closed and budgets slashed. The defense industry experienced massive disarray.

Averting Catastrophes

The most memorable year in modern history for wild cards was probably 1941: German troops invaded the Soviet Union in June, and Japan attacked the U.S. forces stationed at Pearl Harbor six months later. Both events caught their victims by surprise. Neither the Soviets nor the Americans expected the attacks, and both were woefully unprepared.

Why didn't anybody warn the governments of the victim nations about the forthcoming attacks? Actually, there were warnings, but they were brushed off by key leaders, if not by all their subordinates. The British warned the Soviets repeatedly of the German buildup along their eastern border and of Hitler's planned assault, but Stalin, a master of deceit and betrayal, failed to recognize that his duplicity was no match for Hitler's. When the German attack came, Stalin went into seclusion; only with difficulty did his aides get him to rally from his alcoholic despondency to lead the nation's defense. Similar warnings of the coming Japanese attack on Pearl Harbor reached American ears, but they too were largely disregarded by the controlling authorities. When the attack came, America as a whole experienced total surprise and shock.

Wild cards are by definition unexpected, but they are not necessarily uncommon. Over the course of a century, there are probably several thousand events that might be viewed as wild cards in the global arena, and many hundreds of millions in the lives of individuals and organizations. Few people go through life without experiencing at least a couple of wild cards.

Petersen deplores the common assumption that we can neither predict nor prepare for wild cards. He argues that they can, in fact, be anticipated and prepared for and that it is extremely important to do so, because they can threaten the capabilities of human systems. In his book about wild cards, *Out of the Blue,* Petersen writes:

> The chance that we could avert a future catastrophe or at least prepare strategies for dealing with it is reason enough to examine wild-card possibilities. Wild cards may trigger a chain of events that is much worse than the initial event itself. For example, a major natural disaster could produce a global epi-

demic, which could lead nations to close their borders, causing the collapse of the airline industry, and so on.

The rapidly growing technological prowess of humans has, for the first time in history, produced new classes of wild cards that could potentially destroy the whole human race. These new kinds of wild cards are simply too destructive to allow to happen, and therefore require active attempts to anticipate them and be proactive in dealing with their early indicators.

Petersen offers three basic rules for dealing with wild cards:

- Thinking about a wild card *before* it happens is important and valuable. The more that is known about a potential event, the less threatening it becomes and the more obvious the solutions seem.
- Accessing and understanding information is key. Identifying early warning signs, understanding the structure of a wild card, and developing potential responses all require sophisticated and effective information gathering and analysis.
- Extraordinary events require extraordinary approaches. "We are moving into a new period when potential events may outstrip our current ability to understand and deal with them," Petersen believes. "These events look so big, strange, and scary because our usual methods of problem solving are not up to dealing with them. New approaches are needed."

Petersen's position seems to be supported by the following brief analysis of the September 11, 2001, terrorist attacks.

The Terrorist Attacks of September 11, 2001

When a bizarre or unusual event is suggested as a future possibility, most people do not want to consider it seriously since they regard it as either impossible or, at best, extremely unlikely. For example, on September 10, 2001, most people would have scoffed at the suggestion that the World Trade Center's famed twin towers, once the tallest buildings in the world, might be destroyed by Islamic terrorists steering hijacked airliners on a suicide mission.

In retrospect, however, in this case as with most wild-card events, we can identify developments and conditions that foreshadow the surprise happening. In some cases, the surprise should not even have been a surprise; the fact that it was arises from people's general unwillingness to think seriously about future events they believe are unlikely. In the case of the German attack on the Soviet Union in 1941, Stalin should have anticipated Hitler's betrayal.

In the case of the attack on the World Trade Center, futurists had come quite close to suggesting that precise event as a possibility that needed to be considered. *The Futurist* magazine, for example, published a number of articles describing the dangers of terrorism in the years leading up to the September 11 attacks. A 1987 article by terrorism expert Brian Jenkins mentioned the possibility of "aerial suicide attacks." And a 1994 article by futurist Marvin J. Cetron specifically identified the World Trade Center as a "choice target" from the terrorists' perspective.

"Targets such as the World Trade Center not only provide the requisite casualties but, because of their symbolic nature, provide more bang for the buck," wrote Cetron. "In order to maximize their odds for success, terrorist groups will likely consider mounting multiple, simultaneous operations with the aim of overtaxing a government's ability to respond, as well as demonstrating their professionalism and reach."

Cetron added another forecast, which proved, unfortunately, even more prescient: "Despite all this, terrorism will remain a back-burner issue for Western leaders as long as the violence strikes in distant lands and has little impact on their fortunes or those of their constituents. Until a country's citizens believe that terrorism poses a significant threat, traditional economic and political concerns will remain paramount. The industrialized nations will be too busy jockeying for access to markets and resources to be concerned with the less immediate problems."

Could the Attacks Have Been Anticipated?

Let's suppose we had been security officers charged with preventing terrorist attacks, and we had just read Jenkins's article warning of "aerial suicide attacks." How might we proceed to evaluate this warning?

One approach might be backcasting: We might assume that a terrorist gang would actually attack by air. Then we could try to create a variety of scenarios to explain how they might accomplish this feat by means of a plausible sequence of actions.

We begin by assuming that terrorists are unlikely to own their own aircraft. Could they buy one? Perhaps, but the cost would be enormous and many questions would probably be asked. Could they steal one? Yes, in fact, they have frequently hijacked aircraft in the past. Could they hijack a military bomber and load it with bombs? They would have to be awfully clever and lucky to get into an Air Force base, seize a plane, load it with bombs, and fly it to a target. Success would be unlikely, and smart terrorists would know it.

But hijacking an airliner is clearly a possibility. The United States has some safeguards to prevent people from carrying weapons onto aircraft, but some kind of weapon might be smuggled aboard, especially if the terrorists can somehow slip through the security checkpoints. An individual might have some difficulty intimidating the passengers and crew, but a group could probably do it even with modest weaponry. Getting into the pilot's cabin seems possible. So taking command of the plane seems feasible. But would the pilot follow instructions? Probably not if asked to do something suicidal. Could a terrorist be trained as a pilot to take over? Yes, in fact, a number of members of terrorist groups have been trained as pilots.

But how can an aircraft cause destruction if it has no bombs to drop? It can simply crash into its target. Such a crash should wreck a building; a skyscraper would be especially vulnerable. Of course, everybody on the plane would be killed, but if you are ready to die yourself and the victims are perceived as the enemy, that is an added benefit. Scores of terrorists have carried out suicide missions by detonating bombs strapped to their own bodies.

So we now envision a group of terrorists hijacking an airliner and crashing it into an enemy target. But what target might it be? If we had read Cetron's article, we would already have one target to think about—the World Trade Center. In fact, Islamic terrorists did attack the Center in 1993, but their car bomb failed to destroy the building.

Our reasoning might lead us to this scenario: A group of terrorists hijack an airliner and crash it into the World Trade Center. Such a feat would be outrageous or even "impossible" in the minds of most Americans, but it would be both logical and possible for an Islamic terrorist who believes he will go straight to heaven upon committing the deed.

In researching the issue, our futurist might review the previous terrorist attack on the World Trade Center. One fact that emerged at the trial of the 1993 terrorists was that the Center's towers were built to withstand the crash of certain airliners, but not of the bigger ones already flying in the New York vicinity. On September 11, the four planes hijacked by the terrorists were all of the size required to destroy the towers.

Further analysis of terrorist methods and goals would have resulted in greater refinement in our scenario, but what we have already is remarkably close to what actually occurred. What we don't have, at this point, is the idea that it would involve four airliners and at least two separate targets. However, Cetron suggested that multiple targets might be selected for an attack. So we might stress the possibility of a larger, wider attack involving more terrorists and multiple planes and targets.

This retrospective look at the World Trade Center attacks suggests that they could reasonably have been anticipated as a distinct possibility. But could they have been prevented, and, if so, how? Clearly, if the authorities believed that the attack was likely, measures could have been taken. One action that was not taken was making sure that terrorists could not get into the pilots' cabin after takeoff. (Israel previously had implemented that safety measure.) Tighter immigration controls, improved identification systems, better security at airports, and other measures might well have frustrated the September 11 terrorists.

Future Catastrophes

The September 11 attacks, though shocking and tragic, were not as terrible as certain catastrophes that *might* occur in the future. Here are six examples:

- *Nuclear war:* Future wars may well involve nuclear weapons, since a number of countries already have them or could obtain them. An atomic war between India and Pakistan might easily produce 100 million or more dead due to the high population in those nations. Illnesses due to radiation might occur all over the Indian subcontinent and beyond.
- *A global financial collapse:* The international financial system collapsed in the early 1930s, depressing economies around the world. The United States experienced the worst depression in its history. Desperation among Germans provided support for the Nazis. Militarism surged in Japan. Globalization, telecommunications, and the Internet now

have linked financial systems to each other more closely than ever. This may make the world more subject to a chain reaction of bank and business failures that leaves little economic strength anywhere.

- *A devastating global plague.* New and resurgent diseases, such as AIDS, SARS, and drug-resistant tuberculosis, are already killing thousands of people each year, but something much worse could lie ahead. We know this from history: The Black Death, which was probably bubonic plague, first devastated people in Asia and then traveled to Europe, where it depopulated many nations between 1347 and 1351. A similar plague today, when we have far higher populations and closer connections between them, might result in hundreds of millions of deaths.

- *Worldwide religious war:* Angered by Islamic terrorist attacks, Jews and Hindus might begin desecrating mosques and assassinating imams. Muslim mobs might respond with counterattacks on synagogues and Hindu temples. Christians sympathizing with the Jews and already angered by attacks from Muslim extremists might then set off an atomic bomb in Mecca, causing global war between religious faiths. Religious wars can persist for centuries.

- *Institutional meltdown:* A breakdown of international order leads to widespread collapse of key institutions that maintain our civilization—banks, government agencies, business corporations, schools, etc. Authorities cannot stop the spreading collapse of the complex global systems providing food, electricity, transportation, etc. The breakdown leads to chaos, desperation, and increasing mortality due to starvation, disease, and violence.

- *Environmental collapse:* Excessive exploitation of environmental resources eventually touches off a chain reaction of adverse environmental changes that make the earth uninhabitable. Dust and pollutants shut out the sun's rays, causing a global die-off of plants and animals. Humans fight desperately over dwindling stocks of food. Diseases break out everywhere. Survivors are reduced to savagery.

Eight Future *Benestrophes*

Some years ago, a group of young people tried to invent a word that would be the direct opposite of a catastrophe, since the English language lacks such a word. They eventually came up with "benestrophe" (pronounced ben-ESS-tro-fee). The word did not catch on, but let's use it here since we need just such a term. As stressed earlier, a wild card is not necessarily bad; it can be marvelous. So to balance the potential catastrophes, here are some benestrophes.

- *War fades from history:* Effective peace-keeping machinery is finally developed, and war is finally consigned to the garbage can of history. Such an eventuality may not be as fanciful as many people think: Modern communications and transportation have brought the peoples of the world into intimate contact with each other. Little by little, the nations are joining in a wide variety of different transnational institutions. Eventually, the institutions are strong enough to prevent wars.

- *Energy that is almost free:* Scientists are searching for better ways to produce energy very cheaply as well as in ways that will cause little or no environmental harm. The extraordinary energy of fusion was demonstrated by hydrogen bombs, but success in using this power source for electricity has eluded the researchers—so far. Other sources of energy include solar power, wind power, and tidal power. Really cheap energy could enormously boost the standard of living, because energy—in one form or another—is required for every human activity.

- *A happiness pill is perfected:* Alcohol, marijuana, cocaine, and other substances have the power to make people feel— temporarily—much better or even euphoric. Scientists are rapidly discovering the basic neurochemical causes of pleasure and other feelings and finding ways to control them. People subject to depression already take drugs to keep them from it, but people want real happiness or even euphoria. As scientists discover more about the brain's "pleasure centers" and how they respond to chemicals, harmless drugs may someday enable people to feel content—perhaps even ecstatic—while performing dull but necessary tasks.

- *Death becomes an ecstatic experience:* We are all brought up to think of death as something tragic if not extremely painful, but it does not have to be. If drugs are developed that can effectively produce real euphoria, people suffering from a terminal illness could go to hospices where they would be given "ecstasy drugs" that are too risky for use by people not already dying. Hospices then could make dying the most pleasant experience of a person's life—the ultimate reward for a life well lived.

- *Permanent human settlements in space:* The development of towns and cities on the moon, Mars, or elsewhere in space will open a new era of human exploration, settlement, and adventures in new realms. As the universe opens up to human travel and settlement, young people will find exciting new opportunities along the expanding frontiers. Overpopulated nations will have a place to send their excess people, thus reducing crowding and other problems frustrating the alleviation of poverty. Earth's natural resources would be under less pressure from human inhabitants.

- *Drugs to boost human intelligence:* Physicians already are using drugs to prevent mental retardation in certain children as well as the brain deterioration suffered by aging adults. Scientists now are gaining the knowledge needed to boost intelligence in other ways through drugs and diet. An increase in human intelligence would mean that we could have extremely capable people running our institutions: Progress on all fronts would speed up, because smarter people would make more scientific discoveries and would be able to apply them more effectively to solving social problems.

- *A really effective "youth treatment" is found:* Future medical procedures may not just slow the aging process but actually reverse it. Old people might regain their youthful vigor and appearance. A ninety-year-old great-grandmother could look as young and beautiful as a Hollywood star and be as strong and vigorous as a twenty-year-old. Current medical progress suggests that breakthroughs in understanding the aging process may be imminent, so some of today's young people may live for centuries.

- *A "world brain" is constructed:* The United States and Japan are racing to build supercomputers capable of solving unimaginably complex problems. Eventually, there may be a huge global network of supercomputers, capable of solving all kinds of baffling problems, helping to create a better life for people everywhere.

And here is a happy thought: Scientists, scholars, and others are working now—in many different ways—to make all eight of these benestrophes really happen! Don't be surprised if several are achieved within the next fifty years.

A Century of Wild Cards?

Benestrophes raise more questions than catastrophes, because people agree more easily on what would be really bad than on what would be really good. This attitude may arise partly from people's instinctive distrust of change, which surfaces quickly unless people are fully convinced the change will be beneficial to themselves. Even then they may be uneasy because they haven't already experienced the benefits of the change.

So many people would question whether the benestrophes suggested here would really be beneficial. Here are sample objections:

War has resulted in many benefits to humanity; it's even possible that without wars humans would never have made the technological progress that eventually brought civilization. What would replace war as a goad to human progress?

Free energy might make us so rich we would become layabouts, never doing much of anything. We would lose many of the values that give some nobility to human existence.

Happiness produced by chemicals would deprive us of our interest in anything except pleasuring ourselves. We would degenerate completely.

By making death enjoyable, people might want to die as quickly as possible. The earth would be depopulated.

Settlements in space would distract us from solving our earthly problems.

A society dominated by geniuses might be horrendous. Intelligence does not make people kind and virtuous; many criminals are brilliant—and even more dangerous because they are clever enough to escape punishment.

Making everybody young would be a step toward making everybody the same. The strength of society comes largely from the diversity of people's abilities, attitudes, and other characteristics. And do we really want to live on and on, century after century?

If a world brain were constructed, humans would lose their dignity or even, perhaps, be reduced to slaves waiting on the world brain.

The number of wild cards per century seems to be increasing due to rapid advances in technology and the consequent changes in human societies. The twentieth century gave us airplanes, television, atomic bombs, space travel, computers, and many other wild-card developments. Based on the record, we have reason to expect more wild cards during the twenty-first century than in any previous century.

Wild cards will help to make our current century the most exciting ever. No matter how imaginative we are, we cannot anticipate all the extraordinary possibilities that the future holds for us. The wildest fantasies of today may be the facts of tomorrow, and our human potential is not only greater than we think but greater than we *can* think.

To deal with wild cards and other challenges of a rapidly changing world, we need the ability to invent new solutions to emerging problems for which we have no ready-made answers. That means we need to be really creative. So, in the next chapter, we will see how we can think more *creatively* about our future as we try to make it really better.

10

Inventing the Future

Developing scenarios requires us to think *creatively* about the future, since we must develop ideas about things that have not happened but *might* happen. Futurists and others have refined a number of techniques for creative thinking, and we can benefit from the tricks they discovered. Most of these techniques can be used for a number of purposes, but they are particularly applicable to making important decisions that put demands on our creativity as well as our knowledge and logic.

Let's begin by reviewing some of the techniques that creative geniuses have used to get their ideas.

The Secrets of Creative Geniuses

Early in his career, Isaac Asimov, an author who often wrote about the future, discovered an effective way to generate new ideas, and it led to his best-known work, the science-fiction trilogy, *Foundation*. The inspiration for *Foundation* came while Asimov was riding the New York subway to see his editor, John Campbell. Here is how it happened, in Asimov's own words:

> On this subway ride I had no story idea to present him with so I tried a trick I still sometimes recommend. I opened a book at random, read a sentence, and concentrated on it until I had an idea. The book was a collection of Gilbert and Sullivan plays, which I just happened to have with me. I opened it to *Iolanthe* and my eye fell on the picture of the fairy queen kneeling before Private Willis of the Grenadier Guards. I let my mind wander from the Grenadiers, to soldiers in general, to a military society, to feudalism, to the breakup of the Roman Empire. By the time I reached Campbell I told him that I was planning to write a story about the breakup of the Galactic Empire.

Asimov's technique closely resembles the method long used by religious people to solve problems. When troubled about something, they open a Bible at random and meditate on the first verse they see. Often, the verse will start them thinking in a new and fruitful way about their problem. The same effect can be achieved by opening up a dictionary and putting one's finger down randomly on a word. If this word doesn't suggest a solution for the problem, try another.

The reason such techniques work is that they force us to think in new ways about our problems. It is easy to obsess over a problem: The same thoughts race around and around in our heads without producing any useful new ideas. So we need to force our own thoughts out of their isolation into an encounter with other ideas. Randomly opening a book and focusing on whatever we find forces our thoughts in a new direction: Often we can discover new possibilities for solving our problems by using this simple technique.

Michael Michalko, a consultant on creativity, made a special investigation of the methods that history's great creative geniuses have used to generate their ideas. The result was a list of eight ways that anyone can use to think like a genius—or at least come up with creative ideas. Here they are:

1. *Look at a problem in many different ways.* Leonardo da Vinci believed that the first way he looked at a problem was too biased toward his usual way of seeing things, so he would look at the problem from one perspective, then another, then another; with each change, his understanding would grow.

2. *Make your thoughts visible.* Galileo used diagrams to explain his ideas, whereas his contemporaries used only conventional verbal and mathematical approaches. Diagrams can be a powerful way to present ideas and stimulate new thinking.

3. *Produce a lot.* Much of what geniuses produce is worth little, but since they produce a lot, they are more likely to produce some real winners. Thomas Edison held 1,093 patents, still the record. He gave himself a quota of one minor invention every ten days and a major invention every six months! Asimov, who was described as a "writing machine," wrote more than 450 books before his heart failed him at the age of seventy-two. Mozart produced more than 600 pieces of music before he died at thirty-five.

4. *Combine things in new ways.* Einstein's famous equation, $E=mc^2$, brought three well-known concepts (energy, mass, and the speed of light) into a new relationship with each other.

5. *Force relationships.* Samuel F.B. Morse was trying to figure out how to produce a telegraphic signal strong enough to transmit all the way across the United States. One day he

saw horses being exchanged at a relay station, and that gave him the idea that a traveling signal could be given periodic boosts of power.

6. ***Think in opposites.*** This seems to be a very common trait among the supercreative. They constantly turn thoughts inside out: What if we grew younger rather than older? What if we had to eat dessert *before* the main course rather than after? Nobel Prize winning physicist Niels Bohr thought that the juxtaposition of opposites allowed one's thoughts to move to new levels.

7. ***Think metaphorically.*** Aristotle thought people who had the capacity to perceive resemblances between two separate areas of existence had special gifts.

8. ***Prepare for the benefits of chance.*** While Edison was searching for a way to make a carbon filament for his electric light bulb, he happened one day to be toying with a piece of putty, turning and twisting it. Suddenly the answer hit him: Twist the carbon like rope. In October 1879, after more than 1,200 experiments, Edison lit a lamp with a carbonized thread as its filament. The following year, his electric light bulb went into commercial use for the first time.

The Role of Chance in Creativity

The key role of chance events in stimulating creativity seems to arise from the fact that a great creation is an unusually successful *system,* and, as with other systems, success depends critically on a very large number of specific elements being arranged in precisely the right way. If a single element is missing or out of place, the system doesn't work.

Someone once asked Isaac Stern, the celebrated violinist, why all professional musicians seem to play the same notes yet some of the musicians sound wonderful and others do not. "It isn't the notes that are important," Stern replied. "It's the intervals between the notes." A false interval can be as damaging in music as a false note. Similarly, the same joke can produce hilarity or groans depending on the timing of the joke teller. A gifted comedian can evoke roars of laughter just by pausing at the right moments.

Creative success depends not just on having the right elements but in having them in the right relationship to each other. A successful discovery or creation can be forestalled by a single missing part of the puzzle or a tiny misarrangement of the parts. Discovering a successful arrangement of parts often occurs due to one or more favorable chance events that push the inventor or storyteller's thoughts in a new and fruitful direction.

The needed intervention of chance is often provided by events in one's normal life, like the putty in Edison's hands. The chance event introduces a new thought that pushes the conscious mind toward a novel line of inquiry. Suddenly, unanticipated connections are made in one's thinking, and a new idea is born.

The chance event is often purely mental; that is, there may be no external circumstance that triggers it. Simply by mentally searching through old memories, people may "accidentally" stumble over something that stimulates a train of thoughts, leading to a solution for the troubling problem. Mental searching—simply allowing our thoughts to wander where they will—is easiest when we are undisturbed and relaxed, perhaps listening to calming music.

A good night's sleep can also help us to solve a difficult problem, according to recent scientific experiments in Germany. "Sleep, by restructuring new memory representations, facilitates extraction of explicit knowledge and insightful behavior," reported Ullrich Wagner and his colleagues.

A dream may help. Dmitri Mendeleyev, the Russian chemist, was struggling, in 1869, to make sense of the chemical elements: It did not seem to make sense that elements with very different atomic weights had similar properties. Mendeleyev cudgeled his brain for three days and nights struggling for an explanation. But he noticed a curious thing: When he tried to arrange the elements in some kind of order, the result suggested his favorite card game, solitaire (patience), in which cards are laid out both according to number and according to suit. Still brooding, he fell asleep at his desk. "I saw in a dream a table where all the elements fell into place as required. Awakening, I immediately wrote it down on a piece of paper." Mendeleyev had just discovered what he called the Periodic Table of Elements, a discovery that gave chemists the awesome ability to forecast the properties of elements that had never been discovered! Today a copy of the Periodic Table hangs in chemistry classrooms around the world.

But dreaming or quiet meditation will not necessarily turn up the key idea needed to solve a problem. Our thoughts may need to be pushed in a new direction by an external event, and creative geniuses (and creativity consultants) use special techniques for stimulating minds to search in new directions for an idea that will lead to a creative train of thought. Who would have thought that the game of solitaire would lead to the greatest discovery in chemistry?

Chance only partly explains the success enjoyed by Edison, Asimov, and Mendeleyev. More important was their passion for their work: They toiled long and hard to bring their ideas to fruition. "Genius," said Edison, "is 1 percent inspiration and 99 percent perspiration." Mendeleyev worked so hard on chemistry that he took time for a haircut only once a year! Asimov worked from 8 a.m. to 10 p.m. every day of the week and took no vacations willingly. He did, however, tolerate frequent interruptions, including those times he met with admirers at meetings of the World Future Society.

Dining with the Society's president before one meeting, Asimov revealed what may be the most important secret of really creative people: They find nothing else more exciting than creative work. To explain his own astounding productivity, Asimov said that other writers do not really like writing! "They like getting ideas and they like having their books published, but they don't like what comes in between. I *like* what comes in between!"

This would come as no surprise to psychologist Mihaly Csikszentmihalyi, who says that creative people all love what they do. "It is not the hope of achieving fame or making money that drives them; rather, it is the opportunity to do the work that they enjoy doing. ... The process of discovery involved in creating something new appears to be one of the most enjoyable activities any human can be involved in."

The thrill of making a discovery (even when its value is unrecognized by anyone other than oneself) offsets the enormous labor and suffering that creative people often endure. Archimedes, the greatest inventor of the ancient world, was so excited when he made one discovery that he is said to have jumped out of his bath and run through the streets, still naked, to announce triumphantly to his family, "Eureka" ("I have found"). People today may still use his exclamation when they find something they have been looking for, and the same Greek word—*heuriskein* in the infinitive—gives us the modern word *heuristic,* which can refer to anything that helps us to make discoveries.

The Science of Discovery

Heuristics, the science of discovery, now gets increasing attention from business, because companies must innovate furiously to survive in a fast-changing world. Managers have developed a ravenous appetite for ideas that will result in new and profitable goods and services.

Serious efforts to stimulate people's creativity began emerging in the 1950s, when New York advertising executive Alex F. Osborn developed what he called "brainstorming" as a way to get ideas for ad campaigns. He described his technique in his book *Applied Imagination* (1952), which got wide attention in the business community. Brainstorming became the best known of the idea-creating techniques and remains probably the most-widely used even today.

Brainstorming, as developed by Osborn, has four basic rules for generating ideas during a brainstorming session: (1) Defer judgment on any of the ideas, (2) Try to develop a lot of ideas and not worry about their quality, (3) Strive for unusual ideas, and (4) Build on other people's ideas.

During a brainstorming session, the leader—often a professional consultant—encourages participants to offer ideas related to the problems to be solved. Wild ideas are encouraged, and criticism of any idea is strictly forbidden, since the initial goal is to come up with as many ideas as possible, not to select the best. One member of the group records all the ideas, and after one or more brainstorming sessions, an evaluation meeting is held to consider the ideas proposed. The ideas may be sorted, ranked according to priority, and forwarded to whoever is in charge for possible action. Brainstorming earns special praise in James M. Higgins's book *101 Creative Problem Solving Techniques* (1994). "You cannot imagine the synergism resulting from this method unless you try it," Higgins enthuses.

Brainstorming can be used for a wide diversity of problems, though it does not work well with broad and complex problems or those requiring a trial-and-error approach, Higgins adds.

But new ideas are not always welcome. In most organizations, people who prefer the old way of doing things are likely to outnumber those who prefer the new—at least among the primary decision makers. Managers may say they want innovative ideas, but they generally don't want to make major changes in their general way of doing business.

"Creativity is inherently disruptive, and creative behavior does not lend itself to smooth management of routine," explains Michael Schrage, co-director of MIT Media Lab's EMarkets Initiative. "There are probably more organizations suppressing good ideas internally than there are organizations starved for creative insights."

Basic Tools for Shaping the Future

We tend to think of writing as communicating with others, but it is an invaluable tool for communicating with ourselves, helping us think creatively about the future (or anything else).

Writing down our thoughts on paper allows us to review them later. Each time we review them we can try to build up those initial ideas or improve them in some way. Because we are not the same person now as we were before, we don't have the same thoughts. The second or third time we return to what we have written down may give us a valuable insight or idea.

Most of us occasionally prepare a "to do" list, which is almost essential to shopping because it can remind us about various chores that we can easily forget.

But a list can serve many other purposes besides reminding us of what we were supposed to remember. A "to do" list helps us to decide which tasks should get priority. When we look at the list, it may also prod us to think how we going to accomplish our different tasks. We can add those ideas to our list. By thinking repeatedly about the same task, we often can get better ideas than the ones we started with.

Less common than "to do" lists but also useful are lists of reasons for making a certain decision. A pro-and-con list is really two lists: reasons for doing something and reasons for *not* doing it. If the decision is important, we may want to return to the list again and again as we methodically work toward a thoughtful decision. Each time we return to it, we may be able to revise it and add more thoughts.

Using a list of reasons can help us to ensure we make a decision in a well-considered, creative way. When we feel we have gotten all the ideas we can, we can then work toward a definite decision by having an internal debate with ourselves, using the two lists as talking points.

Benjamin Franklin, Charles Darwin, and other leading creative thinkers have used lists to think through important decisions. When Darwin needed to decide whether to marry Emma Wedgwood, he carefully made a list of reasons for marrying and not marrying. The arguments for marriage seemed persuasive, and he did marry her. The couple lived happily for the rest of their lives, producing eight children.

Making a list of thoughts or ideas is often an excellent way to start thinking seriously about a problem. It moves us beyond simply generating ideas to seriously critiquing them, and the end result can be a well-thought-out decision about something that will importantly affect our future.

Another simple but powerful technique for thinking creatively about the future is a diary. Keeping a diary is now easier and more useful than ever, thanks to computers. A diary typically is a more-or-less daily recording of anything noteworthy that happened, plus any thoughts that we have. Recording both the events in our lives and what we thought creates an autobiography that we can return to again and again. One of the first steps in thinking about the future is to consider what has happened in the past that we felt happy or sorry about. By noting these "prouds" and "sorries," we gain a better understanding of ourselves and what we really want to do with our futures.

Glenn T. Seaborg, one of the most productive chemists of all time, kept a very careful journal of his search for atomic element 94, which he and his colleagues eventually discovered in 1944. It was plutonium, an element used in the atomic bomb dropped on Nagasaki in 1945. Seaborg's team also discovered americium and curium. He won a Nobel Prize for his work, but, more impressively, he became the first living chemist for whom an element has been named (seaborgium, element 106). Would he have found his way to those elusive elements without a diary? Probably not.

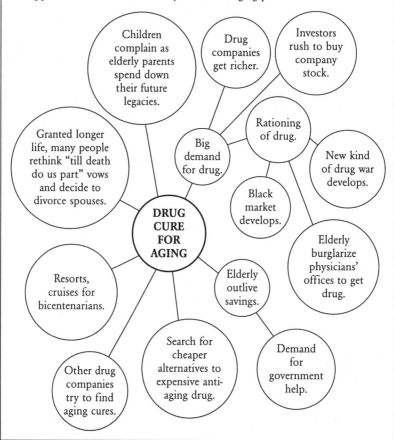

IDEA MAPPING
"A cure for aging is discovered."

Idea maps are a simple but useful tool for thinking creatively about anything. On a sheet of blank paper, write in the center what you want to think about (in a very few words). Draw a circle around what you have written. Around that circle put down whatever ideas flow from your original, central idea. The idea map shown here was used to anticipate what might happen if scientists discover a way to halt the aging process.

In the idea map:

Children complain as elderly parents spend down their future legacies.

Drug companies get richer.

Investors rush to buy company stock.

Granted longer life, many people rethink "till death do us part" vows and decide to divorce spouses.

Big demand for drug.

Rationing of drug.

New kind of drug war develops.

DRUG CURE FOR AGING

Black market develops.

Elderly burglarize physicians' offices to get drug.

Resorts, cruises for bicentenarians.

Elderly outlive savings.

Other drug companies try to find aging cures.

Search for cheaper alternatives to expensive anti-aging drug.

Demand for government help.

Mapping Our Ideas

Lone individuals as well as groups can brainstorm by mapping out their ideas on paper, blackboard, or other medium. You begin by writing down what you want to think about, then draw a circle around it. Next you try to think of relevant things and draw a circle around each of them with a line connecting each to the central circle. Add further ideas in circles and draw connecting lines. The result is something that can be described as a "idea map," but can also be described as a "thought map" or "mind map."

As with group brainstorming, a thought mapper should not criticize the ideas initially but simply write down as many as possible. Idea mapping is an excellent technique for generating new ideas; it is especially useful for identifying all the issues and subissues related to a problem, as well as potential solutions and the pros and cons of those solutions. Thought mapping also works well for outlining presentations and papers.

You can use this technique to think about almost anything, including any aspect of the future. In such a case, the thought map may be referred to as a *futures wheel* or *futures web*. For a futures wheel, you simply write a possible future event and put a circle around it. Then you add possible consequences of the future events and put circles around each of those. Add a line to connect each of the surrounding circles to the postulated future event. Then you can try to think what might be the secondary consequences of your initial ring of consequences. For example, we put in the center the idea that people born in the year 2000 or later will, on average, live to be at least 100 years old. What will be the first-order consequences, the second-order consequences, and so on? We might think that current retirement at sixty-five will be impossible because there won't be enough workers to support all the retirees. As a consequence, retirement may be postponed to the age of eighty or so. As a further consequence, more efforts will be made to make sure people over sixty-five are able to avoid disabilities until later ages. Futurist Richard Slaughter describes using a futures wheel as "a simple but powerful technique."

Planning a Pleasant Evening

A very simple problem—how to spend our time next Saturday night—can allow us to explain a few useful futuring techniques. Let's assume that we all agree that we want to have dinner and see a movie or play. In discussion, we also decide on three restaurants and four plays or movies we would all like to see. So we list our options.

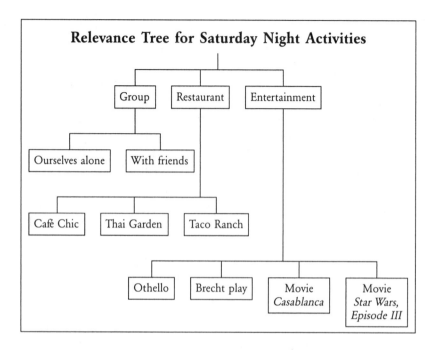

We next decide that it might be helpful to diagram our options so that we can see our choices a little more clearly.

One use of this type of diagram, known as a relevance tree, is to create a visual display of the choices that we need to make. By using a relevance tree, it is often easier, especially in complex decision making, to have the choices made clearly available and also to help a number of people focus on the decisions that need to be made.

A relevance tree, like other diagrams, provides a valuable alternative to text as a way of presenting information. As Galileo and other creative thinkers discovered, a diagram helps both to communicate information to others and to stimulate one's own creativity. The importance of using non-textual communication increases with the amount of information that we must deal with. The Saturday Night example is ultra-simple, whereas a relevance tree for even a modest-size business operation can be highly complex.

Progress in Futuring

We have now concluded our review of a few futuring methods that can help us to find our way in today's complex, rapidly changing world. There are, of course, many other techniques, and we cannot look at them all, but one approach has always been extremely important: Knowing about important things that happened in the past, and relating them to our current circumstances. So in the next chapter we will look at what the past can tell us about the future.

11

The Past as a Guide to the Future

Futuring can be thought of as the art of converting knowledge of the past into knowledge of the future. We can do this using the tools that nature has given us—our memory, intelligence, and imagination—as well as the methods discussed in past chapters. In this chapter, we will look at other ways in which knowing what happened in the past can help us to anticipate what may happen in the future. Let's begin by considering a simple example of how knowledge of the past can be used to help us with a very practical problem—how to safeguard our money.

The Madness of Crowds
In the 1990s, enthusiastic investors rushed to buy the stocks of Internet companies. Everybody knew the Internet was growing by leaps and bounds, so it seemed perfectly obvious that people who invested in Internet companies would make lots of money. Nobody seemed to care that the dot-coms were hemorrhaging money and had inexperienced managers, high expenditures, little revenue, no tangible assets, and no solid path to profitability.

As Internet stocks rose in value, investors who had not yet bought the stocks noted the trend and rushed to buy, pushing prices still higher. A "buyers' panic" began when people who normally had little interest in the Internet or stocks got the notion that they were missing out on the opportunity of a lifetime. They, too, rushed to buy lest they miss out on the golden opportunity to make a fortune.

Normally, short-sellers deflate overpriced stocks by borrowing shares of those stocks and immediately selling them in the expectation that prices will fall and the stocks can be bought back later at lower prices. But the short-sellers avoided the Internet stocks because investor psychology had become so wild. Their decision to avoid the stocks removed a normal check on rising prices. As a result, overpriced Internet stocks got more overpriced, then wildly overpriced, and eventually insanely overpriced.

But in March 2000 prices of Internet stocks began to weaken and then plunge, vaporizing billions of dollars of investor wealth. As stock prices continued to drop, the companies tried desperately to cut their costs and earn revenues, but to little avail. In the aftermath of the stock collapse, 135 *major* Internet companies closed their doors; no count was reported for the smaller companies that were also wiped out, but they likely numbered in the thousands. Survivors such as Yahoo!, Amazon.com, ETrade, and Priceline.com saw their values plunge to a fraction of what they had been. Meanwhile, hundreds of billions of dollars of investor wealth had been converted by the dot-coms' owners, managers, and employees into luxurious homes, lavish clothes, sports cars, wine cellars, and spectacular parties.

During the dot-com craze, seasoned investors avoided the Internet stocks because they sensed that a mania was in progress, and a financial mania generally ends badly for investors. Typically, such manias end unexpectedly when buying weakens, causing prices to dip, then plunge as shareholders panic. Trying to jump into such a frenzy and sell out before prices crash is extremely risky, since it's uncertain how high values will go before suddenly collapsing. Your investment might be wiped out immediately—or you might make some paper profits and then lose everything before you get around to selling out. Knowing financial history helped legendary investors Bernard Baruch and Joseph P. Kennedy preserve their fortunes during the catastrophic crash of prices on the New York Stock Exchange in October 1929. While stock prices were still soaring, Baruch and Kennedy sold stocks, and the cash they received became more valuable than ever after stock prices plunged.

Baruch and other successful investors have credited their success, in part, to Charles MacKay's classic work *Memoirs of Extraordinary Popular Delusions and the Madness of Crowds*, originally published in 1852. MacKay described Holland's famous tulip bulb craze, which briefly caused speculators to pay stupendous prices for tulip bulbs in 1636-37. MacKay also wrote about the South Sea Bubble, which arose from wild speculation in the stock of the South Sea Company in 1720. Among its victims was Sir Isaac Newton, widely regarded as the greatest scientist in history: "I can calculate the motions of the heavenly bodies," Newton commented ruefully, "but not the madness of crowds." Probably few Internet investors ever read MacKay's book or Charles P. Kindleberger's more recent *Manias, Panics, and Crashes: A History of Financial Crises* (1989). A half-hour reading either work might have saved them their nest eggs.

The Internet mania demonstrated the importance of history as a tool for anticipating future events. History can help us in many ways as we explore the future and try to cope with our daily problems. One way it helps, as illustrated by the dot-com mania, is that it gives us models for understanding new situations. The way it works is simple in principle: If we know that a certain type of situation has occurred in the past, we can anticipate that it will develop as such situations have developed in the past. With this knowledge, we can anticipate what will happen in the new situation, enabling us to make a better judgment about what we ourselves should do. That's how Baruch and Kennedy became richer than ever after the stock market crash of 1929. When stocks crashed, cash and gold soared in value.

How will we know when the next mania begins? If we can recall how a "bubble" developed in Internet stocks and then burst, as bubbles will, we have a useful tool to apply whenever we learn about rapidly rising prices for some commodity. When the Internet mania began, seasoned investors noticed the unusual exuberance of less experienced investors trying to buy Netscape and other offerings of Internet stocks and raised their guard. As prices soared for any stock ending in ".com," almost any investor familiar with financial history should have sensed that a mania was in progress and anticipated that it would ruin many investors.

The frenzied excitement over Internet stocks was very much like the mania for Chicago real estate in the 1830s, Florida real estate in the 1920s, stocks in the 1920s, gold and silver in the 1970s and early 1980s, or biotech stocks in the early 1990s. And let's not forget the famous California gold rush of 1849: Far more miners went broke than struck it rich. The people who made money were mainly those who sold things to the prospectors, who went broke trying to get rich quickly.

Practical Lessons from Financial History

Here are a few things that financial history can teach us to help make our financial futures more successful.

- *Watch out for manias, and remember this:* A mania may be hard to recognize in its early stages. As in the case of the Internet stocks, there are generally plausible reasons for believing that a certain class of commodities will increase in value, so it is easy to rationalize a decision to buy. However, if investors seem overly excited or prices rise steeply over a short period, we may suspect that a mania is in progress. And let's not forget that a mania can strike almost anything that is bought and sold: During Holland's tulip bulb mania in the 1600s, a single tulip bulb might be worth a fortune.

- *If you already own a commodity that becomes subject to a mania,* your best bet may be to sell it and enjoy your profits. If you don't own the commodity, it's best not to buy it during a mania, because you never know when prices will stop rising and quickly collapse. Warning: It may be difficult to restrain yourself from buying when your friends are bragging about how much money they are making by buying the commodity.

- *The crash that ends a mania is likely to be much faster* than the previous buildup of values, but you can be pretty sure of one thing: You won't know when it has started, and by the time you decide to sell, it will likely be too late to prevent a heavy loss, though it may still be better to sell because prices are likely to plunge still further, sometimes to zero.

- *Diversify your investments.* This is the advice of every financial adviser, but is often neglected even by the cleverest investors. History teaches that every category of investment—from real estate to hog bellies and collectibles—goes through periodic downswings that can dramatically reduce its value. Unfortunately, people can easily forget to diversify when their imagination is distracted with dreams of future wealth flowing from an investment currently soaring in value.

- *Use leverage with care.* Borrowing money to buy a stock or a house is often desirable, but the risks must be carefully weighed: One can easily fall into serious difficulties due to borrowed money. William C. Durant, who united a numbere of automobile companies to form the General Motors

Company in 1908, later borrowed money to support GM's stock when it declined. But, the stock continued to fall, and Durant was ruined. The former master of the universe went to work running a bowling alley.

The last two rules—diversify your investments and use leverage with care—seem to be among the most important to preserving one's wealth. Poor William Durant neglected both of them.

Many more lessons can be drawn from financial history, and learning them can be very helpful to anyone's finances. But few investors bother to read financial history—or any history, for that matter—and their wealth suffers for it. If you are ignorant of history, you will be unduly influenced by your personal experience, which is extremely limited. You will not benefit from the experiences of other people who, down through history, have faced circumstances similar to yours.

Another lesson of history is that people often draw the wrong lesson from their personal experiences. After being traumatized by the stock market crash of 1929 and the subsequent collapse of the U.S. banking system, many avoided banks as well as stocks for the rest of their lives. So what *did* they do? They kept their savings in cash and hid it in mattresses and the walls of their homes. But a little knowledge of financial history would have warned them that keeping all one's money in cash can also be a costly mistake, because inflation has ruined one currency after another.

The clearest lesson of financial history is that no investment offers complete safety: U.S. government securities and currency are often touted as "risk-free," but no one who knows financial history would trust such a claim. Since 1940, the dollar has lost more than 90 percent of its value, and it continues to depreciate. History offers no comfort whatsoever regarding the safety of paper money. The U.S. dollar once was a promise to pay the bearer in gold or silver, but no more. Now the only thing the government will offer in exchange for your dollars is more dollars, so the dollar has become, in effect, an "I owe you nothing."

The American dollar is still generally regarded as the safest type of paper money, however, because other countries have an even worse record for preserving the value of their currency over the long term. Since the Chinese invented paper currency (and suffered the first inflation), currency after currency has become worthless. However, the lesson of history is not that we should never trust paper currency, but that we must recognize that paper money, like any other investment, sometimes loses its value. Our best safety thus lies in diversifying our investments, so that when one or more fail, we still have something left. Often, that something will be rising in value while other items are falling.

The simple truth that emerges from the past is that we live in a world full of risks, and the challenge is to learn how to assess them carefully and choose only those that are really worth taking. Diversification and other strategies can reduce our financial risks but can never eliminate them entirely.

Using History in Decision Making

Thucydides, the greatest of the ancient Greek historians, can also be regarded as possibly the first futurist, because he did not write his histories simply to recount events for the entertainment of readers, but rather to provide guidance for the future. Thucydides believed that foresight was the most important skill for people to have when they make important decisions. Foresight depends on knowing what happened in the past because similar things were likely to happen in the future. Accordingly Thucydides attempted to be absolutely factual in reporting what happened in the past: "I have written not for immediate applause [like his rival Herodotus!] but for posterity, and I shall be content if the future student of these events, or of other similar events, ... finds my narrative of them useful."

In military schools around the world, students still read Thucydides' history of the Peloponnesian War—a war fought between the Greek city-states Athens and Sparta between 431 and 404 B.C. Today's students are preparing to fight wars using robotic aircraft and perhaps thermonuclear missiles, yet military leaders recognize that the students will make more effective officers if they know what happened in a war fought thousands of years ago with spears and shields.

Since Thucydides' time, political leaders have turned, again and again, to history for guidance in making the decisions that shape the future of nations. Among American presidents, Woodrow Wilson was a political science professor who drew on history for his lectures. Abraham Lincoln modeled his Gettysburg Address on the ancient Greek leader Pericles' tribute to the Athenians who died in the Peloponnesian War. Harry Truman, who considered the Greek historian Plutarch one of his most trusted advisers, had to make some of the most momentous decisions of history, such as dropping atomic bombs on Japan, supporting the creation of Israel, and sending U.S. troops into South Korea to help defend it against a communist invasion.

American leaders have relied on history since the very beginning: The nation's Founding Fathers—John Adams, Thomas Jefferson, and James Madison—consciously sought to abide by the lessons of history in creating their new government. One lesson they all absorbed was that a people could easily lose its rights to a dictator. Guided largely by the ancient historian Polybius, the founders went to enormous pains to create a unique system of government in which power is carefully divided so that it cannot easily coalesce under an oligarchy or dictator. As a result of this foresight, based quite consciously on the painful experiences of the past, the U.S. government has never had a tyrant at its helm.

Whether they lead nations or businesses or just themselves, people making decisions can find useful guidance in what past leaders have done and what the consequences were, and this knowledge can be enormously useful in deciding what will work out best in today's situations. However, busy decision makers may find it easier if the lessons of history are identified and explained in a brief, straightforward manner.

This "bottom line" approach to history was practiced most famously by Niccolò Machiavelli in *The Prince*. This book is a practical guide for rulers based on the experience of past rulers. Machiavelli (1469-1527) hoped that his book would help Lorenzo the Magnificent, then ruler of Florence, to understand how to hold and exercise power.

While writing *The Prince*, Machiavelli would imagine that he was actually in the presence of the great figures of the past. He even wore his formal courtly dress so that he would be comfortable in their presence, and they would not think him unworthy of asking them questions. Happily, the imaginary figures treated him respectfully. "I ask them the reason for their actions," he reported. "Out of kindness, they answer me."

Based on "their" answers, Machiavelli developed a set of policies that a ruler should adopt to ensure the success of his reign. Machiavelli's frequent citations of historical incidents as support give *The Prince* much of its authority and interest for readers. Since Machiavelli's death, his book has been bedside reading of such famous rulers as France's Cardinal de Richelieu, Prussia's Frederick the Great, German statesman Otto von Bismarck, and France's Georges Clemenceau. Today, *The Prince* is often read by U.S. corporate executives, but they are more likely to prefer modern writers, citing more recent historical experience, particularly in the business world.

Creating a Better Future

We don't have to know much history to recognize that truly horrible events occurred in the past; we must therefore assume that there will be more horrors in the future unless we develop ways to prevent them. Studying past horrors is perhaps the first step toward preventing future recurrences, because we can begin searching for effective means of prevention and mitigation. History offers us much encouragement in thinking that serious efforts to safeguard the future world from nightmares can be very worthwhile even if not a hundred percent effective. For instance, we now have—thanks to past efforts—effective preventives and cures for many diseases, such as polio.

The investigation of past events can often be very helpful to the future because it can help so much to prevent future disasters. If we cannot completely prevent a disaster, perhaps we can find ways to reduce its likelihood and also the pain it causes.

The Great Depression of the 1930s—the most profound and terrible economic downturn in American history—has remained a mystery to this day even though it has been studied for years. Economists are still debating its causes: Was it due to the 1929 crash on the New York Stock Exchange? Or was misguided monetary policy to blame? Or could it have been the moves in Congress to restrict imports, which led to the Smoot-Hawley Tariff Act of 1930? All of these factors may have played roles in causing the Depression, but uncertainty about the event lingers; debate often resurfaces when people start worrying that current weakness in the U.S. economy may lead to Great Depression II.

We know from history that economic activity increases and decreases over time, but the timing and amplitude of the cycle varies unpredictably. One reason is that these movements reflect individual decisions made by, literally, almost everyone in the world. Due to the sensitivity of complex systems, the cry of a baby in the Congo could cause a crash of stock prices on Wall Street (as explained in Chapter 5, on systems).

So we cannot either predict or prevent another Great Depression, but the investigation into the causes of these economic disasters has not been useless: Economists are fairly well agreed on certain measures that may be helpful when a recession or depression threatens. For example, one of the most frightening events of the 1930s was the collapse of the banking system. Economists now believe that similar disasters can be prevented by having the Federal Reserve prepared to add liquidity (money) to the banking system when the stock market crashes and panic starts to spread. The extra money (and reassurance from the Fed) enables people and institutions to meet their financial obligations, so the financial system does not freeze up. After asset values recover, the Federal Reserve System can mop up the excess money to forestall future inflation.

"This was done beautifully by the Federal Reserve System after the October 1987 crash, a splendid operation," says economic historian Kindleberger. The newly appointed Fed chairman, Alan Greenspan, earned plaudits from everyone, and his success can be attributed in large part to his wide-ranging knowledge of what happened in America's financial past. Historian John Steele Gordon says the Greenspan-led intervention was only the second time in history that the U.S. government has moved so decisively to prevent a stock market disaster from producing an economic depression. The only previous such instance was Alexander Hamilton's intervention in 1792. In other cases, such as the crashes of 1837, 1857, 1873, 1893, 1907, and 1929, the financial collapse ushered in an economic depression.

America—and the world—can be grateful to Greenspan and his knowledge of financial history.

The Recent Past as a Guide

While knowing what happened in the distant past can be useful, it may be even more important to understand the recent past, because recent circumstances normally are more like those of our own day. Unfortunately, the media give us only spotty reports about recent events, and unless we make a serious effort we are not likely to be well informed and even less likely to really understand the bits of information we have picked up. The media now stress entertainment more than significance, and it's hard to find—amid reports on sports, scandals, Hollywood personalities, etc.—informative articles providing a broad-gauge, long-term perspective on important recent changes in our world and judicious suggestions about what may result from them.

However, a few books do provide general discussions of recent trends and make a conscious attempt to relate them to the future. Among well-known authors of these overview books are John Naisbitt, Marvin Cetron, and Alvin Toffler. Their major books have offered readable summaries of major social and technological trends together with anticipations about where the trends may be leading.

Naisbitt's approach, exemplified in such books as *Megatrends* and *Megatrends 2000,* is to discuss ten selected trends in each book. Cetron does not use the "Top Ten" technique as an organizing device, but, like Naisbitt, focuses on a modest number of topics to avoid overwhelming readers with information. Cetron's major books, *Encounters with the Future* and *American Renaissance,* are unique in that they make quantitative predictions and forecast specific events, which he believes are likely to occur by given dates; these forecasts are backed up by sound, detailed analysis of current trends and events. Neither Naisbitt nor Cetron offers a broad theory of humanity's social development, but Alvin and Heidi Toffler do. Operating more in the grand style of the macrohistorians, the Tofflers view human society as going through a series of "waves." The first wave began with the development of agriculture; the second, with power machinery in the eighteenth century; and the third, with computers and advanced communications systems during recent decades.

These authors summarize a great many current changes in technology and society, making it easy for readers to see big patterns. So much is happening in today's world, and people have so little time to become informed, that there is a widening knowledge gap that may pose serious problems for democratic societies dependent on the people to make responsible public choices. In 1900, people might have hoped to keep up with events by reading newspapers, but as the amount of news increased and the time to absorb it declined, people turned to news magazines as a means of staying current. However, a number of thoughtful people recognize their own growing ignorance of what's happening in the world and are trying to make themselves better informed by means of these "newsbooks."

Naisbitt, Cetron, and the Tofflers may be regarded as pioneers in the art of describing major social and technological trends in a manner accessible to busy people. What a reader gains from their newsbooks is a better understanding of significant world trends and a very rough picture of the future. The newsbooks' real value may be less in their specific anticipations than in conveying to readers a general sense of the emerging forces and issues that are shaping our future. By doing so, they render a valuable service.

In addition to the newsbooks providing overviews, there are also a few journals, such as *The Futurist*, that specialize in reporting on recent trends, forecasts, and ideas about our future, and there are many books that discuss trends in specific areas: economics, technology, demography, etc.

Special mention must be made of the remarkable two-volume *Encyclopedia of the Future* (1996), compiled by George Kurian and Graham T.T. Molitor. Kurian is a noted encyclopedia editor and Molitor a well-credentialed futurist, so they made an excellent team and successfully assembled authoritative articles on a very wide range of topics. The finished work, running 1,116 pages, includes a timeline projecting forthcoming events as far out as the death of the universe. Molitor and Kurian later compressed the two volumes into a single volume entitled *The Macmillan Compendium: The 21st Century.*

The Encyclopedia of the Future provided a magnificent diversity of thinking about the future and set a standard for other such encyclopedias. However, it also suggested some of the problems with overviews of the entire world and its future: (1) Despite its thousand-plus pages, the information provided is infinitesimal compared to the incredible complexity it attempts to describe and anticipate. (2) Each article reflects the perspective of a single individual; a different expert would have offered a very different view. (3) One cannot really see the world as a whole, much less the future world, by means of looking at this encyclopedia. To grasp the encyclopedia as a totality, one would have to read all the articles and then somehow create a conception of the world from that. Despite those basic problems, the *Encyclopedia of the Future* constitutes a constructive step toward making people better informed about the world's future.

What a reader gains from reading the literature dealing with recent trends and where they may be headed is a general sense of change, of human progress, of emerging opportunities and dangers, of hopes and fears. So the books prepare us psychologically for the fast-changing world that lies ahead. But we must also recognize that—based on what we learn from history—today's views of the future will seem quaint when examined fifty or more years hence. Today's literature about the future is not created for the people of the future but for us today; we must not judge these works by the standard of permanent perfection but by the more reasonable standard of being useful to the contemporary world. By this standard, they succeed.

The Value of the Long View

By looking back and identifying the patterns in past events, we gain a powerful tool for knowing what *might* happen in the future. We can even learn a surprising amount from the very distant past. Based on what happened over the many eons of earthly history, we can anticipate, for example, the following:

One or more major asteroids or comets will strike the earth in the future, wreaking colossal destruction, unless we develop the technology to prevent it. Though such collisions are rare, they can be truly awful and, as things stand, we are likely to do no better than the dinosaurs. We might escape this fate by developing a system for deflecting celestial objects, but right now we are defenseless. The little good news about this danger is that our improving technologies could make us much better prepared than in the past to undertake a defensive system against asteroids and comets.

Earth's animals and plant species will be very different in the longer term future from what they are now—and so will humans, if we survive. In the nineteenth century, scientists discovered that plants and animals evolved from one type of organism into another. This process has never stopped: Many animals and plant species are becoming extinct today, and new forms are evolving and taking over the niches left behind by life-forms becoming extinct.

Earth's climate will change considerably in the years ahead. The climate has shifted frequently in the past, and so has the composition of the atmosphere. The earth has gone through both warming and cooling phases through the centuries. Studies of ice cores—samples of fossilized ice—also show shifts in the dust and pollen in Earth's atmosphere, indicating that the very air we breathe is changing subtly in character. Eons ago, the earth had an atmosphere that would have been deadly to humans if there had been any around at the time.

We cannot understand our current circumstances or assess future developments without the perspective that history and our own memory of the past can give us. In the present, our senses are filled with information from the world around us, but the value of this information is largely momentary; after that, its usefulness plunges because very little remains relevant and important. Yet the vividness of sensory experience and recent events can easily mislead us. We fall into the trap of thinking that things we have been experiencing will continue indefinitely into the future. That was the mistake made by the investors who believed that Internet stocks could only go up in price because that was what those stocks had been doing recently.

So if we lack the perspective that comes from knowing history, we easily mistake a short-term shift for a permanent condition. We assume that things will remain indefinitely what they are now. History and scientific research teach us that *nothing* is really permanent; everything changes as time passes. Mighty corporations perish, along with the people who built them. Buildings fall to ruins. Nations collapse. Gods die along with those who believed in them. The science of one generation is trashed by the next. Whatever survives is changed. Languages and cultures must adapt lest they die out. The rock-ribbed mountains wash slowly into the sea. History warns us about their impermanence and provides useful lessons in humility as we consider the future.

Humility is especially needed when we attempt to anticipate what will happen in the future, as we shall see in the next chapter. When it comes to predicting the future, the record shows that even the smartest people can make themselves look like utter fools.

12

Predicting the Future

People often seem ready to listen to anyone who claims to know what will happen in the future. Through history, they have resorted to palmists, seers, crystal-ball gazers, astrologers, Ouija boards, and diviners. In recent decades, seekers after predictions have turned to economists, rocket scientists, financial analysts, and many other professionals for enlightenment.

But is it really possible to predict the future? Yes, No, or Maybe—it depends on exactly what we mean by the question. For some people, it means to know in detail and for certain everything that is going to happen in the future; clearly no one has that power. On the other hand, ordinary people make predictions in everyday life, and we are probably right more often than wrong in our normal, short-term forecasts about things we are familiar with. We may not know who will be the pope a hundred years from now, but we can forecast that we will probably go to sleep sometime within the next twenty-four hours and will probably have a meal or two during that same period. If we put our minds to it, we might come up with a few longer-term predictions, such as what sort of things Americans will be doing on the next Fourth of July (Independence Day). We might even be able to say something about what we ourselves expect to be doing five years from now. Naturally, we could be very wrong, but being wrong a good part of the time is an inescapable part of human life.

So a reasonable *one-word* answer to the question "Can we predict the future?" is Sometimes. Most of what will happen is beyond our power to predict. Yet we can forecast some future events fairly accurately. Not even a top expert in forecasting can know who the U.S. president will be thirty years from now or what the Dow Jones Industrial Average will be at 12 p.m. eastern standard time on January 15, 2050. The world changes so much over long periods of time that it's quite possible there won't even be a president thirty years from now or a Dow Jones Industrial Average in 2050.

But despite the severe limitations in our power to forecast future events, anticipating the future is critically important to our health, well-being, and even our lives, for a very simple reason: Assumptions about the future are required for rational decision making. We may not even be aware of the assumptions we are making about the future, but without them we would lack a rational basis for choosing one action over another. The fact is that we cannot even get out of bed in the morning without forecasting subconsciously that we will not fall through the floor. (This prediction represents a reasonable extrapolation from our experience.) We are so used to making this sort of prediction that we hardly think of it as a forecast.

It's when we have difficulty deciding what will happen, especially in the long term, that we find it tempting to make the blanket judgment "You can't predict the future." But it would be more correct to say that it is often—but not always—impossible to develop a prediction for some future situation on a rational basis. The person who will be president of the United States thirty years from now is presumably alive today, since the Constitution requires that a President be at least thirty-five years old, but there is no scientific way to identify the individual who will occupy the White House then.

We can learn a lot about forecasting by reviewing past attempts to anticipate future events, and that is our task in this chapter. These historical examples have been selected for their interest and for their ability to shed light on the forecasting process. This review will give readers a background for judging forecasts and thinking about the future.

Let's begin by recognizing the fallibility of forecasters: Time and again, the leading lights of a nation, the wisest of the wise, the best and the brightest have looked like fools when they tried to predict the future. So the first lesson in forecasting is: Be humble.

However, as you read the section ahead, remember that each mistaken prediction, no matter how laughable, highlights an instance in which an accurate forecast might have been overwhelmingly valuable. In many cases, skilled and open-minded forecasters might have achieved useful insights where untrained, closed, or biased minds did not.

Follies of Forecasters

In the fifteenth century, King Ferdinand of Spain appointed a committee to review Columbus's plans to sail west to the Indies.

The learned committee spent four years studying the proposal, and then reported that Columbus's idea was absurd: Even if he managed to get to the other side of the earth, the committee opined, he would never be able to get back. Besides, added the committee, Saint Augustine had already revealed that there was no land on the other side of the world. If it had been left to the committee, America might still be occupied only by Native Americans.

Skepticism also greeted Samuel Morse's claim that he could transmit messages by means of electricity. After the inventor demonstrated his telegraph to members of the U.S. Congress in 1842, many congressmen questioned Morse's sanity. One senator confided, "I watched his countenance closely to see if he was not deranged."

By the end of the nineteenth century, people had something else to scoff at—flying machines. Lord Kelvin, the physicist who presided over Britain's Royal Society, stated flatly in 1896 that "heavier than air flying machines are impossible." Simon Newcomb, one of the most distinguished scientists of his time, declared in 1902 that the demonstration of the impossibility of "a practical machine by which man shall fly long distances through the air" is "as complete as it is possible for the demonstration of any physical fact to be."

In 1903, the *New York Times* sneered at flying-machine experiments as a waste of time. Only a week later, the Wright brothers successfully flew their craft at Kitty Hawk, North Carolina. The Wrights themselves were somewhat surprised that they had actually done it: In 1901, Wilbur Wright had told his brother Orville that man would not fly for another fifty years.

After the brothers succeeded in flying, Wilbur Wright swore off predictions, but the *New York Times* went right on getting the future wrong. In 1920, it ridiculed Robert Goddard's rocket experiments and suggested that even a high-school student should know that a rocket cannot propel itself through space since it needs something better than a vacuum to push against. In 1969, as *Apollo 11* was about to reach the moon, the *Times* belatedly ran a correction: "It is now definitely established that a rocket can function in a vacuum. The *Times* regrets the error."

The contrition of the *Times* was exemplary, but readers of its archives can find other instances when an apology might have been appropriate. For instance, when television was introduced at the 1939-1940 New York World's Fair, the *Times* declared, "The problem with television is that people must sit and keep their eyes glued to the screen; the average American family hasn't time for it."

Technology has progressed relentlessly through the twentieth century despite a withering crossfire from skeptics and naysayers, not to mention the frequent cluelessness of the experts themselves. Lee De Forest, the radio and television pioneer, declared in 1926 that, while television was technically feasible, "commercially and financially, I consider it an impossibility, a development of which we need waste little time dreaming." Albert Einstein said in 1932: "There is not the slightest indication that [nuclear] energy will ever be obtainable. It would mean that the atom would have to be shattered at will."

After both the United States and the Soviet Union had working atomic bombs, people everywhere in the late 1940s thought atomic war was imminent. In his novel *Nineteen Eighty-four*, George Orwell talked about "the atomic wars of the 1950s" as if they were an established fact. To escape them, Orwell himself went to live on a remote British island "not worth a bomb." But despite persistent fears, no atomic wars came in the 1950s or the following decades.

Fear of nuclear war ebbed after the Cuban missile crisis of 1962, but the Cassandras found other future catastrophes to worry about. With world population soaring, they said, there soon wouldn't be enough food to go around. In 1967, a book appeared with the dire title *Famine—1975!* But fears of famine abated when the green revolution's high-yielding grains led to food surpluses. Even India, which experienced a real famine in 1943, became a food exporter.

The doomsayers found another cause for alarm in 1973, when the Organization of the Petroleum Exporting Countries (OPEC) quadrupled the price of oil, sparking fears of permanent global shortages of energy. President Carter warned Americans that they would have to give up their gas-guzzling automobiles and wear sweaters to avoid freezing in their homes. But the higher prices for oil made it economically practical to bring on new sources of energy and to invest more in conservation. So by the 1980s, the oil shortage had become the oil glut.

Throughout the twentieth century, economic and political forecasters contended for top honors in the faulty-forecast competition. Again and again, the economy has boomed when it was supposed to collapse (or the reverse), and the stock market has regularly frustrated financial forecasters by going up whenever the forecasters neared agreement that it was bound to go down—and vice versa. The extraordinary fallibility of stock market gurus is so notorious that it has produced a school of "contrarian" financial analysts, who try to make money by betting against the consensus of market forecasters.

In the 1950s, most people were convinced that Japanese goods would always be inferior. U.S. Secretary of State John Foster Dulles even advised the Japanese to export their products to the Third World because they were not up to U.S. quality standards. Even in the 1960s, American automobile manufacturers laughed at Japanese cars. As late as 1968, *Business Week* declared, "The Japanese auto industry is not likely to carve out a big slice of the U.S. market for itself." By the 1970s, Japanese cars and other goods had seized such a large share of world markets that U.S. gloom-mongers had started warning Americans of a Japanese economic takeover. Yet the Japanese juggernaut fell apart during a severe depression in the 1990s.

One of the most famous blunders of the political forecasters was their near certainty that Thomas Dewey would defeat Harry Truman for the U.S. presidency in 1948. George Bush was said to be a shoo-in for a second term as president in 1992, but Bill Clinton shoved him out after economic woes clouded Bush's Gulf War success.

Virtually the entire forecasting community participated in one of the most significant lapses of the century: the general failure to anticipate the collapse of the Soviet system and the end of the Cold War. The United States had poured billions of dollars into gathering information about the Soviet Union, but intelligence agencies like the CIA failed to recognize that the Soviet system was collapsing. Observers have noted that the agency's budget depended largely on U.S. fears of Soviet strength, suggesting that the CIA had a strong motive to keep Congress and the American people worried about Soviet power.

The self-interest of forecasters may also have played a role in the collapse of the Texas oil and real estate economy in the early 1980s. During the 1970s, the Texas economy boomed as the price of oil soared; money poured in, and real estate prices soared. One energy forecaster, Dale Steffes of Houston, became a pariah by warning that the price of petroleum was going to collapse. He turned out to be right, and many people would have benefited if they had acted on the basis of his forecast. Instead, many lost fortunes, because they had, without fully realizing it, bet the ranch on continued high prices and failed to sell out in time.

A forecast may be seen to fail even it is largely correct. A forecast typically includes a number of elements, any one of which may prove to be wrong. So even if a forecaster is right in the main, some details may prove embarrassing. Wary of being wrong, many forecasters try to avoid specifics. "Never give them both a date and a number," forecasters often advise each other, only half jokingly. If you forecast that so-and-so will be elected president next year, you will look silly if he isn't. But a vague forecast is often worth little. Most clients prefer a forecaster who is willing to take reasonable risks in his forecasts by being fairly specific. Errors in forecasts are easier to forgive than vague blather.

A forecaster in 1900 might have correctly anticipated that the U.S. population (then 76 million) would increase in the twentieth century, but people would not have been very impressed if he did not suggest how much it would grow by what date. An added 100,000 people would be trivial; but 100 million would be enormously significant—especially if it were going to happen very quickly. Both timing and magnitude of a development are needed if a population forecast is to be useful. But any forecaster who provides both a number and a date is likely to err in forecasting population more than a few years ahead. A 1966 report in the *Wall Street Journal* quoted experts as projecting that world population in the year 2000 would grow to more than 6 billion, a very good call; but the projection for the U.S. population was for 340 million, about 20 percent too high. The forecasters probably assumed that the high birthrates of the baby boom (1946-1964) would continue; instead, birthrates collapsed in the late 1960s, resulting in the "birth dearth." Still, the 1966 forecast for the U.S. population was probably good enough to help decision makers at the time.

For more insight into why forecasts so often go wrong, let's look at the "postponed miracles"—the long-promised technological wonders that keep us waiting ... and waiting ... and waiting.

Miracles That Were Postponed

It's easy to understand why people back in 1900 were skeptical about "flying machines." The airplane was a truly startling invention, because it departed from all previous human experience and seemed to challenge God in Heaven. What is more puzzling is that we are often told to expect certain wonderful things in the future, but these wonders never seem to arrive.

The personal helicopter is one of the miracles of the future we're still waiting for. It became a popular vision of the future back in the 1940s. Newspapers and magazines talked enthusiastically about how people would commute to their jobs by air rather than having to drive on streets and highways clogged with traffic. Yet today almost no one has a helicopter sitting in his backyard. Somehow the personal helicopter has never really gotten off the ground. Thank God, many people would say.

Since the beginning of the twentieth century, there have been stories about video telephones that would allow us to see the person we were talking to, but even today very few of us have this technology. We were also told, in the 1950s, that we would have three-dimensional television, but that too still has not arrived. Clearly, people who believe that a technology will soon appear can be as wrong as those who doubt it.

It required little imagination to predict the personal helicopter or the picture telephone; but it did require at least some imagination to take proper account of the obstacles they faced. Since the helicopter was a reality in the 1940s and the builders of helicopters were eager to push sales, people could easily imagine themselves flying by helicopter from a suburban backyard to a heliport on a skyscraper. The technology also made for an appealing image in the Sunday supplements. However, further thought might suggest that thousands of whirling choppers in the air would be a nightmare for city officials, police, and almost everyone else. Today, helicopters remain not only expensive but very noisy; only very wealthy people can afford one, and they cannot easily get permission to fly it from most residential areas.

The videophone was envisioned at least as early as the 1900s, and it became technically feasible in the form of closed-circuit television by 1929. AT&T offered videophone service commercially in 1965 from locations in New York, Washington, and

Chicago. However, a three-minute Picturephone call cost $15, and few people used the new service, so AT&T stopped offering it. Since then, the videophone has continued to progress, both technologically and in actual usage, but slowly. In the early years of the twenty-first century, relatively few homes could boast a videophone. On the other hand, prices were falling, and Internet-based video was becoming both cheaper still and highly practical where broadband service was available. It is not unreasonable to think that—at long last and no kidding—something closely resembling the videophone will soon become common.

What delayed the videophone? One reason, which surfaced during AT&T's test of its Picturephone, is that most people did not seem to have much need for a videophone. Some firms used it to interview job candidates and to show certain goods, such as designs. But the high cost and inconvenience of having to go to a special location for marginal benefits kept users away.

Like many other technologies before and since, the videophone was trapped in a vicious circle: Potential customers refused to buy because it was too expensive, too inconvenient, and too klutzy for whatever benefit they might hope to get out of it. And with few customers for their offerings, industry refused to invest heavily in improving the technology. AT&T had monopoly power at the time, and had little to fear from competitors.

The standoff between companies waiting for demand before investing and potential customers refusing to buy goods that offer too little benefit can continue more or less indefinitely unless there is a catalyst for change. This catalyst may be the emergence of a significant group of customers willing to pay a high price for the technology because it offers a benefit that they view as worth the money. A catalyst for the videocassette recorder was the ability of television viewers to record over-the-air programs for later viewing. No other technology offered this service, which customers perceived as something actually worth going into debt to obtain.

For the Internet, electronic mail proved a killer application; neither the post office nor the telephone offered the convenience and speed of electronic mail, so many people were delighted when computers provided that service. Computerized communications also found a ready welcome in the financial world, where people's livelihoods depend on fast-changing security and commodity prices; they, too, were willing to pay handsomely for the new technology. Regardless of why they were motivated to become linked up through computers, these early users created a growing market for computer services of all kinds, thus helping the computer industry to improve quality, develop new services, reduce prices, and locate more customers.

But it is worth noting that the U.S. government financed the early development of both the computer and the Internet, and this government funding was justified by military, not civilian, requirements. So a forecaster who tried to predict the coming of the computer and the Internet would probably have had to take account of international political and governmental factors. In a sense, he would have needed to anticipate U.S. involvement in World War II and the Cold War, because if America had not been frightened by foreign nations during the 1939-1945 period, the funds for developing the early computers probably would not have been forthcoming. Without the Cold War, the Defense Department would probably never have had the money that went to finance the Arpanet, parent of the Internet.

A new technology must overcome huge odds to achieve success. Around the world, people have ideas for making our lives richer, happier, and easier, but the obstacles to realization are fierce and numerous. A new technology must not only do something that people want done, but do it better—at least in some respect—than other systems. It can be faster, safer, cheaper, or whatever, but people want a clear personal benefit to themselves before they buy a new product.

Even if a new invention can provide an important benefit, people often fail to recognize it, especially during the development stage. The first Xerox machine, now in the Smithsonian Institution, looks like a crudely made child's toy. It's easy to understand why IBM and other companies rejected it, missing an opportunity to make many billions of dollars.

The Xerox machine needed a genius, Chester Carlson, for its invention, but it also needed a different sort of genius to recognize its potential and produce it for the market. Happily, Carlson found a champion in Joseph Wilson, president of the Haloid Corporation. Wilson bet his company on the machine, and it became such a runaway success that the company changed its name to the Xerox Corporation.

If a new technology promises major benefits to users, a company may test it. If it continues to look promising, market tests may be made. Even if the benefits are real, people may refuse to buy because the price seems too high. Few people were willing to purchase a videotape recorder when the price was thousands of dollars; after the price fell to hundreds of dollars, millions rushed to buy.

There are many thousands of inventions waiting for a chance to make it big in the marketplace. A few will succeed; the rest will fade away because people find little use for them or think they are too costly, too dangerous, or just too tacky. Some may find niches somewhere: Moving sidewalks have never caught on in city areas, though they have been dreamed about for many years. Cost and other factors have prevented their use, but the concept has found an application in airports as a means of speeding passengers to waiting planes.

The miracles of technology that are postponed, temporarily or permanently, help us to understand a fundamental principle in thinking about the future: Many things that appear possible or probable to us today will simply never happen. They are like seeds that fail to mature, because they get blocked by one obstacle or another. Potentiality always exceeds actuality; innumerable possibilities of the future perish before achieving reality. Only a few manage to become part of our lives.

In contrast to the technologies that fail to achieve the importance their advocates expected, other technologies surprise by being far more important than anyone ever dreamed. This was the case with the computer.

The Computer: A Stealth Technology

Nobody seems to have predicted the computer as we know it today. Science-fiction writers churned out page after page about robots and spaceships without saying anything about computers. Even after the computer became a reality in the 1940s, most people didn't think it was of much importance. And when it had achieved impressive success, they could not imagine that even more wondrous success lay just ahead.

So the computer could be described as history's greatest stealth invention. It repeatedly defeated the radar screens of the forward thinkers and astounded even its wild enthusiasts with its achievements. The question for us is, What can we learn from this puzzling case of forecaster blindness?

When the computer was hatched in U.S. scientific laboratories in the 1940s, it was something worse than an ugly duckling. It wasn't cute at all; it was just a tangled mass of metal frames, wires, and vacuum tubes that filled a room. The scientists at Harvard and MIT claimed their clunky metallic monster could perform certain mathematical calculations that would take a very long time if done by humans. That was no big deal for most people.

By the 1950s, the monster had proved it could help in maintaining records. That was useful, perhaps, but not exciting. The computer was not doing anything that an ordinary human couldn't do, the experts said, but companies and government agencies soon figured out that they could save money if computers could replace a lot of clerical workers. Agencies like the Census Bureau, and even some big companies, began to buy computers. Still, sales were very slow. To sell a single computer in the 1950s, IBM would often have to send in its chairman (and master salesman) Thomas J. Watson Jr. to convince skeptical managers.

Though computers were becoming faster and more reliable, they remained far too expensive for ordinary folk or small businesses. They were also too big: In 1949, *Popular Mechanics* had prophesied optimistically, "Computers in the future may weigh no more than 1.5 tons." Even the minicomputer, which became the darling of the 1970s, was so big and expensive that it was almost unimaginable that people might actually have a computer at home. When someone raised the issue with Ken Olsen, president of the Digital Equipment Corporation in 1977, he assured them that "there is no reason for any individual to have a computer in their home."

But even as Olsen spoke, the microchip had begun to achieve breakaway success outside the established computer industry. To the amazement of old-time computer engineers, a wafer no bigger than a baby's fingernail could substitute for a massive mainframe computer. Computers now could be truly small—and also cheap. The tiny chip of silicon made it possible for a guy in a garage to build a computer, as Apple creator Steve Wozniak and many others actually did. Working largely on the West Coast, far from the old-line computer companies, thousands of unsupervised youngsters began experimenting with the microcomputers. Computers had broken free and were now "running wild," as Adam Osborne put it in his book describing the phenomenon.

To the consternation of the suits at IBM, microcomputers proliferated wildly, moving both into smaller businesses and into people's homes. Computers were now beyond the control of the IBMers or anyone else. IBM quickly developed a microcomputer of its own, but the parade was passing it by. By the 1990s, an upstart company named Microsoft had a higher market value on Wall Street than IBM. Meanwhile, computers had gained increasing ability to communicate with each other, thanks to standardized protocols, and the rapidly developing Internet made possible a radical restructuring of almost every human activity from retailing to education. Like the computer itself, and the microcomputer, the Internet has been a stealth technology, a phenomenon that seems to have developed with little fanfare until it was well established.

One explanation for the general failure to anticipate the invention of the computer is people's general ignorance of the world and its possibilities. We constantly focus on what we know, forgetting that we know only a tiny, tiny bit of what is actually happening. Furthermore, as time passes, events that appear to us totally fantastic and wildly improbable occur with alarming frequency. So it was easy, in the 1940s or 1950s, for even well-educated people to be quite unaware of computers.

A 1940 forecaster assigned the task of identifying the most important technologies of the next fifty years almost certainly would not have included the computer, though it actually appeared only four years later due to a "wild card" event—the Japanese attack on Pearl Harbor. The U.S. military needed a system capable of making a huge number of mathematical calculations very quickly. That provided a killer application for a device that could provide that capability, and the computer held out that promise. Moreover, the customer would pay for its building, thus overcoming a key hurdle for untried technologies—initial funding for development.

In retrospect, it seems likely that if the United States had not become involved in World War II the computer would not have developed when it did. Even if an astute technology forecaster in 1940 had recognized that a device like the computer *might* be developed, he would also have to make the judgment that the United States would be motivated to provide the funds needed for its development. It would have taken an enormous leap of imagination, plus considerable information and good judgment outside the field of technology, to recognize that military concerns would soon provide that impetus.

Even if he had forecast the initial development of the computer, the forecaster might not have anticipated the computer would become the subject of intense development by private companies to serve customers who saw a growing number of uses for the computer. So we can easily understand why a forecaster surveying the technological horizon in 1940 would have failed to identify the computer as one of the most important technologies of the following decades.

In 1950 or even 1960, the promise of the computer remained unclear. By the mid 1960s, however, computers were moving into large organizations everywhere, IBM had become the darling of Wall Street, and the press was filled with stories about how computers might be used in fields ranging from archaeology to zoology. Enthusiasts talked about the wonderful things that computers would do in schools, libraries, and other areas of society. Yet the prophets' imagination still lagged behind reality. If forecasters had taken account of the improvements in the computer, they might well have anticipated— perhaps as early as 1960—the microcomputer and the massive entry of computers into homes and offices that occurred during the 1980s. But this does not seem to have happened.

The microcomputer depended on the microchip, which did not exist in 1960, but a technology forecaster might have simply assumed that some way would be found for the trend toward smaller, less expensive computers to continue. With the assistance of research and technology laboratories, technological capabilities tend to increase despite frequent obstacles, some of which seem to present permanent limitations. But again and again, a new method or system arrives just when it's needed if the trend is to continue. So simply by assuming that computers would continue to get more powerful, smaller, and cheaper, a 1960 forecaster might well have imagined a computer small enough to sit on someone's desk and sell at such a low price that even ordinary people could buy them. But it was hard to do so due to what can be called "paradigm paralysis." Computers in 1960s were huge and expensive; if a computer were small and fairly inexpensive, it simply wouldn't be a computer as it was known then. As well, both the industry and computer experts had an enormous stake in the mainframe computer of the era: They had little or no desire to see it supplanted by an upstart rival. The development of smaller computers would wreck the business they were in, depreciating the value of engineers trained in the older technology as well as the value of the companies making them.

So instead of talking about minicomputers or microcomputers, computer people enthused about computer terminals, which would connect a distant user to a central mainframe computer. The traditional computer industry found this solution quite appealing since, it would mean more business for their mainframes.

Looking back, we can understand how computers could enter society without attracting much attention from the general public during their early years. However, a knowledgeable forecaster might have anticipated much of its subsequent development, because it followed the path of other successful technologies toward general improvement and adjustment to meet user needs—by achieving greater power, more durability, smaller size, lower cost, etc. A forecaster who assumed that the computer would follow this path might have anticipated a number of its future uses, provided that he clearly understood both the capabilities of the computer and the potential applications in government and businesses. However, few people, then or now, have both types of understanding. A forecaster could easily go wrong because he did not really understand how the technical capabilities of the computer could provide so much value to the economy. The forecasting task was made even more complex by the need to find specific uses in specific businesses: Sales are made to individual customers, not to industries and certainly not to the general economy.

Forecasting under these conditions probably must be largely intuitive: After learning as much as possible about the capabilities of the emerging technology, a forecaster today would probably want to search for potential beneficiaries of the technology. These tasks could be quite time consuming but might identify some important users who would finance further development of the technology.

But forecasting technology, and most other things, is generally difficult beyond the next few years. As for forecasting what life will be like a hundred years from now, there may not be much at all that we can say with confidence. If we insist on trying, we may do no better than a group of people in 1893 who tried to anticipate what life in 1993 would be like.

Today's World as Envisioned a Century Ago

As part of the fanfare for the 1893 World's Columbian Exposition in Chicago, seventy-four prominent Americans wrote brief essays for newspapers on what life would be like a century later, in 1993. Industrialists George Westinghouse and W.R. Grace, reformer Henry George, politician William Jennings Bryan, members of President Benjamin Harrison's cabinet, and other luminaries went on record with their hundred-year forecasts. Today, many of these forecasts are hilarious because they have proved so ludicrously wrong.

Treasury Secretary Charles Foster confidently predicted that the railroad would still be the fastest means of travel in 1993. A few fellow essayists saw possibilities in air travel—by balloon. Senator John J. Ingalls declared that, by 1993, "it will be as common for the citizen to call for his dirigible balloon as it now is for his buggy or his boots."

Journalist Walter Wellman correctly forecast the coming of the airplane, but he thought it would be powered by electric batteries. Turning to urban transportation, Wellman saw no future for subways; instead, Americans in 1993 would ride in elevated trains moving along glass-enclosed tracks. The overhead transit system would not only spare Americans the horrors of subterranean transportation, but would shelter pedestrians from rain and snow.

Curiously, the 1893 forecasters failed to anticipate motor vehicles, which were to revolutionize travel in the decades just ahead. Postmaster General John Wanamaker was convinced that the U.S. mail in 1993 would still travel by stagecoach and horseback rider. He conceded, however, that urgent communications would be transmitted by telegraph and telephone.

If the 1893 forecasters had been right, the workday now would last only three hours. Transcontinental mail would be transmitted in pneumatic tubes. Laws would be so simplified that there would be no work for lawyers. The clergy would wear jewelry at services. Religion would have solved the alcohol problem. The Protestant churches would be united. There would be little crime because criminals would be prevented from breeding.

Perhaps most startling to us today is the extraordinary optimism that 1893 forecasters felt as they envisioned our era. Their great hero was Thomas Edison, who was then mass-producing miracles that benefited millions of ordinary people as well as the privileged. Enthusiasm for the new technologies nourished hopes of similar improvements in society, and even in man himself. Senator W.A. Peffer predicted that war would be abolished in the years ahead, unemployment would disappear, poverty would fade, and justice would be dealt to everyone. "Men will grow wiser, better, and purer," he declared.

Joaquin Miller, famed for a stirring poem about Columbus discovering America, thought humans in 1993 would be "handsomer, healthier, happier too, and ergo better." Lawyer Van Buren Denslow agreed that the race would be handsomer, healthier, longer-lived, and happier.

Our predecessors' enthusiasm for our present age makes many people smile today. Why? Was their optimism naïve? Clearly wishful thinking and special pleading for their social goals influenced the 1893 forecasters. But the more-pessimistic attitudes of today may also represent the fashion of an age. We now combine a blasé acceptance of the wonders of technological progress with a cynical peevishness because we still have problems to worry about. Optimism now is greeted with accusations of naïveté or of heartless callousness to suffering and injustice.

The 1893 forecasters also fell victim to two fundamental problems in long-range forecasting: The first is that important developments occur constantly all around the world, but they may not appear significant, and most people may remain totally unaware of them. By 1893, some Europeans had experimented for years with automobiles; gasoline-powered cars were successfully run in Germany in the 1880s. But our 1893 forecasters either had not heard about these "horseless carriages" or did not consider them important. If we today attempt to forecast a hundred years into the future, our forecasts, too, will likely be undermined by current developments we are unaware of.

The second problem is that recent events, especially those we experience personally, dominate our thinking about the future.

The railroads were developing feverishly in the 1880s and 1890s; it took little imagination to think they would become faster and more widespread in the years ahead. So one forecaster was quite certain that by 1993 travelers would be able to ride in a railway train all the way from Chicago to Buenos Aires. Yet, this seemingly safe prediction has never been validated, and we are left to wonder how many of the future developments that we ourselves consider certain will never happen.

Forecasting a hundred years ahead is clearly a challenge; but what about thirty years?

Today's World as Envisioned a Generation Ago

The first regular issue (February 1967) of *The Futurist*, then a newsletter and now a magazine published by the World Future Society, offered numerous forecasts about what would happen in the following decades. Thirty years later, the editor decided to assess how well they had withstood the test of time.

The forecasts were reasonable projections based on social and technological trends in the 1960s. The forecasters themselves were recognized authorities and responsible leaders. Some had standing as futurists: Science writer Arthur C. Clarke, computer pioneer John Diebold, and U.S. Vice President Hubert Humphrey were among the first members of the World Future Society (founded in 1966), and all three later participated in Society meetings.

Among the numerous statements about the future in the February 1967 issue, about forty were so clear and specific that they could be judged either right or wrong by 1997, mainly because the authors had been brave enough to specify the date for realizing the forecast they made. The editor eliminated certain forecasts from consideration because he lacked the knowledge to judge their accuracy. That left thirty-four to be judged.

Of the thirty-four forecasts qualifying for evaluation, the editor awarded twenty-three hits and eleven misses. This could be counted a good score, since anyone who could consistently win two out of three bets at a casino would soon break the bank. But why were there so many wrong forecasts by intelligent, influential people?

One obvious reason was that the forecasters failed to anticipate the slowdown in space exploration. In the 1960s, the

United States and the Soviet Union had been rapidly increasing their outlays for space exploration. If funding had continued to rise at the same rate, there might indeed have been a permanent base on the moon by the late 1980s. However, congressional support for the space program weakened after the moon landing had been achieved, and the Nixon administration had other priorities. An astute forecaster might have anticipated the funding cutbacks, and even if funding had risen, technical problems might have kept several space forecasts from realization; the landing of humans on Mars still looks years away. But in the ebullient 1960s the moon and even Mars seemed well within human grasp.

Though clearly wrong in many specific forecasts, the forecasters could be judged correct in their general view of the future: They foresaw a society making dynamic technological progress, expanding into the oceans and space, enlarging its economy, and curing ancient ills. And that describes reasonably well the overall thrust of American society during the thirty years from 1967 to 1997.

Still, the study illustrated why forecasts often cannot be judged either correct or incorrect years after they are made. Most of the erroneous forecasts could not have been judged wrong if the forecasters had not given a date by which time the prediction was to be realized. This recalls the praises of an admirer of Leon Trotsky, a leader of the Russian revolution: "Proof of Trotsky's farsightedness is that none of his predictions have come true yet."

Coming to Judgment

What lessons can we draw from past efforts to predict the future?

First and most obviously, we must recognize our general ignorance of what will actually happen in the future, especially anything beyond the very near term. Even if we think we are making a certain or nearly certain forecast, we can be utterly wrong. Remember, *anybody* can be wrong. If geniuses like Newton and Einstein can be wrong, so can we.

Another lesson we might draw is that forecasts are not *always* wrong; in fact, they may prove surprisingly correct. This is just as well, since we continue to depend heavily on forecasts in our everyday lives, even if they are frequently wrong. Though we laugh when meteorologists are wrong about the weather, we still want their forecasts when we are planning our activities. We know that weather forecasters are reasonably accurate in their short-term forecasts and we are willing to forgive their lapses, because we recognize that they are certainly more likely to be correct than we ourselves are.

Useful forecasts can be made for certain events, though most of the future lies completely beyond our powers of prediction. Our forecasting ability declines rapidly as we try to look deeper and deeper into the future. Professional futurists rarely forecast more than fifty years into the future. If they do, clients are properly skeptical.

Forecasts are normally probabilistic in character, and the likelihood of a forecast failing rises as it becomes more precise and detailed. For example, a forecast that nanotechnology will be applied extensively in medical technologies may be useful and correct, but a forecast that nanotech repairs on hearts will make transplants unnecessary by the year 2030 is likely to be prove erroneous.

Finally, we need forecasts in order to make rational decisions: If we are organizing a picnic, we want to know the weather forecast. It is also useful to know what we cannot reasonably forecast because the occurrence of certain types of future events is fundamentally unknown and uncertain. If someone informs us that it will definitely not rain in Chicago three months from now on July 12, it's useful to know that he cannot reasonably give us any such assurance, since it is impossible to predict Chicago weather three months ahead. On the other hand, a weather forecaster might reasonably state the probability of rain falling on Chicago on July 12 based on the average rainfall on previous July 12s.

Progress in Forecasting

None of the people making the predictions discussed here was a trained forecaster, though many had extensive education and experience in various areas. Their forecasts were largely intuitive—educated guesses based on their own knowledge and imagination. In recent years, as we shall see later, researchers have developed new methods for forecasting, and universities are now training students in these techniques. So it is reasonable to anticipate that forecasts will become increasingly sophisticated in the future. Computer and telecommunications technologies are also showing their usefulness in forecasting.

But will this mean that forecasts made today will not look foolish in a hundred years? Don't bet on it. Progress in forecasting may be offset by the increasing pace of technological and social change. Though we lack a set of agreed-upon indicators of change that would allow us to measure the speedup, most scholars seem agreed that change is accelerating. Faster change clearly makes forecasting more difficult: Imagine if all the change in *both* the nineteenth and twentieth centuries had occurred in the nineteenth. A forecaster in 1800 might have forecast the development of railroads from what was known about steam engines and, if very, very clever, he might have made a guess at aircraft. He would have had little or no basis for anticipating computers or atomic bombs. It would have been possible to conceive of mechanical brains and ultra-powerful bombs, but there was no plausible path to achieve the extraordinary power actually demonstrated by computers and atomic bombs.

With so many unexpected changes in the twentieth century, some people see science fiction as offering the best forecast for the future. It is true that science-fiction writers described feats of space travel long before the Apollo program; Jules Verne, for example, described a space rocket in his 1865 novel *From the Earth to the Moon*. But science fiction, though often drawing on science, consists of fantasies that make no claim to being forecasts. Since science-fiction writers produce innumerable fantasies, it is possible to find fictional parallels to subsequent technologies or events in the real world. But fiction is not prediction: A forecast must be presented as something that will actually happen in the future. Unless that claim is made, it is not really a forecast at all. Furthermore, the insight into the future of science-fiction writers has been called into question by science-fiction writers themselves.

"Science routinely prods science fiction," according to Isaac Asimov, who wrote both science fiction and science fact. "One has only to read the science fiction written in the late 1930s to see how abysmally blind it was to what was about to happen. Story after story talks about radium as the wonder metal of atomic energy; not one talks about uranium. Story after story talks about robots; not one talks about the computer. Science fiction is very occasionally prescient, but for the most part it is a humble follower of science."

Asimov himself made quite a few successful forecasts during his lifetime (1920-1992). Not only was he the best-known prophet of the age of robots, but he also showed his talent in more mundane predictions. In 1964, he anticipated correctly that medical authorities would eventually discover that tobacco smoke contributes to cancer among nonsmokers. Sure enough, research later confirmed the ill effects of "latent smoking," and it became a major issue in the 1980s. However, when Asimov received a World Future Society award in 1986, he did not exult in his forecasting successes, but recalled a bad mistake he once made: After successfully predicting the pocket calculator—what it would look like and what it would do—Asimov forgot all about his prediction and wrote a whole book about how to use the slide rule! The slide rule book came out the same day the first pocket calculator hit the market, making slide rules obsolete.

Asimov's experience exemplifies an important rule in forecasting: Never forget that the future is smarter than you are. In other words, our ability to anticipate the future is very limited, while the future itself contains infinite possibilities. So one of the surest forecasts we can make is that the future will continue to give us plenty of surprises.

Knowing our limitations is, of course, important in futuring, and one of them is that our thinking about the future and our attitude toward it are shaped by the times we live in. We will see this clearly in the next two chapters as we trace the history of serious thinking about the future.

Serious here means "non-magical." In ancient times, and to a large extent even today, people turned routinely to magic— esoteric practices like astrology and divination—when they wanted to know something about the future. However, a few used methods that would gradually lead to more scientific ways of thinking, and much is owed to key figures in the development of the fields of history, philosophy, and science as we shall see in the next chapter.

In the next two chapters, we will also be looking for answers to a question posed by the 1893 forecasts discussed in this chapter: Why were people at the end of the nineteenth century so confident about the future? And that raises the question, Why did people stop being so optimistic?

13

How the Future Became
What It Used to Be

The idea of progress owes much to the Greek philosopher Plato, who stressed the importance of having the right ideas—not just the correct facts about past events. Good ideas can lead to a better world.

We can improve our ideas by means of a critical inquiry into our current beliefs as well as whatever ideas we develop in the course of our inquiry. In a series of written dialogues, Plato showed how this could be done, and his method of critical inquiry is still used in serious decision making.

Plato also made another important contribution to thinking about the future: He developed the concept of an ideal society in which there would be perfect justice. We now would call his ideal society a utopia, but Plato developed his concept before there was a word for it. His ideal society is described in his greatest work, *The Republic,* in which he seeks to answer the question, "What is justice and how can we achieve it?" Plato suggested that, in the perfect city, wisdom and love of wisdom would dominate. Passion and love of glory would be subordinated to reason.

Since Plato's day, his vision of a better future society has not only fascinated readers but stimulated many of them to come up with their own ideas for a better way to organize human societies. "It is no extravagance to claim, that the entire body of utopian fiction is little more than a series of variations on Plato," comments British historian I.F. Clarke. "As the first in the field he was able to present—once and for all—the basic dilemma that puts power and passion into the dullest utopia—the eternal conflict between individual desires and public necessities, between the happiness of the citizen and the security of the state."

But the really exciting thing about Plato's idea of an ideal community was that it demonstrated that people could imagine a better future society, discuss with others how it might work, and then—perhaps—actually create it! Human life might be improved in a really big way.

The Idea of Progress

Utopia got its name when, centuries after Plato, Sir Thomas More (1478-1535) followed in Plato's tradition by writing a description of a land called Utopia (Greek for "no place"). In More's concept, Utopia had such features as community of goods, a national system of education, and work for everybody. Modern readers may be surprised to find that More's ideal community also included monarchy and slavery, but like all utopias it reflected the culture in which the author lived. At the same time, More's version of monarchy was startlingly modern. Each city in Utopia had a "prince" who was elected by the elected representatives of the people from a list of four men nominated by the people of the four quarters of the city, according to historian-futurist W. Warren Wagar. The prince served for life unless he had to be deposed for "aiming at tyranny." Except for the life term, it's pretty much like the parliamentary system now in place in the United Kingdom, Wagar says.

A century later, in Shakespeare's time, Sir Francis Bacon developed a utopia along different lines from More. Bacon's *New Atlantis* described an ideal science-based community located on the imaginary island of Bensalem, which has a research institute known as Solomon's House at its center. All the island's citizens seek "the knowledge of causes and secret motions of things, and the enlarging of the bounds of human empire, to the effecting of all things possible."

Bacon's utopia reflected his belief that the purpose of knowledge, including natural philosophy, or science, is to improve human life. Knowledge should not be pursued purely for speculative satisfaction, as many of his contemporaries thought. In his book *Novum Organum* ("The New Tool" in Latin), he pointed out that three inventions unknown to the ancients—printing, gunpowder, and the compass—"had changed the appearance and state of the whole world; first in literature, then in warfare, and lastly in navigation; and innumerable changes have been thence derived, so that no empire, sect, or star appears to have exercised a greater power or influence on human affairs than these mechanical discoveries." Never before had the beneficial impacts of new technology—or what Bacon called "profitable inventions"—been so clearly recognized and proclaimed.

Bacon's ideas were too radical for most people of his age. Europe's universities subscribed almost exclusively to Aristotelian scholasticism—essentially Christianity, as defined by Thomas Aquinas, plus Aristotle's views of the natural world. But Bacon did have some readers, and his thinking gradually took root in the intellectual world.

Later in the seventeenth century, many of Europe's scholars crossed swords in a lively literary war known as the Quarrel of the Ancients and Moderns. The issue was whether modern people were the equals of the ancients or inferior to them. The great leaders and writers of the seventeenth century had admirers who thought that some of their contemporaries could reasonably be compared with Augustus and Sophocles. Essentially, the proponents of the Moderns were challenging the domination of intellectual life by Aristotle and other ancients. Scholars were celebrating the achievements of the greats of antiquity while ignoring what contemporary Europeans were doing. The perception that the people of the past were greater than those of the present implied that humanity had actually *regressed* from a golden age—a view that conflicted with the idea of progress.

Entering the fray as a champion of the Moderns, French scientist Bernard de Fontenelle published a book entitled *Dialogues of the Dead* (1683), which described an imaginary discussion between the ancient philosopher Socrates and the modern French essayist Michel de Montaigne. Socrates says he expects that the age of Montaigne will show a vast improvement over his own, because people will have profited by the experience of many centuries. Montaigne says that it is not so, and towering figures like the greats of antiquity are no longer to be found. Socrates protests, arguing that antiquity is enlarged and exalted by distance. "In our own day," he says, "we esteemed our ancestors more than they deserved, and now our posterity esteems us more than we deserve." By challenging the widespread view that humanity had declined from a past "Golden Age," Fontenelle and other Moderns prepared the way for more positive visions of the future.

Meanwhile, Bacon's ideas continued to gain ground. By the mid-eighteenth century, Bacon had a zealous following in intellectual circles. In 1750, A.R.J. Turgot, later to become famous as an economist and statesman, read a paper on the "Successive Advances of the Human Mind" to a conference of clerics at the Sorbonne in Paris. Turgot argued at length in favor of the new theory of progress and ended with a burst of enthusiasm:

> Open your eyes and see! Century of Louis the Great, may your light beautify the precious reign of his successors! May it last forever, may it extend over the whole world! May men continually make steps along the road of truth! Rather still, may they continually become better and happier!

Fontenelle was the first scholar to formulate the idea of the progress of knowledge as a complete doctrine, according to historian J.B. Bury, author of *The Idea of Progress*. Bacon and the champions of the moderns had prepared the way but, says Bury, "the theory of the progress of knowledge includes and acquires its value by including the indefinite future. This step was taken by Fontenelle."

Meanwhile, other French scholars had set to work preparing an encyclopedia that Bacon had suggested, and they explicitly credited him by using the title he had proposed. The first volume of *Encyclopedia, or Reasoned Dictionary of Sciences, Arts, and Trades* appeared in 1751; it eventually ran to twenty-two volumes, many containing engravings that showed how people actually worked with the latest preindustrial technologies. One series of plates shows how horses powered the machines used to roll metal ingots into thin strips that could be stamped into coins. Another series showed a carriage factory with no power machinery at all.

Completing this enormous project proved extremely difficult, partly because the French government and Roman Catholic authorities constantly harassed both the editors and contributors. The principal editor, Denis Diderot, was jailed for a time. But the work went on, and as the successive volumes emerged from the press they influenced thinking all over Europe. People began to think in broad terms about the way in which society's goods were being produced, so it prepared the way for Adam Smith's groundbreaking economic text *The Wealth of Nations* (1776) and stimulated the Industrial Revolution, which was just getting under way in England.

Science and the Industrial Revolution

The Industrial Revolution, which began with the steam engine, brought the railway, the steamship, the electric telegraph, and innumerable other inventions. The new technologies provided tangible evidence for Bacon's view that new technology, assisted by science, could improve human life. Benjamin Franklin reflected the growing enthusiasm for technological progress in a 1780 letter to fellow scientist Joseph Priestley:

> The rapid progress true science now makes occasions my regretting sometimes that I was born so soon. It is impossible to imagine the height to which may be carried, in a thousand years, the power of man over matter. We may perhaps learn to deprive large masses of their gravity, and give them absolute levity, for the sake of easy transport. Agriculture may diminish its labor and double its produce; all diseases may by sure means be prevented or cured, not excepting even that of old age, and our lives lengthened at pleasure even beyond the antediluvian standard. O that moral science were in a fair way of improvement, that men would cease to be wolves to one another, and that human beings would at length learn what they now improperly call humanity.

Franklin's letter was only a momentary excursion into anticipating what might happen in the future, but a few years later there appeared one of the greatest classics in the history of speculation about the future, a book that correctly foretold many of the developments of the nineteenth and twentieth centuries, and may still foretell the developments in the twenty-first. This classic work is the Marquis de Condorcet's *Sketch for a Historical Picture of the Progress of the Human Mind*.

Condorcet (1743-94) was a great admirer of Francis Bacon and even wrote a paper, "Fragment on Atlantis," in which he carried Bacon's idea of a research institute, Solomon's House, to its logical conclusion—a world research center. Still more influential on Condorcet was his friend Turgot, who had delivered the eloquent paean to progress at the Sorbonne in 1750. Turgot had also written a book in which he viewed history as the story of progress from superstition and barbarism to an age of reason and enlightenment. Condorcet took Turgot's basic concepts, extended them to every area of human activity, and used them as instruments to deduce what the future might be like.

The victory of the Americans in their war for independence and the increasing intensity of the movement against slavery heightened Condorcet's natural optimism and confirmed his faith in progress. He felt that he was living through "one of the greatest revolutions of the human race." Indeed, he never lost his optimism even though he composed his book in 1793, when he was a fugitive from the 1793-94 reign of terror imposed by French revolutionary Maximilien de Robespierre.

Probably no other prognosticator has survived the test of subsequent history so well for so long as has Condorcet. He anticipated that the colonies of the New World would become politically independent of Europe; today almost all are. He said they would make rapid progress because they could profit from the knowledge that Europe had acquired, and so they have, though some much more so than others. He predicted that slavery would eventually disappear; it has, almost everywhere. He predicted that science would make rapid progress, that farmers would produce more and better food on the same acreage, that people would have more leisure, and that birth control could become widespread.

Condorcet's *Sketch* has won praise for its accuracy from S. Colum Gilfillan, a twentieth-century sociologist who studied technological change. Gilfillan credits Condorcet with formally originating and using the extrapolative method of prediction and for being one of the first to make conditional predictions—that is, forecasts of what is likely to happen *if* something else occurs.

The Triumph of the Doctrine of Progress

The doctrine of progress, a controversial idea in the seventeenth century, became widely accepted in the eighteenth century and the conventional wisdom in the nineteenth. By that time, progress was visible everywhere—in the new steamboats and locomotives, in the steady march of economic development across the Americas, in the fantastic new discoveries of physics and chemistry, in innumerable inventions like the cotton gin and the grain reaper, in the burgeoning factories pouring out an ever increasing quantity of goods, and in the development of programs for social welfare.

The common people shared in the increasing prosperity. Nineteenth-century life was harsh by today's standards, but living conditions had advanced markedly over the eighteenth century. In 1750, two-thirds of the children born in London died before they reached the age of five, carried away by the privations and maladies that made life a constant battle for survival. With the coming of the Industrial Revolution, swift advances in agriculture, medicine, manufacturing, and other areas rapidly reduced the rate of infant mortality. As the age-old scourges of famine and plague retreated, Europe's population doubled— from 140 million in 1750 to some 266 million a century later.

The railroad became a dramatic symbol of progress in the early nineteenth century. This was progress that everybody could appreciate. Between 1830 and 1850, railway transport spread throughout Great Britain and was introduced on the Continent. The poet Alfred Lord Tennyson, a traveler on the first train from Liverpool to Manchester in 1830, was so inspired that he wrote a poem celebrating progress. The narrator of this poem, "Locksley Hall," is disappointed in love but finds consolation in thinking about the future achievements of mankind:

> ... I dipt into the future, far as human eye could see,
> Saw the Vision of the world, and all the wonder that would be.
> Saw the heavens fill with commerce, argosies of magic sails.
> Pilots of the purple twilight, dropping down with costly bales:
>
> ...
> ... the war-drum throbbed no longer, and the battle flags were furled
>
> ...
> ... In the Parliament of Man, the Federation of the World.

Tennyson was not alone. Railroads created excitement and joy for people in all walks of life. The arrival of a train in a town was a noteworthy event, and riding on one, however slow and bumpy the journey, was a thrill that almost everyone could appreciate. Passengers became proselytizers for railroads and progress.

Science Fiction and Utopias

Speculation about where progress might lead became increasingly common in the nineteenth century. Denmark's Hans Christian Andersen, who used his lively imagination to write much more than fairy tales, entertained adult readers in 1852 with speculations about the tourists of the future. Andersen foresaw young Americans crossing the Atlantic in steam-driven flying machines. He suggested that the tourist slogan would be "See Europe in Eight Days."

The occasional speculations of writers like Andersen were soon eclipsed by France's Jules Verne, who achieved stupendous popularity by writing books about people using the wonderful technologies that would be available in the future.

Verne did not set out to be a fiction writer, but his interest in science led him to write a scientific treatise on controlling the altitude and navigation of a balloon. Publishers rejected his effort, but one suggested he turn it into an adventure story. Verne did, and the immediate popularity and financial success of *Five Weeks in a Balloon* (1863) turned Verne from writing science fact to writing science fiction.

For the next forty years, until his death in 1903, Verne turned out some sixty books. By the time *Twenty Thousand Leagues Under the Sea* was published in 1870, Verne had become established as the great prophet of his time. He became so popular that when *Around the World in Eighty Days* appeared as a serial in a newspaper, *Le Temps*, the Paris correspondents of foreign newspapers would cable the text to their home offices.

"Verne's success as a forecaster appears to be due in no small measure to the fact that many of his readers were inspired to realize the inventions and feats he dreamed about," commented William T. Gay, then the utopias editor of *The Futurist*, in a 1971 article. "Youthful aspirants to careers in science felt that they had a technical manual on how a flight to the moon could be accomplished. And the characters were so humanized that each young reader could imagine himself as one of the participating scientists or one of the world hero astronauts."

It can be argued that Verne did more than any other single individual to make the moon landing of 1969 a reality. Pioneering rocket scientists have acknowledged the inspiration they received from books such as *From the Earth to the Moon* (1865). Konstantin Tsiolkovsky, the Russian "father of astronautics," once said that the "great fantastic author Jules Verne ... directed my thought along certain channels." Tsiolkovsky's American counterpart, rocket pioneer Robert Goddard, read Verne's novels while he was in high school.

Other writers used fiction to show the social as well as technological progress that would be achieved by future societies.

Edward Bellamy's wildly popular novel *Looking Backward 2000-1887* (1888) was perhaps the first predictive utopia to reach a world audience. Within fourteen months of its publication, the book had sold an astounding (for the time) quarter of a million copies in the United States alone. *Looking Backward* was rapidly translated into most of the European languages, and Bellamy Clubs, bent on putting the author's ideas into practice, sprang up in many countries.

The narrator of *Looking Backward*, Julian West, awakens in Boston in the year 2000 after having fallen asleep in 1887. (A long sleep was the way for fiction writers to get characters into the future before H.G. Wells's first novel, *The Time Machine*, 1895, provided a technological solution.) West finds that the civilization of 2000 has electric lights, clean air, full employment, retirement at age forty-five on a good income, and community centers with enclosed sidewalks for protection against the weather. (None of these existed in Boston in 1888, and retirement at forty-five on a good income even now seems like an impossible dream, except for a lucky few.)

Serious nonfiction attempts to forecast the future also appeared during the nineteenth century. One interesting example was *A Look at the Great Discoveries of the 20th Century: The Future of Electrical Television* (1892). The German author, Max Plessner, discussed the possibility of using the power of a selenium cell to translate light into electric current, which could then be reproduced as sight or sound, after transmission through space by electric wire, or through time by a phonograph or a photographic recording.

In 1892, Charles Richet's book *In 100 Years* presented a statistical projection of the growth of world population between 1892 and 1992 and argued that, as a consequence of the decline of European birthrates, the two most powerful nations in 1992 would be the United States and Russia. "Their combined population will probably be around 600 million, which will be much larger than that of all Europe," Richet wrote. This forecast was not too wide of the mark, but Richet was less successful when he tried to forecast the future of colonial empires. Here Richet's chauvinism appears to have clouded his judgment: The French would remain in North Africa, he opined, but Egypt would shake itself free of "British despotism." Turning to energy, Richet forecast that oil would replace the decreasing supplies of coal. He also suggested that it might be possible to exploit solar energy and the internal heat of the earth, but he was not hopeful.

By the 1890s, faith in future human progress had become part of the conventional wisdom. In the words of historian W. Warren Wagar, progress became "the religion of modern man. Long after he lost touch with transcendence, he continued to believe that history recorded his own gradual approach to perfection." That breathtaking vision of humans becoming ever more perfect in an ever more perfect world explains the extraordinary optimism of the American leading lights who participated in the 1893 forecast discussed in Chapter 12.

The Collapse of Optimism

The twentieth century dawned auspiciously, with both Europe and America enjoying peace and prosperity. This relatively untroubled period when people could truly relax and enjoy themselves came to be known in France as *la belle époque* or "beautiful epoch." Other nations shared in this halcyon era. England's King Edward VII reigned over the mightiest empire ever known. Both Britain and France had set aside their centuries-old rivalry and achieved an *entente cordiale* or "cordial understanding." Meanwhile, America's industry boomed, and U.S. influence had stretched across both the Pacific and the Caribbean. Ocean liners, railroads, telegraph, and telephone were binding the world together. And as science and technology forged ahead, European civilization "enlightened" the dark corners of the earth.

With things going so well, the future looked bright, and people took pleasure in speculating about the good things yet to come. In December 1900, the *Ladies' Home Journal* published a remarkable article entitled "What May Happen in the Next 100 Years" by journalist John Elfreth Watkins Jr., son of the curator of technological collections at the U.S. National Museum (now the Smithsonian Institution). Watkins did an admirable job of anticipating future technological wonders; he also enthused about the future blessings to come: free university education, free medical and dental treatment, free eyeglasses, simplified English, cheap transportation, and other good things. There seemed to be only one cloud in the sky: terrifying new weaponry such as aerial warships and forts on wheels with giant guns that could shoot twenty-five miles or more. However,

Watkins's readers, mostly American, probably thought these new war-making devices need concern only the Europeans. No nation would dare challenge America following its decisive victory over Spain in 1898.

Most of the early-twentieth-century writers who speculated about the wonders of the future are now forgotten, but one, Herbert George Wells, contributed so much to thinking about the future that he merits comparison with Sir Francis Bacon. Unlike Bacon, however, H.G. Wells emerged from the lower class. The son of a maid, he lived in poverty during his early years and had to fight his way to success. Throughout his life, he spoke with a lower-class accent, which grated on Britons schooled at Cambridge and Oxford but did not show in his writings.

Wells's first excursion into the future seems to have occurred in 1885 when he read a paper to his college debating society. The subject of his paper was no less than "The Past and Future of the Human Race." Later he wrote both fiction and nonfiction discussing the future. *Anticipations* (1901), a collection of essays, predicted the decline of horse-drawn vehicles, the coming of motor trucks, and the importance of aviation in warfare. "Once the command of the air is obtained by one of the contending armies," he said, "the war must become a conflict between a seeing host and one that is blind."

Wells explicitly called for a science of the future in a lecture given at the Royal Institution of Great Britain on January 24, 1902. Most people, he said, are wedded to the past, but the future was being discovered and people were increasingly shifting their thinking toward it. "It is into the future we go; tomorrow is the eventful thing for us," Wells declared. "There lies all that remains to be felt by us and our children and all that are dear to us."

People's failure to look forward, Wells suggested, was because most believed the past is certain, defined, and knowable, and only a few people thought that it is possible to know anything about the future. "It is our ignorance of the future and our persuasion that ignorance is absolutely incurable that alone gives the past its enormous predominance in our thoughts," he wrote. "But through the ages, the long unbroken succession of fortune tellers—and they flourish still—witnesses to the perpetually smoldering feeling that after all there may be a better sort of knowledge—a more serviceable sort of knowledge than that we now possess."

Wells pointed out that science has discovered the past—through studies of rock strata and fossils—and might also enable the discovery of the future. "Is it really, after all, such an extravagant and hopeless thing to suggest that, by seeking operating causes instead of fossils and by criticizing them persistently and thoroughly as the geological record has been criticized, it may be possible to throw a searchlight of inference forward instead of backward and to attain to a knowledge of coming things as clear, as universally convincing and infinitely more important to mankind than the clear vision of the past that geology has opened to us during the nineteenth century?"

If the specialist in each science is in fact doing his best now to prophesy within the limits of his field, Wells asked, "what is there to stand in the way of our building up this growing body of forecasts into an ordered picture of the future that will be just as certain, just as strictly science, and perhaps just as detailed as the picture that has been built up within the last hundred years to make the geological past?" In his own mind there was little doubt about the answer:

> I believe quite firmly that an inductive knowledge of a great number of things in the future is becoming a human possibility. I believe that the time is drawing near when it will be possible to suggest a systematic exploration of the future. And you must not judge the practicability of this enterprise by the failures of the past. So far nothing has been attempted, so far no first-class mind has ever focused itself upon these issues. But suppose the laws of social and political development, for example, were given as many brains, were given as much attention, criticism and discussion as we have given the laws of chemical combination during the last fifty years—what might we not expect?

Wells moved beyond Jules Verne's interest in the immediate use of potential technology to a concern for technology's long-term consequences, and his writings showed how future changes in society might be anticipated through a combination of scientific knowledge and imagination.

When Wells spoke in 1902, the world did seem to be improving steadily and rapidly—at least from a European standpoint. With economic progress, societies could afford to be more generous toward their less-fortunate citizens, who were now becoming better educated. So people were pleased to hear that things might continue to go well in the future, and it was exciting to think that maybe, just maybe, the good things to come could be predicted in advance so people would envision the future with optimism. Unfortunately, subsequent events did not favor optimism about the future.

The Impact of World War I

World War I, which began in August 1914, was the worst cataclysm that Europe had experienced since the Black Death. The war shattered the easy optimism that had burgeoned during the nineteenth century. Suddenly the future, which had once been a repository of unalloyed hopes, became a sink for dark and sinister fears. The generation of young men who were bombing, shooting, and gassing each other on the Western Front represented the hope of France, the joy of Britain, and the pride of Germany. If they were not killed or maimed at the front, they often returned home to joblessness.

Yet, terrible as the war itself was, the consequences of the war were even worse. These included the Russian Revolution and the development of a totalitarian Communist empire, the rise of Fascism in Italy and Nazism in Germany, World War II, the Holocaust, rockets carrying bombs, and atomic bombs. All this proved so traumatic for civilization that its lighthearted hope for the future—the easy enthusiasm for the future that one finds expressed in the optimism of people who lived in the 1890s and early 1900s—has never returned.

During the eighteenth and nineteenth centuries, rising doubts about the reality of a better future life in heaven had been compensated by increasing faith in the secular paradise that was being built on earth. But during and after World War I, many people became convinced that the world was not really progressing at all and that there would never be an earthly paradise. The idea of human progress came to be viewed as a snare and delusion: After all, automobile factories were now making armored vehicles equipped with cannons to kill people. Airships carried bombs, and the science of chemistry was being applied to the manufacture of poison gas.

Wells, who had written enthusiastically about the future before World War I, wrote more soberly afterwards. "Human history," he wrote in *The Outline of History* (1920), "becomes more and more a race between education and catastrophe." By the end of World War II, Wells was convinced that the race was over, and catastrophe had won. In his last book, *Mind at the End of its Tether* (1945), he despondently declared: "The end of everything we call life is close at hand and cannot be evaded. ... There is no way out or round or through the impasse. It is the end."

Meanwhile, the collapse of optimism had already led to a new literary genre, *dystopian* fiction. The first great dystopian work was Eugene Zamiatin's *We*, written in Russia just three years after the Revolution. *We* describes a future in which the world has one great nation, the United State, populated by people whose names are numbers, whose God is "We," and whose devil is "I." The United State offers stability, perfection, and happiness, but the narrator, whose name is D-503, gradually discovers opposing forces who incarnate chaos, passion, energy, and rebellion. At the end of *We*, the Well-Doer who heads the United State puts down the revolution by performing lobotomies on all the Numbers, including the narrator, whose last words are "Reason must prevail."

We was not published in the Soviet Union and remained little known in the West for many years, but other dystopian writings gained a wider audience. Among the best known are Aldous Huxley's *Brave New World* (1932), George Orwell's *Nineteen Eighty-four* (1949), Kurt Vonnegut's *Player Piano* (1952), and Anthony Burgess's *A Clockwork Orange* (1962).

Pessimism could also be seen in the publication, between 1918 and 1922, of Oswald Spengler's *The Decline of the West*, which provided a ponderous intellectual justification for despair. Cultures rose and fell through history, going through a series of stages, Spengler argued, and the Western world was now on a downward slope. Events now seemed to favor Spengler's grim outlook.

Though the world's hopes recovered a little during the middle and late 1920s, they were again dashed by the stock-market collapse of 1929, the Great Depression, and the rise of aggressive governments in nations like Germany, Japan, and Italy.

During the 1930s, people's concerns focused mostly on the urgent issues of economic depression, totalitarian governments, and military aggression, but interest in the more distant future occasionally found expression.

The New York World's Fair, which opened in 1939, used the theme, "The World of Tomorrow," and the official guidebook explained that "the Fair may help to build the better World of Tomorrow by making its millions of visitors aware of the scientific knowledge and the forces and ideas at work in the interdependent society of today and by demonstrating the best tools that are available."

The theme center of the fair featured a gigantic obelisk called the Trylon and an eighteen-story-high globe known as the Perisphere. Visitors entering the Perisphere at its base were carried up inside by "the longest moving stairway in the world." Beneath them they could view a huge model of "Democracity"—symbol of "a perfectly integrated, futuristic metropolis pulsing with life and rhythm and music."

But as impressive as Democracity was, it could not compare to the scale-model world of the future in the General Motors pavilion. Known as the Futurama, this model of the future America was the largest and most realistic scale model ever constructed, and it became the sensation of the fair.

People had to wait in line for four hours or more for a chance to see the Futurama. Then, they got only a ten-minute ride through the model world, but the vision was stunning—unlike anything anybody had ever seen before. The model included 500,000 individually designed houses and 50,000 automobiles, of which 10,000 were in operation over superhighways, speed lanes, and multi-decked bridges. The Futurama exhibit enabled visitors to see how superhighways and other infrastructure would greatly enhance the value of an automobile, so it had instant appeal for drivers, actual and would-be. It was also an automobile manufacturer's vision of paradise, and enraptured car drivers could be expected to lobby governments to spend more public money for superhighways and other infrastructure helpful to motor vehicles. But realization of GM's driver's paradise had to wait. In 1939, several months after the fair opened, World War II broke out.

The Death of Progress?

The year before the World's Fair opened in New York, Britain's Science Fiction Association began publishing a magazine called *Tomorrow: The Magazine of the Future*, with H.G. Wells as its prophet. The magazine included forecasts of coming technological developments as well as articles on science fiction. *Tomorrow* managed to publish only a few issues before its editors and writers had to march off to World War II. But, during its brief existence, *Tomorrow* raised again the torch that H.G. Wells had lit early in the century. In the Spring 1938 issue, Professor A.M. Low suggested that Britain should have a Minister for the Future: "It will be the duty of the Minister to collect data from all over the world, to tabulate, correlate, compare and calculate. He will be like a spider sitting in a web, drawing towards him all knowledge, and working out, on scientific lines, the effect that the latest developments and discoveries will probably have upon the human race," he wrote.

Meanwhile, a more-sinister idea from Wells was about to bear fruit, and it had far greater impact. His 1913 novel *The World Set Free* had featured the liberation of atomic energy and the development of atomic bombs. The book had come to the attention of physicist Leo Szilard in 1932 while he was in Berlin. The following year Szilard was a refugee in England, and a speech by Lord Rutherford pooh-poohing the possibility of liberating atomic energy on an industrial scale made him think again of Wells's predictions. In 1934 Szilard worked out the theoretical equations that could govern a self-sustaining chain reaction, releasing enormous amounts of energy.

Szilard was exploring fission reactions at Columbia University in New York in 1939 when he got word that two German physicists had discovered the fission of uranium. So Szilard and physicist Eugene Wigner persuaded Albert Einstein, a scientist who was internationally prominent, to warn President Roosevelt of the dangers if Germany succeeded in building an atomic bomb. Einstein's letter to Roosevelt led to the United States building its own atomic bombs, and that eventually led to what was the most frightening event of World War II, the dropping of atomic bombs on Japan.

All told, the horrors of World War II exceeded the worst fears of the pessimists: The global conflict killed at least 40 million people, far more than any previous war; introduced new efficiencies into torture and mass murder; and concluded with the use of bombs so terrifying even to the scientists who created them that they became known as "the league of frightened men."

Technology now seemed to be carrying humans toward mass destruction, democratic hopes had been crushed in many nations, and a new barbarism had emerged. Who could now believe in inevitable progress? How could *regress* be prevented? French poet Paul Valéry, who had lived through the *belle epoch* at the beginning of the twentieth century and into World War II, shared a widespread sentiment when he said, "The trouble with our time is that the future is not what it used to be."

But if the future is not to be a vision of inevitable progress, what should be the new vision? Dutch scholar Fred Polak investigated the images of the future that different civilizations have developed. He reported in a two-volume work that the great civilizations of the past always had constructive images of the future, but modern people's "imaging" faculty has been impaired. He attributed this primarily to the rise of de-Utopianism—that is, the tendency to believe that the future offers neither a heaven in the sky nor a utopia on earth. "The task before us," said Polak, "is to reawaken the almost dormant awareness of the future and to find the best nourishment for a starving social imagination."

But after World War II that was not easy. Western civilization had drawn confidence from the vision of inevitable progress, but now the light of progress had faded away. How could people now think constructively about the future? In a bizarre world where mysterious and unforeseen events actually occur, how could we possibly know anything about the future, much less have a positive view of it?

In the next chapter, we will see how people groped for answers to those questions.

14

The Futurist Revolution

World War II and its aftermath could not help but alter people's thinking about the future, but it did so in very different ways depending on where they lived and what their personal experiences were. Many people suffered minor or infrequent inconveniences, but others had soul-wrenching experiences that uprooted their previous ways of thinking and gave them a fundamentally different outlook on life.

The peace that followed the war was so uneasy that it came to be called the Cold War. Rockets and atomic bombs made the future appear more ominous than ever. The very survival of humans was now in question.

To understand how these developments affected thinking about the future, let's recall the great confidence in the future that people had shared around the beginning of the twentieth century. As noted in the last chapter, leading Americans surveyed in 1893 were universally optimistic about the future; their attitude might be described as a bubbly enthusiasm for what the future had in store for the human race. And this attitude was reflected in H.G. Wells's 1902 advocacy of a "science of the future" that would allow people to know in advance about the good things in their future.

Such optimism and confidence in a predictable future vanished during World War I, and it has never returned; instead, pessimism has been periodically reinforced by new traumas that followed. Events had also overturned widespread belief that social forces determine historical trends and individuals have little real influence over the forces of destiny. World War II seemed to demonstrate quite convincingly that individual personalities can have enormous influence, either for better or for worse. Hitler, Stalin, Churchill, and de Gaulle became poster boys for the importance of individuals in determining the future.

Yet out of this bleak and frightening period of war, slump, depression, tyranny, and doomsday weapons, a new vision of the future began to emerge. This new vision seems to have taken shape largely in France and the United States, arising from the very different experiences of the two nations during World War II and its aftermath. We will look first at the French response to their situation and then at the American response.

Can France Have a Future?

The defeated French were humiliated in 1940 when victorious German troops paraded around Paris's Arc de Triomphe, the monument to former victory. The Germans occupied about half of France, including Paris, and created a puppet regime, based in Vichy, to govern the rest of the country. So the war touched each Frenchman very personally.

Recognizing the new dangers in which they lived and the choices forced upon them, the French had to struggle daily with such questions as: Should I join the Resistance against the German occupation and risk imprisonment, torture, death, and the loss of my loved ones? Or should I quietly accept the occupation of France, so that my family and I can survive? Should I try to escape from France? How will my family manage without me? Whichever options one chose, there were risks, and no choice would be free from all danger. Those French who did not risk their lives by joining the Resistance might still be questioned, tortured until they revealed everything they knew, and then killed. Resistance hero Jean Moulin, a young government offical before the French defeat, escaped to England but returned in secret to France to coordinate the French underground guerrillas known as the *Maquis* (underbrush). He died under torture.

The French people were driven to ask basic questions about themselves and their values. Unable to fight openly, they struggled privately with the dilemmas posed by human freedom and the inability to be true to all one's values in making choices. One French writer, Jean-Paul Sartre, articulated the turbulent, but largely silent, self-searching going on among his compatriots. He called the lessons learned from this process *Existentialism*, and promoted it not only in his philosophical works but in novels, plays, and essays that engaged ordinary readers. General Charles de Gaulle once commented, "Touch Sartre, and you touch France."

From Sartre we have an eloquent description of the French experience during the war:

> We had lost all our rights, first of all, the right to speak. We were insulted to our faces every day, and we had to remain silent. We were deported in large groups as workers, as Jews, as political prisoners.... Since the Nazi venom inserted itself even into our thoughts, each free thought was a victory. Since the all-powerful police tried to force us into silence, each word became precious as a declaration of principle. Since we were hounded, each of our movements was like a skirmish with the enemy.

That passage helps explain how and why many of the French developed a strong sense of *personal* responsibility for the future of their country. With France no longer France but only an appendage of Germany, France could really only exist in the hearts of her individual citizens struggling against enemy institutions and having to beware constantly of informers. As Sartre put it: "Everyone of her [France's] citizens knew that he owed himself to everyone and that he could only count on himself; each of them realized, in the most total abandonment, his historic role and responsibility."

Feeling a *personal* responsibility for their country, the French patriots also recognized their conflicting responsibilities, such as those to their families. Many obsessed over questions such as, Is it right to desert my mother in this difficult time in order to join the Free French? Is it right to risk a reprisal against our village if I attack the enemy? In one reprisal, the French village of Oradour was completely "cleansed" of its inhabitants, burned to the ground, and left in hollow ruins.

Sharply conflicting responsibilities forced ordinary individuals to make agonizing choices. As a result, many actually did some serious thinking about the human situation and human values. They gained a new respect for the dilemmas of human freedom and the importance of choice.

Sartre, Albert Camus, and other French writers of the period emphasized that each human being creates his or her own future and participates in the creation of the human future. Each is, in effect, a legislator for humanity as well as the captain of his personal destiny and must therefore take full responsibility for it. He must not try to excuse his actions by saying that he is doing what his employer, his church, his parents, or some other outside force requires. That would be an evasion, because he is always free to refuse to do what they say he should do. Can we excuse those who torture and kill people simply in obedience to an order they have received?

There is no one and nothing that can authoritatively tell you what to do, Sartre proclaimed. In a 1946 lecture, he declared, "You are free. Choose, that is to say, invent. No general system of ethics can tell you what to do." Years later, the phrase "inventing the future" became popular among futurists after it was used as the title of a book by Dennis Gabor, a futurist as well as a Nobel Prize winning physicist. But the concept was clearly expressed by Sartre and other existentialists. Gabor, as a Hungarian, also knew the agonies of Nazi domination.

The concept of the future as something to be invented or created contrasted sharply with Wells's view of the future as inevitable destiny—something that could be predicted by scientists specializing in the future. The existentialists had a sharply conflicting view: The future is undetermined. We humans create it, and we are responsible for what we do.

Planning France's Future

After the occupying troops retreated from France in 1944, the French faced the task of revamping their government, retooling their economy, and rebuilding their institutions. To help them in doing this, they naturally relied on France's long tradition of using central planning, directed from Paris, to achieve an ideal future society. The new French government thus launched a series of five-year plans to revive and stimulate the economy and other areas of government concern.

The planning effort required assumptions about what might happen in the years ahead, and a few French planners became seriously interested in knowing just what assumptions could reasonably be made. Serious thinking about the future seemed essential, and Paris buzzed with ideas about what might lie ahead and what the government should do.

A key figure in French futurism during the 1950s was Gaston Berger, a philosopher, businessman, and educator with wide ranging interests. In 1957, Berger established in Paris the Centre International de Prospective (International Center for Foresight). The following year, the Center published the first issue of a journal, *Prospective*, which contained articles looking at many different aspects of the future. For example, Louis Armand, head of France's nationalized railroad system, contributed an article on the future of transportation.

Berger and his circle, known as the Prospective movement, emphasized that foresight is not the same as forecasting, which they viewed as an extension into the future of trends observed in the past. He explained his views in the first issue of the new journal:

> In what does the Prospective attitude consist?
>
> Its principal characteristic consists obviously in the intensity with which it concentrates our attention on the future. We may be tempted to believe that this is something quite ordinary. But in fact nothing is rarer. As Paul Valéry wrote, "We walk forward with our backs to the future."... On the contrary, we must look it in the face ... grasp its intrinsic nature, and hence apply to it other methods than those which are valid for the present or the past.
>
> This turning of our faces, which seems quite easy and natural, actually requires sustained efforts because it runs counter to our most ingrained habits. Doubtless we often think about the future but we dream about it rather than construct it. Dreaming is at the opposite pole from planning. Instead of starting us off along the path of action, it turns us away from it; it allows us to enjoy in our imagination the fruit of a labor we have not accomplished.

Berger's views reflected Sartre's existentialism in that they emphasized the reality of choice and the need to create one's own future. As Berger saw it, this kind of choice is not limited to individuals but extends also to communities, nations, and all humanity.

Berger and his Prospective group articulated the future orientation that France's planners had been groping for. Though Berger was killed in an automobile accident in 1960, his Prospective movement continued and had a wide influence on French government officials, business leaders, and independent professionals.

Among those active in the Prospective group was Pierre Massé, formerly executive director of the nationalized Electricité de France and then Commissaire Général au Plan (High Commissioner for the Plan). In preparing for the Fifth National Plan, Massé decided to enlarge the forecasting process taking place under his direction and created in 1963 a Committee of 1985, whose function would be to take a broader view of the future of France and its economic goals and social problems. This broader view would provide a horizon for the planners engaged in more immediate and limited forecasting. Massé's initiative created a link between the Prospective group and a number of young technocrats in the various branches of the French government.

By this time, the Prospective group had developed a distinctive approach to studying the future. For one thing, the group's ad hoc study groups were highly interdisciplinary; people from different fields had to work together (just as they later did in working parties created for the French government's National Plans). Another characteristic was their search for factors likely to be important in shaping the future. The study groups did not limit themselves to logical analysis but also used imagination and forecasts to make their analysis of the future as comprehensive as possible and to take full account of what was desirable as well as what could be accomplished. This future-oriented perspective provided a background for the formulation of short-term plans and decision making.

De Jouvenel's Influence

Also active in Paris during the 1950s and moving in the same circles was Bertrand de Jouvenel, a well-known journalist and economist. De Jouvenel had a long-standing interest in international affairs and the future. As a youth, he had accompanied his diplomat father to the peace conferences that followed World War I. He described his reaction as follows:

> ... the Conference of Paris was proof positive that the world could be remade deliberately, and this well or badly. Keynes became our hero for denouncing the inherent absurdity both of interallied debts and reparations and the extension of national debts. A further absurdity, of which I happened to be an indignant witness, was the humiliating manner in which the Treaty of Versailles was presented to liberal representatives of a new German Republic, who were bidden to sign on the dotted line. This was unprecedented; nothing so degrading had ever occurred in the history of civilized Europe. The treaty also included the famous Article 231 that charged Germany with exclusive responsibility for the war—an injustice of which Hitler was to make much.

In the 1950s, de Jouvenel became increasingly concerned about the trend toward authoritarian governments among the world's new nations in Africa and Asia. At a 1958 symposium on the Greek Island of Rhodes, he caught the attention of a young man from the Ford Foundation, Waldemar Nielsen, who later got the Foundation to support de Jouvenel's work.

In 1960, with Ford money, de Jouvenel launched a project dubbed Futuribles. Under de Jouvenel's leadership, the Futuribles group got experts from a great variety of fields to speculate about likely social and political changes in the future. The papers were published from 1961 to 1965 in the *Bulletin* of the Paris-based Societé d'études et documentation économiques, industrielles et sociales (SEDEIS), which de Jouvenel edited. Some 130 papers were produced before Ford support ended in 1966.

In a 1964 lecture, de Jouvenel explained what he wanted to accomplish through the Futuribles project:

> The purpose is to generate a habit, the habit of forward-looking. We feel that as this grows into a habit, we, or our successors, shall develop in this exercise greater skill, thanks to self criticism and mutual criticism. At the outset we encountered in the authors we solicited a great reluctance to embark upon such speculation. They said it was unscholarly, which of course it is, but it happens to be necessary. It is unscholarly perforce because there are no facts on the future: Cicero quite rightly contrasted past occurrences and occurrences to come with the contrasted expressions *facta et futura: facta*, what is accomplished and can be taken as solid; *futura*, what shall come into being, and is as yet "undone," or fluid. This contrast leads me to emphasize: "there can be no science of the future." The future is not the realm of the "true or false" but the realm of "possibles."

At the outset of the Futuribles project, de Jouvenel did not ask the scholars to use any special method for speculating about the future, partly because it was difficult enough to get scholars to think about the future at all. But as the project progressed, de Jouvenel and others became curious about the methods the scholars were using.

To find out how the scholars were developing their forecasts, de Jouvenel and his colleagues organized a methodological conference in Geneva in June 1962. This was followed by a second conference in Paris in July 1963 and a third at Yale University in December 1964. The conferences led a number of American and European scholars to think about methods of exploring the future. For instance, Daniel Bell, a leading American sociologist who was collaborating with the Futuribles project, produced a memorable essay, "Twelve Modes of Prediction—A Preliminary Sorting of Approaches to the Social Sciences," which appeared in the influential scholarly journal *Daedalus* in 1964. Bell systematically defined the modes in which forecasters can operate. Among the twelve modes he suggested are trends and extrapolation, structural certainties, prime movers, and alternative futures or scenarios. Bell linked French futuring to American scholars, and he went on to become a key influence on American futuring, as we shall see later.

Meanwhile, Ford support for the Futuribles project came to an end, so de Jouvenel and his wife, Hélène, founded in 1966 a monthly journal *Analyse & Prevision* and, in 1967, the International Futuribles Association. De Jouvenel served as the Association's first president and Massé as its second. The de Jouvenels' son, Hugues, later took over the association in 1973 and led it into the twenty-first century. The Futuribles Group is now one of the world's leading foresight institutions.

Besides his pioneering work in the Futuribles project, Bertrand de Jouvenel left a lasting contribution to the futurist movement through his book *The Art of Conjecture*, first published in French in Monaco in 1964, then in English in 1967. Today's futurists view this treatise on forecasting and the future as a classic statement of futurist thinking.

The Art of Conjecture not only provided a rationale for thinking seriously about the future, but indicated how one could think about the future. De Jouvenel put into words much that might be viewed today as fairly obvious but whose importance had not been recognized clearly in the past. If people can find out what they are doing when they actually make forecasts (which they do routinely every day), they can begin to compare forecasts and decide which are most likely to be accurate. Clear thinking about the future can lead to wiser decisions.

The Rise of American Futurism

Unlike France, the United States escaped the first two years of the Second World War, remaining officially neutral until the Japanese attacked Pearl Harbor. Though momentarily stunned, the United States quickly mobilized its people and economy and led its allies to complete victory. At the end of the war, not only was mainland America intact, having escaped bombing, but the wartime economy had provided plentiful jobs. Most people suffered only modest hardships, such as rationing and interrupted plans for college. A minority, of course, suffered grievously due to the death or maiming of a family member or other loved one, but many Americans were probably happier during the war than in the peace that preceded it, when jobs were scarce and economic privation was often severe. During the war, people also found a real sense of purpose in achieving victory in a just war against murderous tyrannies.

America triumphed over its enemies in World War II, but the war had paradoxically left the nation feeling even more threatened than before. Before the war the United States had been protected from potential enemies both by two vast oceans that could not quickly be crossed and by the risk of facing the powerful American Navy. But postwar threats to U.S. security came from two wartime developments—rockets and atomic bombs—as well as a wartime ally that had become a dangerous new enemy. The Soviet Union and a vigorous international communist movement was moving aggressively to take control over a large number of nations. The Eastern European countries fell quickly under Soviet domination, and communists had also taken control of China, the world's most populous nation.

America ended the war with a monopoly on nuclear weapons, but, thanks in part to spies, the Soviet Union soon acquired the know-how to build bombs of its own. The Soviets had also brought in German scientists to build rockets. Military people recognized that the Soviets would soon have nuclear bombs and the rockets to launch them.

To protect America, the U.S. Congress appropriated more and more billions of dollars for military preparedness. But what sort of preparations should be made? It was now very clear that technology would likely be decisive in future conflicts, and the question was, Just what sort of defense systems were needed? What were the superweapons of the future—and the defenses against those superweapons?

Foresighted military leaders had already begun to think seriously about future technology. In 1944, H.H. ("Hap") Arnold, commanding general of the Army Air Corps, took the initiative of ordering aeronautical engineer Theodor von Karman to prepare a forecast of future technological capabilities that might be of interest to the military. Von Karman's report,

Toward New Horizons (1947), began a tradition of technological forecasts, which resulted in the permanent Army Long-Range Technological Forecast. Von Karman's report showed that technological capabilities could be forecasted, thus confirming the view expressed by sociologist S. Colum Gilfillan in a 1937 report *Technological Trends and National Policy*. Gilfillan argued that the development of technology should not be viewed as a number of inventions made independently by lone geniuses, but rather as a process, so future developments could often be anticipated. Based on that view and with an abundance of funds, the defense establishment began expanding its technological forecasting capabilities.

The need for serious forecasts of technological capabilities was now viewed as urgent: Starting in 1945, there would be a technological revolution every five years, as Herman Kahn noted in his 1960 treatise, *On Thermonuclear War*. Any realistic attempt to make military plans for future conflicts had to take account of the revolutionary changes in technology.

The growing magnitude of military forecasting is suggested by the Air Force's *Project Forecast*, a 1963 effort that involved representatives from about forty U.S. government organizations, faculty members from twenty-six universities, representatives from seventy major corporations, and personnel from ten nonprofit organizations. The end product was a fourteen-volume report that attempted to blueprint the technological characteristics of forces that could most effectively support the Department of Defense in the post-1970 time period. (Since 1970, the U.S. military has actively pursued its forecasting activities in fields such as terrorism, economic and political issues, and more. However, the work is generally classified.)

In addition to initiating the first big technological forecast by the military, Arnold made another contribution to the study of the future that was even more original and important: He institutionalized the process of analyzing military policy alternatives. Arnold did this by getting the Douglas Aircraft Company to establish, in 1946, a Project RAND (the acronym stands for "research and development") to study the "broad subject of inter-continental warfare other than surface." In 1948, Project RAND split off from Douglas and became the RAND Corporation, with the financial backing of the Ford Foundation; the new corporation's announced purpose was to "further and promote scientific, educational, and charitable purposes, all for the public welfare and security of the United States." RAND thus shifted from merely studying alternative weaponry systems to considering also government policies.

The RAND Corporation's Influence

As the first free-wheeling policy institute or "think tank"—a place where scholars are paid to think freely about future possibilities—RAND was a novelty, and it was soon being imitated. By the 1960s, most advanced nations had think tanks of one sort or another, and the United States had several score. The think tanks were oriented toward scientific methodologies, but they were invariably multidisciplinary and had links to the nonscientific and technological communities. They also had a large degree of freedom in studying their assigned problems, which were often quite broad in scope.

RAND proved of key importance to the development of futuring as a scientific/scholarly activity. For one thing, two of its researchers developed the Delphi method (discussed in Chapter 6). Olaf Helmer, one of the researchers responsible for the Delphi method, later teamed up with Theodore J. Gordon, a Douglas Aircraft engineer, in a major Delphi study of possible future technological developments; widespread use of teaching machines, moon colonies, and computer translation were among the topics examined. The results of this study, in which a number of leading scientists and experts participated, were widely reported. A game based on the study also drew wide attention to the Delphi technique, which provided an easily understood example of how the future might be studied seriously. At the time, futuring was considered to be something that only science-fiction writers and their fans ever did.

Besides pioneering in the development of the Delphi technique, Helmer was a key figure in assembling a group of people interested in establishing an institute that would specialize in futures research on domestic, civil, non-security issues. The organizing committee issued a "Prospectus for an Institute for the Future," dated May 25, 1966.

The Institute's purposes would include:

• To explore systematically the possible futures for our nation and for the international community.

- To ascertain which among these possible futures seem to be desirable, and why.
- To seek means by which the probability of their occurrence can be enhanced through appropriate purposeful action.

The prospectus said that ability to deal effectively with the future "becomes increasingly important as the pace of change accelerates," and added:

> Today, because the resources available to governments are immeasurably greater than ever before, and the courses of action taken by governmental and private agencies are interacting in more intimate and complex ways, we are becoming more concerned over the need to understand what is implied by the alternative courses open to us. The cost and limitations inherent in piecemeal responses and short-term orientation have in recent years become sufficiently apparent for industry and government agencies to accept the idea that policies and programs designed to shape future courses of development must be planned and worked out more systematically than heretofore.

The prospectus also noted that the idea for the Institute arose from a change in attitude toward the future: The fatalistic view that the future is unforeseeable and inevitable was being abandoned. People were recognizing that there are a multitude of possible futures and that appropriate intervention can make a difference in their probabilities. As a result, the promoters argued, the identification and study of possible future developments and the search for ways to influence their probability were becoming an important social responsibility.

The Advisory Council for the new institute included thirty-two persons, mainly people associated with universities and think tanks, but a few with connections to the U.S. government. The group included Helmer, Gordon, and Frank Davidson, an international lawyer active in the "Chunnel" project that later succeeded in connecting Britain and France by means of a tunnel under the English Channel. Davidson would later become the Institute's first president.

The Institute for the Future opened its doors in Middletown, Connecticut, in 1968, and made a large number of studies that earned it an excellent reputation for painstaking analyses of future possibilities and studies of forecasting methods. The Institute later relocated to Menlo Park, California, where it pioneered in exploring such issues as the future of computer conferencing many years before the Internet existed.

The Institute made Mother RAND a grandmother, in 1971, when staff member Theodore Gordon and two colleagues left to set up The Futures Group, a profit-making research organization, in Glastonbury, Connecticut. The Futures Group International has grown to 140 staff members in fourteen countries.

The Hudson Institute may also be cited as part of the RAND legacy. Hudson was founded by former RAND analyst Herman Kahn, whose seminal work was discussed in Chapter 8, along with lawyer Max Singer. After Kahn's death in 1983, the Institute moved to Indianapolis. Under its current president, Herbert London, an educator and former professor of humanities, Hudson has maintained its future orientation and continues to produce thoughtful studies of policy issues.

The Space Age Begins

Concern about national security took a new turn in 1957 when the Soviet Union launched the first satellite. *Sputnik I* incited U.S. leaders to mount a huge effort to recover the lead in space that the Soviets had seized. Billions of dollars soon poured into the space program. The National Aeronautics and Space Administration, succeeding the National Advisory Council on Aviation in 1958, mushroomed into a gigantic agency. Thousands of scientists, engineers, and technicians joined the effort, lured by high salaries and a chance to work on an exciting historic program.

The space race brought a new need for serious technological forecasting, because its administrators had to know what could be done in space and what capabilities would be available in the years ahead. The money pouring into the space program also funded a wide variety of research and development projects. Colleges and universities benefited because the government's space program provided a major source of direct and indirect funding of their programs.

Like the Manhattan Project, the space program was a powerful though unintended force in stimulating the study of the future. Neither of these massive projects was designed as an exercise in futuring, but both demonstrated in an extremely convincing way that it is possible to forecast what can be achieved through technology, and then actually to do what one has decided upon. Furthermore, both demonstrated that people can shape the future by intent, rather than leaving it to chance or fate. Though the realization of humanity's power over its own destiny is not always comfortable, it brings with it a new sense of responsibility. The power of the atom, demonstrated so frightfully but so convincingly, was power at the disposal of man, and this power, though it caused dread, also suggested hope. That hope has since been realized (though somewhat uneasily) through the use of atomic power for peaceful purposes.

The landing of men on the moon was a similar achievement of accurate forecasting. It stimulated people even more powerfully to recognize their own capabilities—and responsibilities—for their own future. "If we can land a man on the moon," people said, "why can't we conquer cancer (eliminate poverty, ensure world peace)?" The Manhattan Project and the moon landings unequivocally demonstrated that people could imagine a future development, evaluate its practicality and desirability, and then set out to realize it. Perhaps never before had the human ability to shape the future—at least in some measure—been so dramatically demonstrated.

The rapid increase of government funding for science after World War II also encouraged serious thinking about the future. The U.S. Congress set up the National Science Foundation (NSF) in 1950; within a few years, the government was handing out hundreds of millions of dollars to fund a wide variety of scientific projects. This support for basic natural science, which grew rapidly during the 1950s and reached startling heights in the 1960s, was unprecedented: Never before had pure research enjoyed such financial support. Vannevar Bush's vision of science as an "endless frontier" offering huge future payoffs had captured a following, and as the economy boomed Congress faced relatively few budgetary constraints. For a time, there seemed to be enough money to finance every scientist available to use it.

But by the late 1960s the supply of scientists caught up with the supply of funds, and hard questions began to be asked about which scientists should get how much money. The subject of science policy began to get serious attention in the government scientific community. Policy makers knew that investments in science have perhaps the longest and most diverse—as well as potentially the greatest—payoffs of any investments that can be made. To decide what scientific research to support, government policy makers need to know what society will require in five, ten, twenty, or fifty years. Hence many NSF staff members, such as Henry David, Charles W. Williams, and Robert W. Lamson, became seriously concerned with trying to understand the future.

Concern was also mounting during the 1950s and 1960s about the unintended side effects of increasingly powerful technology. People were growing more aware of dangers from air and water pollution, solid waste problems, chemical additives, and a wide range of technological impacts. Among the many results of these new concerns were the creation in 1967 of the U.S. Environmental Protection Agency and a congressional requirement that government agencies prepare environmental impact statements for major projects. These developments stimulated further interest in trying to assess the future impacts of technology and in concerns about "quality of life" issues. In 1972, the U.S. Congress created the Office of Technology Assessment to evaluate technologies so that Congress and other agencies could make intelligent judgments. For two decades, OTA operated an invaluable service, for both Congress and the general public, but Congress killed it during a budget-cutting frenzy in the 1990s.

The 1960s also witnessed President Lyndon B. Johnson's Great Society and War on Poverty programs, designed to be massive assaults on social problems in the United States. The programs awakened interest in measuring these problems statistically, so policy makers would know how bad a problem was and could keep track of their progress in overcoming it. A "social indicators" movement became prominent at the Department of Health, Education and Welfare. Social scientists now became prominent in policy-making circles. One of them was the sociologist Daniel Bell, who had collaborated on Bertrand de Jouvenel's Futuribles project.

Bell accepted the government project on social indicators because "I was appalled by the fact that the Kennedy and Johnson administrations had 'discovered' the problems of poverty, education, urban renewal, and pollution as if they were completely new. The real need in American society, as I saw it, was for some systematic efforts to anticipate social problems, to design new institutions, and to propose alternative programs for choice."

Bell had prepared for his government assignment by serving as chairman of the Commission on the Year 2000, sponsored by the American Academy of Arts and Sciences in Boston. Bell hoped that the Commission would begin the design of alternative solutions "so that our society has more options and can make a moral choice rather than be constrained, as is so often the case when problems descend upon us unnoticed and demand an immediate response."

The Commission, whose thirty-eight members included Herman Kahn and urbanist Daniel P. Moynihan, held plenary sessions in 1965 and 1966 before breaking into smaller groups to look at specific aspects of the future. The plenary sessions resulted in a volume, edited by Bell, of reports and papers. The volume was published as the Summer 1967 issue of *Daedalus* under the title *Toward the Year 2000*.

Some members continued to foster thinking about the future after the Commission had wound up its work. Moynihan, for instance, persuaded the Nixon White House to establish a future-oriented National Goals Research Staff, which produced a thoughtful report, *Toward Balanced Growth: Quantity with Quality* (1970).

Futurist Groups Form

During the 1960s, scores of futurist groups sprang up, both in the United States and other countries. In addition to research institutes, a number of associations or clubs developed. In Italy, Aurelio Peccei, an economist and businessman, formed the Club of Rome, an international group of scientists, humanists, planners, and educators interested in looking at the problems of the world from a global standpoint. Elsewhere in Europe, a group known as Mankind 2000 took shape under the inspiration of journalist Robert Jungk. And in Washington, D.C., a group of private citizens formed the World Future Society in 1966. Shortly after its founding, the Society began regular publication of a newsletter, *The Futurist*, which, by 1969, grew into a magazine. By that time, the Society had some 3,000 members (today it has about 25,000). Other publications started in Europe and elsewhere; these included the de Jouvenels' *Analyse & Prevision* in France, as well as *Analysen und Prognosen* (Berlin), *Futuriblerne*

(Denmark), *Futures* (United Kingdom), *Futuribili* (Italy), and *Futurum* (Germany). Meanwhile, Mankind 2000 evolved, by 1973, into the World Futures Studies Federation, currently led by Richard Slaughter of the Australian Foresight Institute.

Futurist Web sites began appearing in the 1990s, along with electronic newsletters for futurists, such as *Futurist Update*, launched by the World Future Society in January 2000. By then, many nations around the world had futurist publications, such as *Tomorrow, Framtider International* (Sweden); *Foresight* (United Kingdom); *Blickpunkt Zukunft (Future View,* Germany); *Futuribles* (France); *Futurics, Technological Forecasting & Social Change, Futures Research Quarterly,* and *Growth Strategies* (U.S.); and many, many others.

The perception that we can explore the future rationally and very usefully is now widespread, though by no means universal. Even today, many scholars remain poorly informed about the futurist movement. But the pioneering work of de Jouvenel, Kahn, Helmer, and other futurists has left its mark, and today most educated people recognize that trends, scenarios, and other methods refined by futurists are useful in serious decision making. The remarkable achievements of the pioneering futurists have provided a foundation for increasingly effective exploration of the future. The task for the twenty-first century is to enable futuring to realize the great promise that it has shown. As adequate understanding and support for futuring develops, we will be able to look forward to the future with a great deal more confidence than we can at present.

One reason for being hopeful is that the futurist movement has provided a serious challenge to the fatalistic attitudes that have long impeded both individual success and human progress. In the next chapter we will see how the futurists have challenged fatalism and why their struggle against this ancient but crippling doctrine is so important.

15

Improving Our Futures

Fatalism is an ancient doctrine that is still very much alive and well today. A singer, Doris Day, summed it up in the refrain to her theme song, *Que Sera Sera:* "Whatever will be will be; the future's not ours to see." Though the song has a beautiful melody, its message is dangerous because it encourages people to believe that they have no control over their futures, and they might as well just do whatever feels good at the moment.

Fatalism is more dangerous than ever because there is so much more that we can now do about our futures than we ever could in the past. Scientists have long challenged fatalism by developing many ways for humans to anticipate or control certain future events. As a result, we now have such things as precise predictions for many celestial events, useful short-term forecasts for the weather, and much better control of our future health than people had in the past.

Futurists, as we have seen, have also challenged fatalism in recent decades by refining methods that allow us to identify and assess possible future events. Now we are ready to look carefully at the underlying reasons we *can* anticipate future events, despite the claim of the fatalists, and why we really can do a lot about our futures. We will also be looking at why we need to think *now* about the future rather than wait until the future becomes the present.

Let's begin by looking at the case of an actual victim of fatalism, so that we can understand why the doctrine is so dangerous.

A truck driver named Jim developed a back problem, which meant he could no longer drive trucks. Jim needed to find a new line of work, but he had no idea what he could do. Eventually, he sought the counsel of Noelle Nelson, a clinical psychologist who often writes about people's views of the future.

Here is how Jim, a fatalist, saw his future:

> I guess I'll be doing pretty much what I'm doing, unless something comes along and I get to do something different. The future is just what happens to you tomorrow, and whatever happens is whatever is going to happen.

Jim needed to understand that, if you don't take charge of your career (and other aspects of your life), "whatever happens" is indeed what you will get, and you may not like the results. "Believing, as Jim did, that the future happens to you, rather than being something you create," Nelson explains, "limits your ability to be proactive, to seek out and thus actualize your chosen future." Jim thought he couldn't do anything about his future, so he didn't try, and his career was wrecked.

With Nelson's guidance, Jim did learn to take control of his future and eventually succeeded in a new line of work. Unfortunately, there are countless other victims of fatalism in today's world because it is changing so rapidly and profoundly. People who fail to look ahead make a perilous error, as Jim's case showed, and often they never manage to make the transition to a new career. We can attribute their failure, at least in part, to their negative attitude toward the future. They don't know the importance of foresight and thinking creatively about their futures. Instead, they fall victim to fatalism, which rationalizes their short-sightedness and discourages them from exploring their future opportunities.

Challenging Fatalism

To avoid a career wreck, a health wreck, or some other kind of wreck, we need foresight, not fatalism, so we must develop our understanding of the future through futuring. We should not have to start thinking about a new career only when we suddenly are forced out of an old one. Nor should we start safeguarding our health only after we suffer a heart attack. Unfortunately, fatalism holds many of us back by persuading us that we can know nothing and do nothing about our future. To break free of fatalism, we must understand its dark appeal.

The emotional appeal of fatalism is easy to understand. The ancient doctrine tells us we are free to do whatever we feel like doing right now because we cannot alter our foreordained destiny. We may as well just relax and focus on any immediate pleasures we can find. There's no point in sweating over onerous tasks in order to achieve long-term goals, because it won't help a bit. So we may as well just be spectators as our future unfolds. Let others struggle in the arena; we will just sit in the stands and enjoy ourselves as much as we can.

Fatalism reduces our shame about our past failures as well as our guilt for continuing to do little to gain success. If the future is predetermined, nobody can hold us responsible for any bad things we do. We were simply victims of circumstances. We couldn't do anything but what we did. Fatalism provides absolution from all sins, failures, weaknesses, or whatever.

Besides its emotional appeal, fatalism is supported intellectually by three half-truths. Like other half-truths, fatalism's half-truths are true in one sense but false in another. The result is that they are highly persuasive, but also highly dangerous.

The half-truths may be summarized as follows:

- *The knowability of the future. The half-truth:* We cannot know anything about the future. *The whole truth:* We can know virtually nothing about the future because the world is bafflingly complex and time stretches out infinitely. BUT—and this is a critically important BUT—the knowledge that we can gain about the future is extremely valuable for improving our own personal futures as well as the futures of our organizations, our communities, and human life in general.
- *The improvability of the future. The half-truth:* We cannot do anything about the future. *The whole truth:* We as individuals have little power to shape the future of the world, much less the universe. BUT we do have extraordinary power to improve our own futures, as countless people have demonstrated. We also have appreciable power to improve certain other people's future.
- *The urgency of the future. The half-truth:* We shouldn't spend time thinking about the future because we have too many immediate problems to deal with. *The whole truth:* It's true that we need to take care of immediate emergencies and other issues requiring immediate action, BUT it's not true that immediate problems prevent us from thinking about the future. We can always find time if we recognize that it really is important and urgent to think about the future.

These half-truths reflect three issues that need to be explored and understood clearly—the knowability, improvability, and urgency of the future. We will look at each of these issues in turn.

The Knowability of the Future

We can acquire some useful knowledge of the future because of the *continuity between the past and the future.* If there were no connection between what happened in the past and what will happen in the future, we would be totally incapable of anticipating future events or thinking about the future at all. All we would do is respond immediately to whatever stimuli our brains received.

In fact, however, there is enormous continuity between the world of the past and the world of the future. Most animals know how to use this continuity to improve their future. They *learn* from past experience how to get what they want in the future. Humans have an extraordinary ability to do this, partly because we are able to use symbols, which free us from the present moment—the here and now—and allow us to mentally recreate past events that we have never witnessed and imagine future events that may or may not someday occur. We develop this ability in childhood, according to studies by Jean Piaget and other psychologists, but it would not be possible to use knowledge gained in the past to improve our future if there were no *continuity* between past and future.

We confirm this continuity each morning when we wake up and discover—surprise!?—that the world looks very much the way we left it when we went to sleep the previous evening. Things still look much the same despite all the talk there is about how fast our world today is changing. It is quite true that the world is changing. Despite the speedup of change, a great deal still remains remarkably constant as time passes. It is this continuity that enables us to use the past to anticipate what may happen in the future.

We can identify four types of continuity between past and future:

- *Continuity of existence:* Much of our physical world survives for long periods of time. We can reasonably expect that many long-lasting realities are likely to continue to be part of our world in the future, at least over the near term. Example: Antarctica has been around for many millions of years. We can reasonably expect it to survive another half century, if not longer, though there will doubtless be many changes in it, some of which will likely be substantial.

- *Continuity of change:* When a change occurs, it may persist over a substantial period of time rather than happen instantaneously. Once we can identify such an ongoing change, or trend, we may be able to project how big the change will be at a later point in time. Example: Travel has increased enormously over the past century, so it seems likely that even more people will be traveling in twenty years than are traveling today, though this anticipation could be derailed by war, economic slump, or other obstacles.

- *Continuity of pattern:* Many changes conform to a certain pattern, so if we recognize the continuity of the pattern, we can anticipate future developments. The development cycles in animals and plants are one example of this type of continuity. Another continuity is the gradual drift of the sun in its course through the sky and the subsequent warming or cooling of the environment. This important observation enabled ancient peoples to predict the seasons, so they would know when to get ready for winter and when they could safely plant in the spring. Futurists use the same principle when they identify precursors (forerunners) of change. For instance a new sport or therapy that achieves popularity in California—known as a forerunner jurisdiction—often will become common elsewhere.

- *Continuity of causality:* There is impressive continuity through time in the functioning of the natural world and in some social relationships. Changes often can be anticipated on the basis of antecedent circumstances. For instance, if a U.S. president dies in office, the vice-president can be expected to succeed to the presidency as provided by the Constitution.

More reliable than human rules are the laws of nature, such as the freezing of water as the ambient temperature drops below 0°C. These relationships are fairly stable over time, enabling scientists to understand and predict events not only on earth but far out in the universe.

People apply these continuities intuitively in everyday life. To anticipate what might happen on a stock market, we might intuitively use the continuities in this way:

- The continuity-of-existence principle suggests that the exchange will still be functioning regularly, that stocks will be traded, and that price quotations and averages will be available.

- The continuity-of-trend principle suggests the prices might be slightly higher because of the long-term upward bias in stock prices.
- The continuity-of-pattern principle warns us not to count on a rise in prices, because stock prices constantly fluctuate up and down. Furthermore, there are periods of months, or even years, when stock prices stagnate: Rather than move up or down very much, they merely fluctuate without any clear trend. To make the situation even more complicated, stock prices often exhibit a persistent downward trend and sometimes collapse.
- The continuity-of-causality principle calls attention to events that are likely to push stock prices up or down. For instance, an increase in inflation suggests a need to raise interest rates—an event that would likely push stock prices down.

But does a knowledge of the continuities connected to stocks enable us to predict what the Dow Jones Industrial Average will be next July 1? Hardly, but it can enable us to develop certain expectations about what is *most likely* to happen. We may, for instance, decide on the basis of the past that the average will probably not be more than, say, 500 points away from where it is now. We might even have a "target" price—a general expectation or "guess" about what the average will be—next July 1, but we should not bet all our money on it!

Here are examples of what we can know *probabilistically* about the future based on its continuity with the past:

- Next January 29, California will experience at least one earthquake.
- Five years from now, the U.S. economy will produce more goods and services than the Belgian economy.
- Ten years from now, a pound of gold will be worth more than a pound of butter.
- Twenty years from now, the world will be able to celebrate its escape from a catastrophic collision with an asteroid.
- Thirty years from now, a year will still have about 365 days.

None of these forecasts is certain, yet they all will likely prove accurate because of things we know probabilistically about our world, specifically:

- California has been experiencing an average of 37,283 earthquakes *each year* or 102 a day, according to the Seismological Laboratory at the University of California at Berkeley. So the odds make it unlikely that the state will escape having even one earthquake next January 29.
- The U.S. economy is many times larger than Belgium's.
- Gold is very scarce and has always been highly valued. Butter is an everyday market item with only a tiny market value compared with gold.
- Major asteroid collisions are extremely rare.
- The year has had 365 days throughout recorded human history, according to the U.S. Naval Observatory in Washington. Back in the age of the dinosaurs, however, there were about 400 days per year.

Though we may feel confident of these forecasts, they are far from certain. California *might* beat the odds and escape an earthquake on January 29. Something *might* destroy the U.S. economy and/or cause the Belgian economy to expand prodigiously. Somebody *might* develop a way to produce enormous quantities of gold at trivial cost. A major asteroid *might* collide with the Earth during the next ten years. Human actions (or something else) *might* cause the Earth's rotation to accelerate or decelerate, meaning there would be significantly more or fewer days per year.

We can make many more such forecasts, but the point here is simply to recognize that we do have a fair amount of probabilistic knowledge about the future, and this knowledge is essential to our ability to function as rational beings.

The Improvability of Our Future

Earlier we noted the importance of seemingly trivial chance circumstances and their ability to shape events in complex, interactive systems. Now we must stress the importance of human choice in determining outcomes.

Humans are not simply pushed here and there by natural and social forces. We have considerable power to consciously assess past events and future possibilities and to respond in ways calculated to improve our future situations. We do this all the time. We are not prisoners of fate but rather largely independent beings with extraordinary power to shape our futures, both as individuals and as organizations. The future does not just happen to us. What we experience now or will experience in the future is largely of our own doing, since we ourselves play such an important part in shaping our futures.

The power of an individual to create his or her own future can best be appreciated if we look at instances where people seem to have been almost totally deprived of any freedom of choice, such as people in jail or people who are physically incapacitated. Such people might seem quite helpless and lacking in any real freedom of choice at all, yet they have often demonstrated remarkable power to remain masters of their own destinies.

Convicts and prisoners of war often make productive use of their time in confinement. They educate themselves and acquire new skills. A library could be filled solely with books written by prisoners or former prisoners who conceived their works in prison. Examples include Martin Luther King Jr., *Don Quixote* author Miguel de Cervantes, and Indian leader Jawaharlal Nehru.

Christopher Reeve, a Hollywood actor who starred in the role of Superman, fell off a horse and found himself totally paralyzed from the neck down. Since his accident, Reeve has played the greatest role of his career by serving as an advocate for the handicapped and as a subject for experiments with new medical treatments. He became Superman in a new and more convincing way than before. Now he is a living example of human courage and achievement under overwhelmingly tragic circumstances.

Reeve insists that Supercourage was not required for what he did. He says, "I never knew how powerful the human mind was until age forty-two when I had my accident. I don't think I am unique. Anybody can do quite a lot by refusing to give in to limitations."

Striking ability to shape one's future productively can also be seen in those individuals brought up in the same family with much the same heredity and life circumstances. Blood brothers and sisters can, and often do, choose radically different futures for themselves.

Brothers William and James J. (Whitey) Bulger grew up in an impoverished Boston family. James drifted into crime, went to prison, escaped, and eventually was put on the FBI's ten Most Wanted Fugitives list. Meanwhile, his brother William went to college, then entered politics, and eventually became president of the University of Massachusetts. (He was forced to resign in 2003 after being accused of concealing information that might lead to his brother's capture.)

Rosa Lee, a shoplifter and welfare recipient in Washington, D.C., had eight children. Six of her children followed her into petty crime and welfare, but two rebelled against the circumstances of their early life and became respectable, hard-working citizens.

What made those two different from the others? Possibly, suggests journalist Leon Dash in his book *Rosa Lee*, it was the fact that they had experienced someone who helped them to develop a positive vision of their future. However, they themselves had to make the difficult choices required to achieve a positive future amid circumstances that lead others into antisocial careers.

Individuals, groups, business firms, and even nations possess the potential to shape their futures creatively and positively. Nations such as Japan, South Korea, and Singapore have shown how a backward country can climb quickly from poverty to prosperity if it commits itself seriously to achieving a new economy and society. Enlightened and dedicated leaders such as Singapore's Lee Kwan Yew seem to play key roles in making it really happen. With such leadership, a small country like Singapore, which belonged to the Third World when it became an independent republic in 1965, today is a prospering nation with First World ranking.

The Urgency of the Future

Continuity makes futuring possible, but rapid change makes it urgent. Despite the continued stability in much of our world, technological and social changes are coming faster than ever. If we do not do more futuring, we will experience increasing difficulty in making the right decisions in a timely fashion. Good decisions depend on good foresight.

In the past, when the world changed more slowly, foresight was much less of a problem than it is today because the world changed much more slowly. Typically, you were born into a small community where you might remain the rest of your life, and you might even live and die in the house where you were born or at least in the same community. Your occupation tended to remain fixed, too, partly because most families were involved in agriculture. If you were a boy, you would learn your father's trade and continue to work in that trade for the rest of your life. If you were a girl, your mother and relatives trained you in household and mothering skills, and you were well prepared to be the wife of a neighborhood boy.

Life is very different in today's fast-changing world. Tradition no longer lays out our futures. We must somehow create our futures by ourselves, trying, as best we can, to fit ourselves and our organizations into a highly complex, swiftly changing global economy that provides extraordinary opportunities for those with good foresight but potential disasters for people who lack it. Sadly, schools and universities are doing poorly in preparing students for the challenging world they face today. Students are being thrust into a bewildering environment with which they often cannot cope. The pace of change poses similar challenges for business organizations, communities, and the world as a whole.

On the other hand, rapid change opens extraordinary opportunities for those who have a future-oriented attitude and know how to explore the possibilities of their future. They can develop realistic plans for achieving success in both work and life in general.

So futuring must not be neglected because we are "too busy" handling current crises and just don't have time. We must not fall victim to colleagues who say, "Why worry about the future until we get to it?" This is mere sophistry—the kind of thinking that leads us to ignore problems until they inflict major damage on us.

The future is urgent because we simply cannot postpone it. Danger and opportunity do not sit patiently in an invisible waiting room until we feel it convenient to deal with them. Quite the contrary. They are likely to rush on us when we are least prepared. In the face of that simple fact, our only reasonable response is to think ahead and prepare as best we can. That means *now*—not some time in the future.

Obviously, we must deal quickly with certain emergencies that require immediate action, such as when there is a fire. But focusing on current problems that often are quite trivial keeps us from seeing more critically important issues. Only too often, a "long-term" concern suddenly becomes an immediate emergency. The managers of the World Trade Center in New York may have thought of terrorism as a long-term problem until the very moment the Center collapsed around them.

The bottom line is that we can develop foresight through futuring. But we cannot accomplish much if we constantly neglect the future because we think we must concentrate exclusively on problems that seem to demand immediate action. The future is urgent because it's all we have left.

Foresight: The Secret Ingredient of Success

The primary goal of futuring—the active exploration of future possibilities—is to develop foresight.

Foresight might be defined as the ability to make decisions that are judged to be good not just in the present moment but in the long run. People with good foresight can think ahead by intuitively futuring—identifying and assessing a wide variety of possibilities and making astute judgments about what will work out best over time. Good foresight depends on good futuring.

Foresight works its wonders invisibly. We must infer its presence from the quality of the decisions that individuals and organizations make. If people are generally successful in their activities, we are likely to judge them as having good foresight, so foresight is often linked to wealth. As Tevye noted in *Fiddler on the Roof*, "When you're rich, they think you really know!"

But since we cannot really see the foresight in people's heads, people's success—in gaining wealth or anything else—is likely to be attributed to something other than foresight. Often, success is attributed to luck or chance, though people often will mutter about some form of chicanery. It's undeniable that chance circumstances play an enormous role in human success in every area of life, as suggested by what we have seen in our review of systems, chance, and chaos (Chapter 5). But trying to understand how chance interacts with human choices in determining success is extremely difficult. We do, however, have a model that may illuminate this interaction—the game of bridge.

In bridge, winners and losers are determined both by the chance distribution of cards and by the choices that people make about how to play whatever cards they are dealt by chance. As the cards are repeatedly shuffled and dealt during play, the competing players must make a long series of choices about how to play their cards. A pair of novice players competing with a pair of expert players may win some games due to superior cards, but as play continues the expert players will eventually come out on top. They can do so simply by making better decisions about how to play their cards than their opponents do. Better choices sooner or later tip the odds of winning decisively toward those players who can anticipate what will likely happen when they play the cards in their hands.

In life, good choices probably are even more determinative of success than in bridge. In the game of life, people with superior foresight can invent an extraordinary number of ways to minimize the effects of any "bad cards" they are dealt and will exploit whatever opportunities are allowed by chance. In some cases, humans can even rewrite the rules of success, as Christopher Reeve did after he became paralyzed. With good foresight, achieved by futuring, we can snatch success from disaster. Meanwhile, those with poor foresight may turn a stroke of luck into a catastrophe. As the astute Duc de la Rochefoucauld observed, "No occurrences are so unfortunate that the shrewd cannot turn them to some advantage, nor so fortunate that the imprudent cannot turn them to their own disadvantage."

But the importance of foresight is commonly overlooked due to its invisibility. Again and again, success will be attributed to luck. General Dwight D. Eisenhower offers a case in point. His excellent planning ability was recognized by his superiors, and he was promoted by two far-sighted leaders, generals Douglas MacArthur and George C. Marshall. After Eisenhower became Supreme Commander of Allied Forces in Europe, he planned and executed history's biggest invasion, which led to the Allied triumph over Germany in World War II. During the two terms in which Eisenhower served as U.S. president in the 1950s, Americans probably felt more content than ever before because they enjoyed both peace and prosperity.

But for all Eisenhower had achieved, many people thought he was just lucky: Critics saw him as a man who idled away his presidency on golf courses and just "happened to be" president during a time of peace. Here is his response:

> The United States never lost a soldier or a foot of ground in my administration. We kept the peace. People asked how it happened. By God, it didn't just happen! I'll tell you that!

Of course not. Eisenhower himself was largely responsible for the peace the United States enjoyed while he was in office. Circumstances alone rarely if ever make war inevitable; the chance success of a terrorist in Sarajevo in 1914 set the wheels in motion for the outbreak of World War I, but the drift to war could have been stopped if political leaders had made different choices.

Eisenhower had the foresight needed to avoid war, and he was in a key position to maintain the peace. By contrast, both his predecessor and successor in the presidency led America into wars in Korea and Vietnam that cost thousands and thousands of lives. Were Harry Truman and John F. Kennedy just unlucky? Historians can debate the issue endlessly, but can we not recognize that America may have enjoyed peace in the 1950s because of a president with the foresight in security matters to achieve it?

Responsibility for the Future

We are made wise not by the recollection of the past but by the responsibility for the future.

—George Bernard Shaw

If we think that luck really determines the fate of nations and our own fate in work and life, perhaps we should make our career decisions by rolling dice and select our political leaders by lottery. But if we recognize that choices really count in determining our future, we must also recognize that we ourselves are largely responsible for our own futures.

In this book, we have scouted along the frontiers of the future in order to understand how we can use futuring to acquire the foresight needed for wise choices. During the years ahead, good foresight will be more urgently needed than ever before in order to achieve personal and organizational success.

We began our scouting expedition by looking at the Great Transformation now radically altering the character of human life, and we noted key supertrends that can help us to understand what is happening. The trends also help us to identify future problems and opportunities.

We went on to look at patterns of change, such as cycles and stages of development, that enable us to anticipate certain future events, and also at the way we can use the concept of systems to understand many of the often bizarre ways in which events are fashioned.

We moved on to examining methods of futuring that enable us to learn about the future and so make good decisions about what we do—techniques such as visioning, scanning trends, developing scenarios, and creating novel approaches to our problems. We also reviewed the ways we can learn an enormous amount from history—knowledge that can help us to create better governments in the future and also protect our pocketbooks.

We also have seen how the twentieth century intensified the need for thinking about the future and led to a futurist movement that has refined more-effective approaches to understanding the future. We now have a considerable toolchest for improving the futures of our organizations and communities and also our own futures. Today we have more power than ever to determine our own future, so we must accept our responsibility for actually making the wise decisions that are needed.

We have focused so far on futuring and foresight as benefiting ourselves and the groups to which we belong. In the next and last chapter, we will investigate the question of whether we have any responsibility for people who have done nothing for us and whom we will never see—the future generations who will inherit the earth from us.

16

Future Generations

"The one way that you cannot avoid thinking about the future," Margaret Mead once said, "is if you have a two-year-old child in front of you. When you think about ten years from now, that child will be twelve; when you think of twenty, that child will be twenty-two and you begin to wonder: What will that child's children be like?"

Today's children put a human face on the future. We instinctively feel responsible for their welfare and try to help them. We also know that today's children will be tomorrow's parents with children of their own, and other generations will follow. So children remind us of the responsibility that we bear for other people, including those others who have not yet come into existence. In this chapter, we will consider these broader responsibilities and how we should deal with them.

Do We Have Duties to the Future?
Native American tribes refer to the future as "the seventh generation yet unborn." This seventh generation will arrive in about 200 years.

"We won't actually meet that seventh generation," notes Oren Lyons, an Iroquois leader, "but our collective actions will determine the kind of life they have and whether or not they can be all we hope they can be.... We have the power to create a world in which the seventh generation will be able to exist as dignified and positive human beings. And we have the responsibility to do our best thinking to bring that world about."

Lyons dedicated his own Native American publication specifically to the seventh generation yet unborn. He asserts that we have a moral duty to them, and it is certainly true that many things bind our generation with both past and future generations. There is, first of all, the invisible chain of causation that links past events and conditions to those in the future. We use buildings, furnishings, and natural resources that have come to us from the past, and we may pass them on to the future. Even our bodies are intimately connected to both past and future, because the atoms that compose them were once used by other people and living things who lived in the past. In the future, those same atoms will be used by still more people and organisms.

From this perspective, our brief existence can be viewed as merely an ephemeral phenomenon in the ongoing transformations of life. In the words of philosopher Robert B. Mellert, "Our lives are the threads out of which the future is woven."

"What I do today," Mellert explains, "lives on after me in my children, and in the children of those to whom I am related in the bond of humanness. My ultimate ideal, then, cannot be limited to self-interest or personal happiness, which will cease at my death."

Other thinkers share the perspective of Mellert and Lyons and wonder how future generations will feel about us, their ancestors. Will they praise us for our technological achievements or will they curse us for such crimes as wiping out thousands of species of plants and animals?

Today, there is growing international concern for those future generations. In 1997, UNESCO's General Conference, meeting in Paris, issued a *Declaration on the Responsibilities of the Present Generations Towards Future Generations.* The Declaration stated, "The present generations have the responsibility of ensuring that the needs and interests of present and future generations are fully safeguarded."

But getting from a pious declaration to effective action is difficult and slow. At its founding in 1945, the United Nations pledged itself in its charter to "save succeeding generations from the scourge of war." But the fact is that, since the charter was adopted, wars have continued, and they are continuing today and will continue into the future until the world has better institutional machinery for resolving conflicts.

Beyond the precincts of UN entities, lawyers and policy makers often debate questions of intergenerational equity, such as the rights of an unborn child vs. the rights of his or her parents. Policy makers worry about the tax burden being placed on future generations by the benefits now promised to retiring workers. In Europe and America, many workers now drop out of the workforce as soon as they can retire while they are still in good health and quite capable of working. Thereafter, they may do little but amuse themselves while their idle lifestyle is supported by young workers, who often are hard-pressed to meet the needs of their dependents.

Former Colorado Governor Richard Lamm, financier Peter G. Peterson, and others have repeatedly warned Americans about the burden that retiring baby boomers will place on future workers. Someday, there may be a tax rebellion in which young workers will be pitted against the idle old who remain in good health.

Some nations, such as Germany and France, are already struggling to contain a growing financial crisis imposed by early retirement and overgenerous benefits for retirees, but cutting back on people's entitlements is politically difficult and sometimes provokes violent responses. In the United States, retirees and people close to retirement wield enormous political influence and have not only secured generous payouts to the elderly but have made it politically dangerous to oppose them. However, a day of reckoning may come for future retirees if a taxpayer revolt prevents the government from making good on its promises to retirees. (Today's young workers may want to protect themselves against this contingency by staying longer in the workforce and building up their personal savings.)

A Pledge to Future Generations

People concerned about future generations might consider making a personal pledge to them. Allen Tough, a professor emeritus of futures studies at the University of Toronto, got this idea while on a bicycle trip above Canada's tree line. He wanted to translate global issues into what an individual might do to improve the future. Most of the changes occurring in the world today are not the doing of a few famous leaders but of billions of people making day-to-day decisions with little thought about how their actions affect the world at large.

Tough's own pledge to future generations includes these points:

- To care about the well-being of future generations. Their needs are just as important as those of today.
- To choose paid work or volunteer work that makes a positive contribution to humanity's flourishing.
- To play my part in halting the deterioration of our environment and support efforts to achieve a sustainable relationship with our planet.

- To support actions, goals, and directions that will help human civilization to survive and flourish over the next few decades. (This includes the well-being of children, cooperation among diverse cultures, better knowledge of world problems and our future, etc.)
- To seek an appropriate balance between my own needs and those of future generations when deciding how to spend my money and time.
- To recognize that I live in an age when some of the most important choices in the history of human civilization will be made.

Tough does not ask that others endorse his pledge, but suggests that they make their own pledges expressing what they believe is important for the future. Tough currently edits the Future Generations Forum sponsored by the World Future Society (wfs.org). The forum also offers an opportunity for people to share their ideas about future generations.

Many years before Tough's project, philosopher C. West Churchman had struggled with the question, "What is morality?" He eventually decided that morality is "what a future generation would ask us to do if they were here to ask." Tough decided to try to find out what future generations would ask by getting opinions from people living now. So he recruited thirteen professors in nine nations to arrange for their students to play the role of people who will be alive several decades from now. The role-playing exercises produced a rich array of ideas, priorities, and messages from which Tough selected key points and blended them into a single message to today's people from tomorrow's generation.

Sample "requests from the future": Reduce nuclear and biological weapons; decrease military forces; reverse population growth; take precautions against possible runaway epidemics or asteroid collision; develop governance tradition emphasizing long-run global perspective; balance governmental budgets; enlarge and disseminate knowledge; reduce child poverty, hunger, neglect, and abuse; increase learning opportunities for people of all ages.

But what about our obligation to today's people? Is it right to accord future generations priority over the living, breathing people of today? Yale sociologist Wendell Bell analyzed the arguments made on behalf of future generations and concluded that the moral choice appears to be a balance between the interests of present and future generations. We have, Bell believes, "an obligation, first, to strive to create the conditions that permit an equal and good chance to every presently living person to live a long (eighty to a hundred years) and good life, and, second, an effort to leave future generations at least as well off as we of the present generation so that they, too, can live long and good lives. Being morally responsible means caring for ourselves, for each other in the present, and for others in the future."

Happily, the interests of both present and future generations sometimes converge, so Bell suggests looking for actions that offer a "double benefit" by enriching both present and future generations. One way, he notes, is through research, technological development, and scholarship, which give to future people increased knowledge and therefore increased power to control the conditions of their lives.

Another way to reconcile the interests of present and future generations is to help today's young people, the generation that links us to the unborn generations of the future.

Helping Young People

Young people today clearly have many problems, but one of the biggest is that so many are fatalistic about their future. As we have seen fatalism discourages people from thinking constructively about their future and thus sets them up for low achievement and failure. This sad fact has emerged from scholarly studies of underachieving individuals and groups. So, clearly, one way we can help today's youth is to see that they are well prepared to think ahead and take charge of their futures.

The need for young people to think about their futures has become urgent because of two major changes brought by the ongoing Great Transformation: First, life choices have become far more complex than they were in the past due to such factors as the proliferation of new opportunities (and concomitant shrinkage of old opportunities), and, second, young people are increasingly left without caring adult guidance while they are making difficult and risky choices involving their careers and often their health and safety.

In the agricultural society of the past, children lived primarily on farms and in small communities where parents and neighbors were always close at hand, well positioned to keep an eye on the young and provide both reprimands for bad behavior and praise for good. Young people now find themselves largely abandoned by both their parents (mothers as well as fathers now work outside the home) and adult neighbors, who now are strangers who happen to live nearby.

Children and youth now form peer groups lacking adult guidance, and they become further separated from the adult world by their absorption in the pseudorealities provided by electronic entertainments and sports. The media entertainments and, increasingly, sports are supported by commercial advertisers, who are only too willing to sacrifice the welfare of the young if it means larger profits for themselves. The growth of peer-group participation and the proliferation of commercial messages reaching the young now displaces and even overrules the messages from parents and teachers—the adults who actually care about the long-term welfare of the young.

So there is a widening gap between the preparation that young people need for their future and the preparation they actually receive. Gone are the days when children could anticipate their future—and even prepare for it—by merely observing and helping their parents and neighbors. Youth can no longer say, "I will become like Father (or Mother)." Now they are likely to doubt that they *could* be like Father (or Mother) even if they wanted to be, which many don't. So youth are left in limbo struggling with the question, "What should I do with my life? How can I have a future?"

Educators clearly have a critically important role here. They can prepare today's young people for the uncertain future by helping them learn what the future world may be like and how they can explore it creatively. Enabling young people to develop foresight can greatly increase their chances for success in our complex and turbulent world. People with good foresight have a kind of mental "map" of the future. The "map" is very vague and rough, but it gives them a starting place for thinking about their own future and making wise decisions about it. Young people who are thus equipped—and some are—can chart a course for themselves that tends to lead to success. Young people who can't chart a course are likely to go nowhere.

Foresight is not a genetic gift but a quality of thought that enables people to anticipate future developments and prepare for them. Young people can acquire foresight by learning how to think about their future, and a number of specific ways to go about this task have already been described. Young people have a special need for *ideas* about the future, because we can't think about something unless we have some ideas to think with. The future world is invisible to us today, so there is a special need to furnish young people with ideas about it. Then it will be easier for them to form a framework of future concepts on which to draw their mental "map" of the future, a map they will need in order to deal with their futures proactively.

The vagueness of our mental maps of the future must not lead us to underrate them. All we know about the world—past, present, or future—exists invisibly, in hidden and mysterious form, within the confines of our craniums, and it is perhaps the most valuable thing we have. But our ideas about the future are pitifully few compared with our ideas about the past. We need to make a serious attempt to build up our ideas about the future, because tomorrow's world will certainly not be a pale replica of the present world, whatever else it may be.

Young people must be encouraged to learn about the major trends now reshaping human life and begin to think about how these trends are influencing our everyday lives, creating new problems and opportunities. As they explore the meaning of these trends in terms of what they themselves might contribute, we can hope that they find a path to success for both themselves and others.

Teachers of adolescents and young adults now can find an appreciable number of materials for teaching students about the future. Simplified versions of such futuring techniques as trend scanning and analysis, scenario building, and gaming can get young people into the habit of thinking ahead, thus enabling them to make better decisions in work and life.

Books available now provide information about current trends. Many such books are described in current issues of *The Futurist* magazine, which is designed to be sufficiently reader-friendly that it can be used by motivated high school as well as university students. Titles of other books are listed on the World Future Society's Web site. The Society's monthly newsletter *Future Survey* describes current scholarly and policy-oriented books that would be of interest to teachers and students in higher education. Professors and teachers interested in the future can take one- or two-day courses on futuring at World Future Society conferences.

The Australian Foresight Institute has identified hundreds of future-oriented courses at institutions around the world. (Visit www.swin.edu.au/afi.) In the United States, for example, the University of Houston at Clear Lake offers a master's program in studies of the future, and the University of Hawaii offers both master's and doctoral programs in futures studies. Sociologist Stephen Steele recently received approval for the establishment of an Institute for the Future at Maryland's Anne Arundel Community College. Individual professors and teachers at many other institutions have also offered courses on the future.

These moves in the educational community are very encouraging but many more are urgently needed. Most educators are preparing students to live in the past, not the future.

Connecting students to the future can encourage them to safeguard their personal futures by enlarging their store of knowledge about the opportunities the world offers for constructive activities that will help them to achieve real success.

Futuring also can make other school work more meaningful. Asking the question, "Where are we going?" leads to interest in how we got to where we are. History becomes relevant to what is happening now or may happen in the future. Science also can become more meaningful by connecting it to the social problems that science can help solve. Young people need ideas about what they themselves can do in the future.

Through futuring, young people can develop the foresight they need to meet the challenges of our rapidly changing world. They become aware of things they need to learn about, dangers they can avoid, opportunities they can grasp if they prepare. This knowledge of future possibilities enables them to become proactive rather than reactive in dealing with challenges. Without such foresight, they are only too likely to become victims of happenstance, unequipped for the world they live in.

What We Can Do

Our feeling of responsibility for future generations arises in no small measure from our recognition of what we owe to the past. Where would we be now without telephones, automobiles, computers, antibiotics, and the countless other things that were achieved by the dedicated efforts of our ancestors? We can never repay our debt to them, but we can convert this debt to the past into an obligation to the future—an obligation that we can meet by adding our bit to the legacy we will leave for the generations that succeed ours.

And there is surely no shortage of problems for us all—both young and old—to work on. Anthony Judge and his colleagues at the Union of International Associations in Brussels have actually been counting and cataloguing world problems since the 1970s. The first edition of their *Encyclopedia of World Problems and Human Potential* listed no fewer than 2,560 world problems. Yet that was only a start. By the time the fourth edition was published in 1994, the number of problems had climbed to 13,000, and the problem hunters were beginning to lose count. Early in the twenty-first century, the total number of problems reached about 30,000. This vast collection of problems now is kept on computers. (See www.uia.org/data.htm.)

To rank as a "world problem," a problem must affect people in a number of nations, but such problems can be highly diverse. Here are a few samples: incompetent management, shortage of animal protein, secret laws, underground economy, illegally induced abortion, acne, and inadequate welfare services for the aged.

Over time, the world's problems change—or at least the ones we are most concerned about do. People in Western nations worry far less nowadays about witches than their ancestors did in the sixteenth and seventeenth centuries. They also probably worry less about the devil, but they have plenty of new worries, such as nuclear terrorism, computer viruses, and AIDS, which didn't trouble their ancestors. On the other hand, there are certain people who do still worry about witches and the devil, so both are listed in the *Encyclopedia* along with newer problems.

We may think our problems today are bigger than those experienced by people in the past, but the fact is that life for the average person has been getting better through the centuries, though there have been many setbacks along the way. Progress was truly extraordinary during the twentieth century, and life improved greatly in countries all around the world, even though conditions in many areas remain appalling.

The improvement in living conditions was demonstrated by means of an interesting experiment in London that led to a four-part British documentary, *The 1900 House*. As part of the celebration of the year 2000, the producers restored a middle-class London house that existed in 1900 nearly to its original condition. They removed any additions made during the twentieth century, as well as the modern furniture, and substituted furniture and appliances from 1900. Then, week after week as television cameras recorded their actions, the new residents—a modern London couple with four children—had to follow all the patterns of life of 1900: buying 1900-type foods and preparing them according to 1900 recipes, wearing 1900-style clothes, doing 1900 chores, and playing 1900 games.

This re-creation of life in 1900 showed that even in the glorious heyday of the British empire, life for a middle-class family in London was hard and dull, with many time-consuming chores and no television, no radio, no motion pictures. Few people today would want to go back to the actual conditions of life in 1900. Though there are still huge disparities between rich and poor, life is much more comfortable today than it was for our ancestors in 1900. Human progress has been real, and it is now up to us to keep it going.

Humanity's New Potential

Realistically, we cannot expect to conquer quickly the thousands of world problems that now exist, so today's young people will have plenty of room to make their unique contributions. And there are exciting new resources available to both young and older people for solving problems.

- *Improving technology.* One example is our new intellectual technology—the computers and communications systems that enable us to collect, organize, and analyze growing masses of information. Increasingly sophisticated software will help us solve countless problems.

- *Accumulating knowledge.* Scientific knowledge continues to accumulate prodigiously in every field, from archaeology to zoology. This growing store of knowledge means that we have a growing database that can help us accomplish almost anything we set out to do.

- *Highly trained people.* We have far more trained people than ever before. It has been estimated that 80 percent of all the scientists who ever lived are alive today.

- *Global institutions.* We have a growing array of international institutions capable of handling global tasks. People in business firms, government, and education have learned how to operate successfully around the world.
- *Economic power.* Today's capital equipment—ships, airplanes, factories, railroads, power plants, refineries, trucks, highways, apartment houses, office buildings, and so on—dwarfs what was available a century ago. If we had the political will, collective humanity now could undertake simultaneously a dozen projects on the scale of the Apollo program.

Our potential for future accomplishments is nothing short of stupendous. We live in an age when the creation of a peaceful, prosperous world has become not only a possibility but a goal that we might be able to reach before the end of the twenty-first century—that is, *within the lifetime of many people now living.* Peering through the clouds of problems that worry us, we can catch glimpses of a magnificent future supercivilization. We have the power to create a civilization so vastly superior to anything known in the past that we have difficulty even imagining what it might be like.

But we also know that the happy future we hope for may never come to reality, because its coming depends on people around the world working more cooperatively than they have in the past and showing much greater foresight and wisdom. We must somehow develop the means of making better collective choices about our future. We need decisions that will move us closer toward that ideal future, and we need good political leadership.

Choosing the future of humanity is a truly awesome task, but that is the responsibility that has been thrust upon us. Choosing our collective future is not simply a matter of selecting our preferred environment from a cosmic menu of alternative paradises. If it were, the choices we face would be far less momentous than they are. The fact is, we could make such poor choices that, instead of getting any sort of desirable future, progress could become regress and civilization could collapse into barbarism and savagery. History contains numerous examples of civilizations that have collapsed, relapsed into barbarism, or simply vanished.

Probably the most reasonable and constructive attitude we can have toward the future is either concerned hope (if you are an optimist) or hopeful concern (if you are a pessimist). The Great Transformation amply justifies our hopes by what it has accomplished and our doubts by what it has cost. As for the future, its risks are balanced by its opportunities.

When we assemble a balance sheet of risks and opportunities, pluses and minuses, the future's bottom line seems elusive: There are too many uncertainties. So perhaps our best policy is to stop worrying whether the future will be as good as we hope or as bad as we sometimes fear and just get on with the task of creating a future that we will try to ensure is good.

Epilogue

A Fellowship of Explorers

Futuring is best undertaken in fellowship with other explorers of the future. That is why the World Future Society exists—to offer a gathering place for all those seeking ideas about the future and tools with which to build it.

Membership in the Society is open to anyone interested in the future and includes subscriptions to the Society's magazine, *The Futurist*, and its e-mail newsletter, *Futurist Update*. Visit the Society's Web site, wfs.org, to join or to learn more about futuring and the future in general.

A special Web page is devoted to posting materials of interest to readers of *Futuring*. Watch that page (wfs.org/futuring. htm) for suggestions about new resources and opportunities for you to learn more about futuring.

The Society's Web site also offers a variety of other features for people interested in the future, including a Future Generations Forum, descriptions of new books about the future, and a list of consulting futurists.

Society members are invited to the group's annual conference where they can hear and meet leading futurists and other forward-looking people. As part of these conferences, the Society offers about a dozen courses dealing with the future, including one or more introductory courses for newcomers.

The Society also offers a Professional Membership program, which includes a scholarly journal, *Futures Research Quarterly*, and annual forums limited to Professional Members.

Other services include a network of chapters in a number of cities and a monthly newsletter, *Future Survey*, that provides reports and assessments of current books and articles dealing with the future and public-policy issues.

The World Future Society is a nonprofit scientific and educational association located in Bethesda, Maryland, in the suburbs of Washington, D.C. The Society acts as a neutral clearinghouse and forum for forecasts, ideas, and other information related to the future. It is a nongovernmental, nonpartisan organization and provides many opportunities for scientists, scholars, politicians, business leaders, and others to share their ideas about the future.

The Society's activities are supported by members and friends who make voluntary contributions of time and money to sustain the Society's operations. The Society is currently seeking funds to provide better support for educators and young people engaged in serious thinking about the future.

For more information about Society activities, please contact:

Membership Committee
World Future Society
7910 Woodmont Avenue, Suite 450
Bethesda, Maryland 20814, U.S.A.
Telephone: 301-656-8274
E-mail address: info@wfs.org
Web site: wfs.org

Notes

Preface

xi Futurists have never agreed on what to call their field. Besides *futuring*, terms enjoying appreciable usage include *futures studies, futuristics, futurology, futurics,* and *prognostics.* For more on the name issue, see "A Field Without a Name: What Shall We Call the Study of the Future?" by Edward Cornish, *The Futurist,* May 1998, and "A Field in Search of a Name," Appendix B, p. 254 of Edward Cornish's *The Study of the Future* (see Bibliography). A 1998 poll of World Future Society members indicated a strong preference for a term using the Latin stem *futur-,* but opinion was very divided about the ending for the word.

xiii For more on the development of futurist thinking and Kahn's work, see Chapter 14.

Chapter 1: Introduction

2 For more on Meriwether Lewis's preparations, see *Undaunted Courage: Meriwether Lewis, Thomas Jefferson, and the Opening of the American West* by Stephen E. Ambrose (New York: Simon & Schuster, 1996), pp. 80-125.

3 Colin Powell was quoted in *Outlook,* published by The Futures Group (Glastonbury, Connecticut), December 1996.

5 Earl Joseph made this point in a brief article, "What Is Future Time?" *The Futurist,* August 1974. Discussing "Middle Range Futures" (five to twenty years from now), Joseph said, "Almost anything imaginable may be brought about in this time frame."

6 For more on Alan Hald's vision, see his article, "When Vision Becomes Reality," in *The Futurist,* November-December 1988.

6 For more on the Bill Gates's visioning, see his book *The Road Ahead* (see Bibliography).

Chapter 2: The Great Transformation

9 Michael Marien used the "era of multiple transformations" phrase in an interview with the author in 2002. Marien's early work on societal issues led him to produce a remarkable work entitled *Societal Directions and Alternatives: A Critical Guide to the Literature,* published in 1976 by Information for Policy Design in Syracuse, New York. Since then, he has edited the monthly newsletter *Future Survey,* which provides bibliographic summa-

ries of books and articles related to the future and public-policy issues.

10   The exact number of countries in the world is uncertain. About 200 nations are recognized by the United Nations.

11   For more on large-scale projects, see books by Frank Davidson and McKinley Conway in the Bibliography.

11   Max Ways's estimates of the pace of change are from his book *Beyond Survival* (New York: Harper & Brothers, 1959), p. 25. His article "The Era of Radical Change" in *Fortune*, May 1964, contained his proposed categories of change.

12   Kurzweil made his comments at a symposium at DePauw University, Greencastle, Indiana, October 5, 2002. Reported by DePauw University News (www.depauw.edu/news).

12   For a discussion of the singularity, see "Exploring the 'Singularity'" by James John Bell, *The Futurist*, May-June 2003. The singularity may be described as the point in time when current trends go wildly off the charts, so that the future beyond the singularity cannot be envisioned.

12   Theodore Modis's forecast for a slowdown in change appeared in his article "The Limits of Complexity and Change," *The Futurist*, May-June 2003.

13   See "The Cultural Ecological Niche," in C. Loring Brace's *Evolution in an Anthropological View* (Altamira Press, 2000).

15   A very engaging recent account of the introduction of steam engines into the coal industry is given in Barbara Freese's book *Coal: A Human History* (Cambridge, Massachusetts: Perseus Books, 2003).

18   Doenitz was quoted in *Tuxedo Park: A Wall Street Tycoon and the Secret Palace of Science That Changed the Course of World War II* by Jennet Conant (New York: Simon & Schuster, 2002).

19   Pelton is executive director of the Arthur C. Clarke Institute and director of the Space and Advanced Communications Research Institute at George Washington University (www.sacri.seas. gwu.edu). Recent articles by Pelton in *The Futurist* include "The Rise of Telecities" (January-February 2004) and "The Fast-Growing Global Brain" (August-September 1999).

Chapter 3: Six Supertrends Shaping Our Future

22   For an excellent brief summary of significant trends, readers may refer to "50 Trends Shaping Our Future," a sixteen-page

report available from the World Future Society. The report was prepared by veteran futurists Marvin J. Cetron and Owen Davies and is updated periodically.

24   Maddison's *Monitoring the World Economy, 1820-1992* was published in Paris in 1995 by the Development Centre of the Organisation for Economic Co-operation and Development.

25   For more on longevity and Jeanne Calment, see "The Centenarians Are Coming" by Cynthia G. Wagner, *The Futurist*, May 1999.

26   The SARS virus almost brought Hong Kong to a halt and created major problems in Toronto and elsewhere. The disease also caused major disruptions in the travel and hospitality industries. See "U.S. Warns Against Asia Travel as Virus Spreads," *Wall Street Journal*, March 31, 2003.

28   Language death is discussed in "Disappearing Languages" by Rosemarie Ostler, *The Futurist*, August-September 1999, pp. 52-56.

28   For more on African cities, see Paul Theroux, *Dark Star Safari: Overland from Cairo to Capetown* (Boston: Houghton-Mifflin, 2003).

28   See Bibliography for more on Toffler's book *Future Shock*.

31   Richard Easterlin's observations on happiness appear in his book *Growth Triumphant: The Twenty-first Century in Historical Perspective* (Ann Arbor, Michigan: University of Michigan Press, 1996). Other researchers following up on his work have found that people's happiness may actually decrease when their living conditions improve if they perceive others doing better than they are. "Does Money Buy Happiness" by Jon E. Hilsenrath, *Wall Street Journal*, January 4, 2002.

32   Suein L. Hwang made her comments in "The TV Employee: Glamorous, Rich—But Totally Off Base," *Wall Street Journal*, October 13, 2002.

33   For the latest information on UN population projections, contact the United Nations Population Fund (www.unfpa.org).

Chapter 4: Understanding Change

37   The projections for male height and longevity are based on an article, "Older, Taller, Bigger," in the *Washington Post*, November 20, 1999, which cites as sources the Population Reference

Bureau and futurist Graham T.T. Molitor, one of the reviewers of this book.

38   Thomas T. Samaras presents the case for shorter human size in "Short Is Beautiful: So Why Are We Making Kids Grow Tall?" *The Futurist*, January-February 1995.

40   Consumers Union of Yonkers, New York, publishes *Consumer Reports*. For more information, go to www.consumerunion.org.

42   Tom Wolfe describes the reception to his novel in "Stalking the Billion-Footed Beast," *Harper's*, November 1989.

42   Ian H. Wilson's group at GE published its report, *Our Future Business Environment*, as an internal GE document in 1968.

44   Though many books and articles have been written about Kondratieff's theory, scholars still argue whether the long-term cycle really exists. In an article published in *The Futurist* in February 1985, Joseph Martino, a research scientist with the Technological Forecasting Group at the University of Dayton Research Institute, concluded: "The Kondratieff Wave may be real, but the evidence for it is weaker than the evidence against it."

46   For more on the stages of technological innovation, see the "Stages of Innovation" section in Joseph Martino's *Technological Forecasting for Decision Making* (see Bibliography), pp. 8-10.

47   Molitor is president of Public Policy Forecasting, a research firm in Potomac, Maryland, that has long specialized in monitoring the development of public issues.

48   Rube Goldberg (1983-1970), a San Francisco artist, became famous for his newspaper cartoons, each of which showed an extremely complicated way to solve a simple problem. For more information, go to www.rubegoldberg.com.

Chapter 5: Systems, Chance, and Chaos

49   For an informative recent history of systems thinking, see Debora Hammond's *The Science of Synthesis* (see Bibliography). Miller's *Living Systems* is described in the Bibliography.

52   Leonard Garment's article "Frank Wills and Deep Throat" (*Washington Post*, October 3, 2000) commented that "Wills's story is a sharp reminder that seemingly inevitable pieces of our political history are in fact the product of accident upon accident.... History is shaped by accidents; but individuals' lives are formed by whether they are able to make use of such accidents." Garment, who was White House counsel in the Nixon

administration, noted how—after making history—Frank Wills failed to make much of the rest of his own life.

52   John Muir's statement appears in *My First Summer in the Sierra*, cited in the *Quotationary* (New York: Random House, 1998).

53   The meeting in Munich and Hitler's decision are described in John Toland's two-volume biography *Adolf Hitler* (Garden City, New York: Doubleday & Co., 1976), pp. 93-94.

56   For more on the sperm-freezing accident see Roger Gosden's *Designing Babies: The Brave New World of Reproductive Technology.* (New York: W. H. Freeman, 1999). Glycerol was the first effective cryoprotectant. Later it was discovered that certain insects protect themselves from low temperature with this natural antifreeze.

57   The fate of the "young mother," Emilio Ortiz, and Jimmy Walsh in the terrorist attacks of September 11, 2001, were reported in "Sketches of the Missing: Hard-Working Early Risers," *Washington Post*, September 14, 2001.

57   The lucky escapes of Monica O'Leary, Greer Epstein, and Joe Andrew were reported in "She Got Laid Off, He Missed His Train; Such Were Lucky Breaks" by Robert Tomsho and others, *Wall Street Journal*, September 13, 2001.

58   James Gleick's 1987 book on chaos may still be the best introduction to the subject. (See Bibliography.)

58   Edward Lorenz presented his paper "Predictability: Does the Flap of a Butterfly's Wings in Brazil Set Off a Tornado in Texas?" to the American Association for the Advancement of Science meeting in Washington, D.C., on December 29, 1972.

60   For a detailed account of Pickett's charge, see *Gettysburg: Day Three* by Jeffry D. Wert (New York: Simon & Schuster, 2004).

60   Pickett's charge is simply one example of how chance shapes events. Professor Peter Bishop of the University of Houston at Clear Lake tells his students about the time during the American Revolution when George Washington's army was almost trapped on Long Island and only managed to escape because a thick fog came in overnight. Otherwise, the British would likely have destroyed the Continental Army and crushed the rebellion. "No Pickett's charge after that!" Professor Bishop adds.

63   Michelangelo described this fantasy in a sonnet. As a true "Renaissance man," he was a poet of considerable merit as well as a painter, sculptor, and architect.

Chapter 6: Futuring Methods

66 Regarding the Cuban missile crisis, a *New York Times* review of *The Kennedy Tapes: Inside the White House During the Cuban Missile Crisis* stated, "It is not hyperbolic to say, as many have, the Cuban missile crisis was the single most dangerous episode in the history of mankind." ("Profile in Caution," Book Review section, October 19, 1997.)

67 Helmer and Dalkey published *An Experimental Application of the Delphi Method to the Use of Experts* in 1953 as an internal RAND document. It was classified "secret" at the time. In 1964 Helmer and Theodore J. Gordon published *Report on a Long-Range Forecasting Study*, also an internal RAND document, that gained wide attention. In 1965 the Delphi procedure was applied to corporate planning at the Thompson-Ramo-Wooldridge Corporation (TRW). For more on Helmer and his Delphi work, see Chapter 14, section dealing with "The RAND Corporation's Influence."

67 The Fort Bragg war games were described in "A Mistaken Shooting Puts Army War Games Under Tough Spotlight" by Chip Cummins, *Wall Street Journal*, February 26, 2002.

67 The games at Fort Polk were reported in "Trial by Fire" by Richard Leiby, *Washington Post*, December 26, 2001.

68 Col. Gardiner described his war gaming in an article "It Doesn't Start in Kashmir, and It Never Ends Well," *Washington Post*, January 20, 2002. Gardiner, now retired from the U.S. Air Force, is a visiting professor at the Air War College and National Defense University.

69 A useful book on business modeling is Michael Schrage's *Serious Play* (see Bibliography).

70 Patrick Brown's fantasies were discussed in "Imagine a Glass Chip..." by Rachel K. Sobel, *U.S. News and World Report*, June 24, 2002.

70 Forrester explained his global modeling methods in his book *World Dynamics* (Cambridge, Massachusetts: Wright-Allen Press, 1971).

71 The National Weather Service prediction was reported in "This Time They Saw It Coming," *Washington Post*, February 19, 2003.

72 An eight-page biography of Jungk appears in Cornish, *The Study of the Future*, pp. 147-153 (see Bibliography).

73   Jungk and N. Müllert describe the workshops in *Future Work-shops* (see Bibliography). See also discussion of "Future Work-shops" in Wendell Bell, *Foundations of Futures Studies*, Vol. 1, pp. 300-305 (see Bibliography).

73   For more on Lindaman, see *Thinking in the Future Tense* by Edward B. Lindaman (Nashville, Tennessee: Broadman, 1978).

74   Lawrence L. Lippitt (Ronald Lippitt's son) describes Preferred Futuring in *Preferred Futuring: Envision the Future You Want and Unleash the Energy to Get There* (San Francisco: Berrett-Koehler, 1998). A closely related technique called "future search" is ex-plained in *Future Search: An Action Guide to Finding Common Ground in Organizations and Communities* by Marvin R. Weis-bord and Sandra Janoff (San Francisco: Berrett-Koehler, 1995).

74   Bezold is quoted from an article, "Visioning Flourishes in Communities and Organizations," *Alternative Futures,* newslet-ter of the Institute for Alternative Futures in Arlington, Vir-ginia, Winter 1994, p. 1.

75   Senge is quoted from his book *The Fifth Discipline*, p. 206 (see Bibliography). Bezold says Chapter 11 of this book is "possibly the best statement yet written on the usefulness of vision for or-ganizations."

75   The Center for the Study of American Business (now the Wei-denbaum Center, wc.wustl.edu) published the results of its study in *Insights from Business Strategy and Management 'Big Ideas' of the Past Three Decades: Are They Fads or Enablers?* by Richard J. Mahoney and Joseph A. McCue (CEO Series Issue No. 29, January 1999). The study reviewed fifty "big ideas," in-cluding strategic planning, reinventing the company, quality circles, benchmarking, re-engineering, and just-in-time.

75   The Nanus quote appears in his book, *Visionary Leadership*, p. 3 (see Biography).

76   Chris Malone's mock conventions were described in "Professor Imbues Students with Political Passion" by Valerie Strauss, *Washington Post*, January 20, 2004. Malone was quoted as say-ing, "When you teach politics, I don't see how you can teach it through a textbook."

Chapter 7: Knowing the World Around Us

80   The Lincoln quote is from a speech given on June 16, 1858, at the Republican state convention in Springfield, Illinois, when he

accepted the Republican nomination for the Senate. (He lost the election to Stephen Douglas.)

82 Brown and Weiner's book *Supermanaging* was published by McGraw-Hill, New York, 1985.

82 "Environmental Scanning: Its Use in Forecasting Emerging Trends and Issues in Organizations" by William P. Neufeld in *Futures Research Quarterly*, Fall 1985.

82 The quote from Edie Weiner is from "Future Scanning for Trade Groups and Companies," *Harvard Business Review*, September-October 1976, p. 14.

87 Martino discussed the influence of breakthroughs on aircraft speed in "Survey of Forecasting Methods," *World Future Society Bulletin*, Vol. 10, No. 6 November-December 1976, pp. 5-6.

Chapter 8: Using Scenarios

94 Kahn's decision to use the term *scenario* is discussed by Gill Ringland in her book *Scenario Planning*, p. 12 (see Bibliography). She says Kahn liked the emphasis the term gave not so much on forecasting but on creating a story or myth.

95 The article by Frank Bartholomew of United Press appeared in the *New York Times*, April 19, 1958, p. 4, headlined, "Soviets Say SAC Flights Over Arctic Peril Peace, U.S. Denies Provocation." A companion article was headlined, "SAC Maintains 15 Minute Alert. Margin Reduced as Result of Soviet Firing ICBM." See also discussion in Theodore J. Gordon, *The Future*, Macmillan Company of Canada, Toronto, 1965.

95 *On Thermonuclear War* was published by Princeton University Press, Princeton, New Jersey. The outraged reviewer was James R. Newman in the *Scientific American*, March 1961.

95 *Thinking about the Unthinkable* was published by Frederick A. Praeger, New York, 1962.

102 For more on the use of scenarios in business planning, see "The Strategic Armament Response to the Challenge of Global Change" by James L. Morrison and Ian Wilson in *Future Vision: Ideas, Insights, and Strategies*, edited by Howard F. Didsbury Jr., a volume prepared for the 1996 conference of the World Future Society (Bethesda, Maryland: World Future Society, 1996).

Chapter 9: The Wild Cards in Our Future

109 The story of Paul's conversion experience (paraphrased) is told in Acts: Chapter 1, Verses 1-9, *The Living Bible* (Wheaton, Illinois: Tyndale House Publishers, 1981).

109 The earthquake in New York City was reported in "In the Midst of Other Woe, A Small Quake in New York" by N. R. Kleinfeld, *New York Times*, October 28, 2001. The epicenter was on Manhattan's east side just north of the Queensboro Bridge.

109 The Indian earthquake occurred in Gujarat on January 26, 2001.

110 Rockfellow discussed his experience in "Wild Cards: Preparing for the Big One," *The Futurist*, January-February 1994.

110 The report by Rockfellow and his colleagues, titled "Wild Cards: A Multinational Perspective," was issued in 1992. It was prepared jointly by the BIPE Conseil (France), Institute for Futures Studies (Denmark) and the Institute for the Future (Menlo park, California, United States), with multiple contributors but no author listed. For more information on Copenhagen Institute for Futures Studies, go to www.cifs.dk.

110 For more of John L. Petersen's ideas about wild cards, see his book *Out of the Blue* (see Bibliography) and his article "The 'Wild Cards' in Our Future: Preparing for the Improbable," *The Futurist*, July-August 1997.

114 Brian Jenkins's article, "The Future Course of International Terrorism," appeared in *The Futurist*, July-August 1987.

114 Marvin Cetron's article "The Future Face of Terrorism," appeared in *The Futurist*, November-December 1994.

114 Also foreshadowing the 2001 attacks was the article "Superterrorism: Searching for Long-Term Solutions" by Glenn E. Schweitzer and Carole C. Dorsch, *The Futurist*, June-July 1999. This article noted that the nature of terrorism was changing: "While low-cost kidnappings and bombings have been the order of the day for decades, high-tech attacks on large numbers of people or on a nation's infrastructure are increasingly likely. The United States is slowly but steadily becoming a target at home."

Chapter 10: Inventing the Future

122 Asimov's memoir about getting an idea for his editor, John Campbell, appeared in *Luna Monthly*, August 1971.

122 A five-page biography of Asimov, checked by Asimov himself, was included in Cornish, *The Study of the Future*, pp. 167-171 (see Bibliography).

123 For more on Michalko's strategies, see "Eight Strategies for Thinking Like a Genius" by Michael Michalko, *The Futurist*, May 1992, pp. 21-25. Another article by Michalko, "From Bright Ideas to Right Ideas: Capturing the Creative Spark," appeared in *The Futurist*, September-October 2003.

124 The author is grateful to Harlan Cleveland for the anecdote about Isaac Stern.

125 The research on sleep by Wagner and his colleagues was reported in *Nature*, January 22, 2004. Wagner is at the University of Lubeck.

125 Mendeleyev's discovery of the periodic table is discussed in the final chapter of Paul Strathern's book *Mendeleyev's Dream: The Quest for the Elements* (London: Penguin Books, 2000).

126 Asimov's comment on other writers not really liking to write was made during a supper conversation with the author in New York in about 1974.

126 Csikszentmihalyi's comments on creativity appear in his book *Creativity: Flow and the Psychology of Discovery and Invention* (New York: HarperCollins, 1996), p. 107.

127 Higgins's book is described in the Bibliography.

128 See Schrage's *Serious Play* (see Bibliography).

129 See Darwin, "This is the Question," pp. 84-85, in *Wing to Wing, Oar to Oar: Readings on Courting and Marrying*, edited by Amy A. Kass and Leon R. Kass (Notre Dame, Indiana: University of Notre Dame Press, 2000).

129 For more on Seaborg as a diarist, see *The Plutonium Story: The Journals of Professor Glenn T. Seaborg, 1939-1946*, edited and annotated by Ronald L. Kathren, Jerry B. Gough, and Gary T. Benefiel (Columbus, Ohio: Battelle Memorial Institute, 1994).

Chapter 11: The Past as a Guide to the Future

134 Historian-futurist W. Warren Wagar says, "E.H. Carr said it well, 'Good historians, I suspect, whether they think about it or not, have the future in their bones. Besides the question: Why? the historian also asks the question: Whither?' *What Is History?* E.H. Carr (New York: Knopf, 1964). Wagar used this citation in an essay, "Past and Future," *American Behavioral Scientist*, Vol.

42, no. 3 (November-December 1998), pp. 365-371, but he added this comment: "Historians, even nonbelievers in progress, should have the future in their bones. They do not, by and large. But they should."

135   Regarding the Internet stock debacle: *Value Line Investment Survey* reported in its June 1, 2000, report, "The majority of the stocks of the Internet industry lost more than 75 percent of their market value over the past year." (From "The Year in Review: 2000" by Terence O'Hara, *Washington Post*, December 3, 2000.)

135   For a first-person account of losing one's savings in the crash of technology stocks in the year 2000, see David Denby's book, *American Sucker* (Boston: Little, Brown, 2004).

135   For more on the mania of investors in technology (Internet) stocks, see "Bursting of the Technology Bubble Has a Familiar 'Pop' to It" by Stephen E. Frank and E.S. Browning, *Wall Street Journal*, March 2, 2001.

135   The short-sellers' reluctance to enter the Internet fray was discussed in "Short Sellers' Long Ordeal" by Kathleen Day, *Wall Street Journal*, December 14, 2001.

135   MacKay was editor of the *Illustrated London News* during the 1840s. His book has been reprinted numerous times because of its ever-timely warnings to novice investors.

135   The quote from Newton appears in Kindleberger's book *Manias, Panics, and Crashes*. (See Bibliography.)

136   See the Bibliography for more on Kindleberger's book.

137   For more on Durant, see Frank and Browning article cited for page 135.

139   The Thucydides quote is from the *Encyclopaedia Britannica*, 14th Edition, Vol. 22, p. 165, subject heading *Thucydides*. Thucydides has also been quoted as saying, "the accurate knowledge of what has happened will be useful because according to human probability similar things will happen again." From *History, Civilization and Culture* by F.R. Cowell (London: Thames and Hudson, 1952), p. 2, cited by Bruce G. Brander in *Staring into Chaos: Explorations in the Decline of Western Civilization* (Dallas: Spence Publishing, 1998), p. 308.

140   Machiavelli described his imagined encounters with historical figures in a letter to his friend Vettori. A section of the letter is quoted in Christian Gauss's introduction to *The Prince* (New York: New American Library/Mentor Classic, 1952).

142   For a discussion of Greenspan's role, see chapter on "The Great Crash (of 1792)" in *The Business of America* by John Steele Gordon (New York: Walker & Co., 2001). Also see Kindleberger's *Manias, Crashes, and Panics*, p. 241 (see Bibliography).

143   See Bibliography for details on the books by Toffler, Naisbitt, Cetron, and Molitor.

Chapter 12: Predicting the Future

148   Numerous collections of faulty forecasts have been compiled through the years. One example is Laura Lee's *Bad Predictions* (see Bibliography). See also her article, "Forecasts That Missed by a Mile," *The Futurist*, September-October 2000.

Other sources for the faulty forecasts listed here include:

"Erroneous Predictions and Negative Comments Concerning Exploration, Territorial Expansion, Scientific and Technological Development" compiled by Nancy T. Gamarra for the Senate Committee on Aeronautical and Space Sciences. Legislative Reference Service, The Library of Congress, May 29, 1969.

Also see "Blunders of Negative Forecasting" by Joseph Martino and "Faulty Forecasting through History," both in *The Futurist*, December 1968, pp. 120-121.

Profiles of the Future, rev. edited by Arthur C. Clarke (New York: Harper & Row, 1973).

152   Dale Steffes's pariah experience was reported in "Energy Forecaster Finds Being Right Isn't Like Being Rich" by George Getschew, *Wall Street Journal*, May 3, 1985.

157   The Olsen quote is from Laura Lee, op. cit., p. 107.

161   The 1893 forecasts are included in a book compiled by Dave Walter of the Montana Historical Society. The book is titled *Today Then: America's Best Minds Look 100 Years into the Future on the Occasion of the 1893 World's Colombian Exposition* (Helena, Montana: American and World Geographic Publishing, 1993). This book was reviewed by Edward Cornish in "1993 as Predicted in 1893: If They Could See Us Now!" *The Futurist*, May-June 1993.

163   For more on the 1967 forecasts in *The Futurist*, see "The Futurist Forecasts 30 Years Later" by Edward Cornish, *The Futurist*, January-February 1997.

Chapter 13: How the Future Became What It Used to Be

169   Plato's critical inquiry method has gotten new recognition in recent years because of its usefulness in reaching reasoned deci-

sions about many practical issues in public policy making, marital disputes, and other settings. Courses in critical inquiry or argumentation are taught at Northwestern University and elsewhere. The Teaching Company (teach12.com) sells a course on argumentation taught by Professor Leo Zarefsky of Northwestern.

169 I.F. Clarke's comment on Plato is from "The Utility of Utopia," *Futures*, Vol. 3, No. 4 (December 1971), p. 396.

170 See I.F. Clarke's article, "More's Utopia: The Myth and the Method," *Futures*, Vol. 4, No. 2 (June 1972), pp. 173-178.

170 Professor W. Warren Wagar's comments were made in a personal communication to the author.

170 For the quote from Sir Francis Bacon and comments on Bacon's thinking, see I.F. Clarke's article, "Bacon's New Atlantis: Blueprint for Progress," *Futures*, Vol. 4, No. 3 (September 1972), pp. 273-279.

170 Bacon is quoted from his *Novum Organum* (1620), p. 129. This quote appears in J.B. Bury's *The Idea of Progress* (see Bibliography).

171 The battle between the Ancients and the Moderns is described in J.B. Bury's *The Idea of Progress*, pp. 78-97 (see Bibliography).

171 The Socrates comment from Fontenelle's *Dialogues of the Dead* is cited in Bury's *The Idea of Progress*, op. cit., p. 100.

172 Turgot is quoted by I.F. Clarke in his article, "1750-1850: The Discovery of the Future," *Futures*, Vol 5, No. 5 (October 1973), pp. 494-495.

172 See Bibliography for more on Denis Diderot's *Encyclopedia*.

173 Benjamin Franklin is quoted by Roger Adams in an article, "Man's Synthetic Future," in the *Annual Report of the Smithsonian Institution*, 1952, p. 230.

173 For more on Condorcet, see description of his *Sketch* in the Bibliography and discussion of his work in I.F. Clarke's *The Pattern of Expectation*, also in the Bibliography.

174 Gilfillan made his comments about Condorcet in "A Sociologist Looks at Technical Prediction" in *Technological Forecasting for Industry and Government* edited by James R. Bright (Englewood Cliffs, New Jersey: Prentice Hall, 1965), p. 15.

174   References to eighteenth-century living conditions are from I.F. Clarke's article "1750-1850: The Shape of the Future," *Futures*, Vol. 5, No. 6 (December 1973), pp. 580-583.

175   The progress of the railroad is discussed in J.B. Bury's *The Idea of Progress*, pp. 326-329 (see Bibliography).

175   Tennyson's poem *Locksley Hall* was first published in 1842 in a two-volume edition of his poetry entitled *Poems.*

175   Andersen's description of future tourists seeing Europe in eight days is from I.F. Clarke's "The Calculus of Probabilities, 1870-1914," *Futures*, Vol. 7, No. 3 (June 1975), p. 239.

176   The discussion of Jules Verne is based largely on "Jules Verne: The Prophet of the Space Age" by William T. Gay in *The Futurist*, Vol. 5, No. 2 (April 1971), pp. 76-78.

177   For more on Bellamy's *Looking Backward*, see the Bibliography.

177   References to Plessner's book *A Look at the Great Discoveries of the 20th Century: The Future of Electrical Television* (1892) are from S.C. Gilfillan's paper "A Sociologist Looks at Technical Predictions" in *Technological Forecasting for Industry and Government*, op. cit., p. 17.

177   The forecasts by Richet are from I.F. Clarke's article "The Calculus of Probabilities, 1870-1914," op. cit., p. 243-244.

178   The Wagar quote is from the dust jacket to his book *Good Tidings: The Belief in Progress from Darwin to Marcuse* (Bloomington, Indiana: Indiana University Press, 1972).

178   John Elfreth Watkins's *Ladies' Home Journal* article, "What May Happen in the Next Hundred Years," was reprinted in *The Futurist*, October 1982, accompanied by a commentary, "John Elfreth Watkins: Forgotten Genius of Forecasting," by Harold G. Shane and Gary A. Sojka, both of whom were then professors at Indiana University.

179   Wells's 1902 address, "The Discovery of the Future," was published in *Nature*, Vol. 65, No. 1684 (February 6, 1902), p. 327.

181   Wells's *The Outline of History* was first published by Doubleday, Garden City, New York, in 1920 and went through many subsequent printings.

182   H. Bruce Franklin described the novel *We* in "Fictions of the Future," *The Futurist*, Vol. 4, No. 1 (February 1970), p. 27.

182   See Bibliography for notes on books by Huxley and Orwell.

182 Kurt Vonnegut's *Player Piano* was published by Avon Books, New York, 1970. Anthony Burgess's *A Clockwork Orange* was published by Random House (Modern Library) in New York in 1962.

182 Oswald Spengler's *The Decline of the West* was published in New York in two volumes, 1926-1928.

184 Professor Low's idea for a "Minister of the Future" appeared in his article "Why Not a Minister for the Future?" *Tomorrow*, Vol. 2, No. 1 (Spring 1938), p. 2.

184 Szilard's role is related by Daniel Bell in *The Coming of The Post-Industrial Society* (see Bibliography), p. 388.

185 See Polak's book *The Image of the Future* (see Bibliography).

Chapter 14: The Futurist Revolution

187 Sartre's comments on the wartime mood of the French are from his article in *Les Lettres Françaises*, September 9, 1944.

187 Sartre's statement about individual freedom is from a 1946 lecture entitled *L'existentialisme est un humanisme* (translated into English as *Existentialism is a Humanism).*

189 See Bibliography for Gabor's book *Inventing the Future.*

189 For more on Berger and his Prospective movement, see *Shaping the Future*, edited by André Cournand and Maurice Levy (New York: Gordon and Breach Inc., 1973).

190 Berger's views of Prospective are from *Prospective*, No. 1 (May 1958), pp. 1-10, reprinted in Section VI of *Shaping the Future*, op. cit., pp. 245-249.

191 For more on de Jouvenel, see biography on pages 132-140 of Cornish, *The Study of the Future* (see Bibliography).

192 De Jouvenel's comments on the Versailles conference and the League of Nations are from his article, "The Planning of the Future," in *The Great Ideas Today*, Encyclopaedia Britannica Inc., 1974.

193 Daniel Bell's essay "Twelve Modes of Prediction" appeared in *Daedalus* (Summer 1964), p. 869.

193 See de Jouvenel's *The Art of Conjecture* in the Bibliography.

194 For more on von Karman's influence on technological forecasting, see Joseph Martino's article "Technological Forecasting in

the U.S. Air Force," *The Futurist*, Vol. 5, No. 6 (December 1971), p. 251.

195 For more on the creation of RAND, see Paul Dickson's *Think Tanks* (New York: Atheneum, 1971), pp. 22-25.

196 For more on Helmer and the Delphi technique, see Chapter 6, section on "Consulting Experts," pages 64-65. Also see Helmer's book *Social Technology* (New York: Basic Books, 1966). Especially noteworthy is the chapter "On the Epistemology of the Inexact Sciences," a paper he wrote with Nicholas Rescher. (Rescher's book, *Predicting the Future*, is in the Bibliography.)

196 See T.J. Gordon and Olaf Helmer, *Report on a Long-Range Forecasting Study*. Paper P2902. The RAND Corporation, Santa Monica, California, September 1964.

200 "I was appalled...." Daniel Bell's comments on accepting the chairmanship of the Commission on the Year 2000 appear in his book *Toward the Year 2000* (Boston: Houghton-Mifflin, 1968).

201 *Toward Balanced Growth* was published by the Government Printing Office, Washington, D.C., 1970.

Chapter 15: Improving Our Futures

203 Noelle Nelson discussed Jim, the truck driver, in "Ideas About the Future," *The Futurist*, January-February 2000, pp. 47-51.

204 Lionel Sosa lists fatalism as one of the values and attitudes that present obstacles to the upward mobility of Latinos in achieving success in American life. He comments: "Individual initiative, achievement, self reliance, ambition, aggressiveness—all these are useless in the face of an attitude that says, 'We must not challenge the will of God.'...." from Sosa's book, *The Americano Dream: How Latinos Can Achieve Success in Business and in Life* (New York: Penguin, 1998). Sosa's work is cited in *Culture Matters: How Values Shape Human Progress* edited by Lawrence E. Harrison and Samuel P. Huntington (New York: Basic Books, 2000), p. 306.

209 The Berkeley Seismological Laboratory (www.seismo.berkley.edu/seismo/) coordinates a network of earthquake monitoring projects including the University of California at Berkeley, Caltech, and the U.S. Geological Survey.

210 The *Washington Post* reported on March 14, 2003, that Reeve had undergone experimental surgery that doctors believe will enable him to breathe regularly without a respirator for the first time since he broke his neck in a horseback accident in 1995.

With the respirator turned off, Reeve was able to talk and to detect odors. "I actually woke up and smelled the coffee," he said. Now the task is to strengthen the muscles of Reeve's diaphragm.

210 The contrast between the Bulger brothers was described in "Brothers and Law" by Wil Haygood in the *Washington Post*, February 3, 2003. William Bulger was longest-serving president of the Massachusetts Senate before becoming president of the University of Massachusetts. His brother, James, was still being sought by the FBI as this book went to press.

211 For more on Rosa Lee, see Leon Dash's book *Rosa Lee* (see Bibliography).

211 The discussion of the urgency of the future reflects a useful insight offered by Wendell Bell in commenting on an earlier draft of this chapter. The author had written that foresight was more important for us today than in the past, but Professor Bell pointed out that foresight has always been critically important in human life. What is different today is that it is harder to obtain the needed foresight. As he explains, when changes are slow, foresight based on yesterday and the day before remains reliable and valid. "Indeed, if tomorrow is just like today and yesterday and if I have a workable, effective understanding of today and yesterday, then I am prepared for tomorrow. Foresight may be no more important to me in periods of rapid change, but it is more difficult to get such foresight because my simple tool of treating tomorrow as I did today is less reliable and valid." I have accepted with gratitude Professor Bell's point and revised the present text accordingly.

214 The Eisenhower quote is from Burt Nanus's article, "Leading the Vision Team," *The Futurist*, May-June 1996.

Chapter 16: Future Generations

217 Margaret Mead is quoted from her article, "Ways to Deal with the Current Social Transformation" in *The Futurist*, June 1974, pp. 122-123.

217 Oren Lyons's words appeared in his article, "The Seventh Generation Yet Unborn," *The Futurist*, March-April 1988. Lyons, an Onondaga Faithkeeper, is a professor at the State University of New York at Buffalo. His essay was originally published in the Native American publication *Daybreak*.

218 Mellert's comment is from his article "Do We Owe Anything to Future Generations?" in *The Futurist*, December 1982.

218 For more information about UNESCO (United Nations Educational, Scientific, and Cultural Organization) in Paris, go to www.unesco.org.

219 Tough described his pledge to future generations in "Making a Pledge to Future Generations," *The Futurist,* May-June 1993. Two years later he speculated on what message future generations might want to send to us in his article, "A Message from Future Generations," *The Futurist,* March-April 1995. See also "Six Priorities from Future Generations" by Allen Tough in *Future Vision: Ideas, Insights, and Strategies,* edited by Howard F. Didsbury Jr. (Bethesda, Maryland: World Future Society, 1996).

220 Churchman is quoted from *Futures Research: New Directions,* edited by Harold A. Linstone and W.H. Clive Simmonds (Reading, Massachusetts: Addison-Wesley Publishing Co., 1977), p. 87.

221 Wendell Bell expressed his views in "Why Should We Care About Future Generations?" in *The Years Ahead: Perils, Problems, and Promises,* edited by Howard F. Didsbury Jr. (Bethesda, Maryland: World Future Society, 1993), pp. 25-39.

225 For more about the world problems encyclopedia, contact the Union of International Associations, www.uia.org.

Bibliography

Only a few of the many books dealing with the future can be listed here. Selection criteria include recency of publication, trustworthiness of the author, readability, and usefulness to nonspecialists. Certain classic works have also been included, as well as a few other books not fully meeting the selection criteria but still likely to be of interest to readers. Information on the most recent books is available on the World Future Society's Web site (wfs.org), which also provides information through *Future Survey*, a monthly newsletter describing and commenting on the latest books and articles dealing with the future and major public-policy issues. *Future Survey* is the best available guide to current literature dealing with the future and is available by subscription.

Anderson, Walter Truett. *All Connected Now: Life in the First Global Civilization*. Boulder, Colorado: Westview Press, 2001.

The author argues that globalization is nothing new. "It is as old as the first migrations out of Africa." He sees it as both desirable and inevitable, a final product of human evolution.

Anderson, Walter Truett. *The Future of the Self: Inventing a Post-Modern Person*. New York: Penguin Putnam, 1997.

This is an example of the numerous thoughtful books in which Anderson probes the social and psychological issues of modern life. *The Future of the Self* deals with how people are changing in the most intimate part of themselves—the self. Other noteworthy books by Anderson include *To Govern Evolution* and *Reality Isn't What It Used to Be*.

Ashley, William C., and James L. Morrison. *Anticipatory Management: 10 Power Tools for Achieving Excellence into the 21st Century*. Vienna, Virginia: Issue Action Publications, 1995.

Designed mainly for business executives, this book discusses ten "power tools," including Surfacing and Challenging Assumptions, Strategic Trend Intelligence System, Issue Life Cycle, Issues Vulnerability Audit, Issue Briefs, Delphi Rating Method, Ten-Step Issue Management Process, Issue Accountability Model, Issue Analysis Worksheet, and Scenario Technique.

Austin, William J. *Strategic Planning for Smart Leadership: Rethinking Your Organization's Collective Future through a Workbook-based, Three-level Model*. Stillwater, Oklahoma: New Forums Press, 2002.

Practical guidance for organizational planning.

Barker, Joel Arthur. *Paradigms: The Business of Discovering the Future.* Reprint edition. New York: Harper Business, 1993.

A business consultant applies Thomas Kuhn's paradigm-shift theory to business innovation.

Barry, Bryan W. *Strategic Planning Workbook for Nonprofit Organizations.* Revised and updated. St. Paul, Minnesota: Amherst H. Wilder Foundation, 1997.

Step-by-step guidance for developing a realistic plan for an organization's future. This handbook includes reproducible worksheets designed to help you develop the plan, involve others in the process, and measure results. Topics covered include the critical ingredients of a sound plan, strategies to address problems and opportunities, a detailed sample of one organization's strategic plan, and information on how various organizations can use strategic planning.

Becker, Ted, and Christa Daryl Slaton. *The Future of Teledemocracy.* Westport, Connecticut: Praeger, 2000.

A detailed discussion of actual experience with "televoting" systems, prospects for the future, and the implications for society.

Bell, Daniel. *The Coming of Post-Industrial Society: A Venture in Social Forecasting.* New York: Basic Books, 1973.

Sociologist Bell argues that people can make meaningful forecasts about the future of modern society if they take the trouble to understand fully the present conditions of that society and the trends visibly at work in it. Scholarly and well-documented, this book offers a thoughtful analysis of a number of major trends that Bell sees at work. This book popularized the term "post-industrial society"—a term Bell used to differentiate the new society from the industrial society without attempting to give it a more specific label until more is known about it. Other scholars, Bell suggests, may be jumping the gun by labeling the new society a "communications society," an "information society," or whatever.

Bell, Daniel, ed. *Toward the Year 2000: Work in Progress.* Boston: Houghton Mifflin, 1968. Reprint, with a new preface, Cambridge: MIT Press, 1997.

This is the first report of the Commission on the Year 2000, formed in 1965 by the American Academy of Arts and Sciences and chaired by sociologist Daniel Bell. The volume summarizes the dialogue that occurred at the working sessions of the Commission in October 1965 and in February 1966. The book also includes a number of papers ranging from Leonard J. Duhl's ideas on planning to David Riesman's *Thinking on Meritocracy*. This book is a highly compact compendium of stimulating ideas, though it is now mainly of historical interest.

Bell, Wendell. *Foundations of Futures Studies: Human Science for a New Era.* Volume 1: *History, Purposes, and Knowledge.* Volume 2: *Values, Objectivity, and the Good Society.* New Brunswick, New Jersey: Transaction Publishers, 1997.

This comprehensive scholarly overview of the most important aspects of futures studies—history, methods, theories, and principal practitioners—brings together the intellectual tools for thinking seriously about the future. Volume 1 deals with the history and purposes of futures studies, basic assumptions and epistemology, methods and exemplars. Volume 2 covers values, practical strategies for judging preferable futures, and the good society. The author, a Yale sociology professor and noted scholar, is evenhanded in his judgments and keen in his insights. This well-referenced volume is strongly recommended as an authoritative guide and belongs in every serious futurist's library. However, casual readers may be intimidated by the academic social scientific approach.

Bellamy, Edward. *Looking Backward, 2000-1887,* 1888.

One of the most popular utopian books ever written, this description of Boston in the year 2000 became an international best seller following its publication in 1888 and led to the establishment of Bellamy groups in many countries around the world. Bellamy, an American journalist, foresaw electric lights, equal rights for women, radio and television, and aircraft. His success as a forecaster, like that of the Marquis de Condorcet, derives largely from his belief in continued progress in technology, growing affluence, and greater individual freedom. Today's readers may not find his book very exciting, in part because of its quaint style and also because many of the innovations he anticipated have become commonplace.

Berry, Adrian. *The Next 500 Years: Life in the Coming Millennium.* New York: W. H. Freeman, 1996.

A British science writer and fellow of Britain's Royal Astronomical Society offers an optimistic and imaginative view of the possibilities of the future, emphasizing technology and outer space.

Bezold, Clement, Jerome A. Halperin, Jacqueline L. Eng, eds. *2020 Visions: Health Care Information Standards and Technologies.* Based on 1992 conference sponsored by the U.S. Pharmacopeial Convention Inc. Rockville, Maryland: USPC, 1993.

This book provides a clear, readable description of the use of futuring as a means of guiding executives and professionals in the pharmaceutical and health-care industries. Bezold is president of the Institute for Alternative Futures in Arlington, Virginia.

Boulding, Kenneth E. *The Meaning of the Twentieth Century: The Great Transition.* New York: Harper and Row, 1964.

This classic work by the late economist and social thinker argues that mankind is in a transition from civilized to "post-civilized" society and needs to avoid four "traps": (1) the war trap ("A major nuclear war would unquestionably set back the transition to a post-civilized world by many generations"); (2) the population trap (attempts to help people through medical services, says Boulding, could lead to disastrous overpopulation); (3) the technological trap ("Technology at the present time, even the highest technology, is largely dependent for its sources of energy and materials on accumulations in the earth which date from its geological past. In a few centuries, or at most a few thousand years, these are likely to be exhausted"); and (4) the entropy trap (borrowing a term from thermodynamics, Boulding suggests that the human potential may gradually diminish). To avoid these traps, Boulding believes that man should use all his intellectual resources to create an image of the future and a set of long-range goals that would reflect the infinite possibilities of the future.

Boulding, Kenneth E., and Elise Boulding. *The Future: Images and Processes.* Thousand Oaks, California: Sage Publications, 1995.

A collection of essays by two scholars who devoted many years to thinking about the future. Topics include images of the future, "future-creating" workshops, and women's and peace issues.

Boyer, William H. *Myth America: Democracy vs. Capitalism.* New York: The Apex Press, 2003.

> The author, a professor emeritus in philosophy at the University of Hawaii, discusses the conflict between corporate power in America and the needs of a democratic society to achieve a just and sustainable future. An activist and community organizer, the author created a movement to provide legal rights for future generations.

Branch, Melville C. *Comprehensive Planning for the 21st Century: General Theory and Principles.* Westport, Connecticut: Praeger, 1998.

> A practicing planner and retired professor of planning explains the basic principles of planning that all complex organizations must consider to embrace and shape change. This is not an entertainment but a reliable textbook offering a useful introduction to planning.

Branch, Melville C. *Simulation, Planning, and Society.* Westport, Connecticut: Praeger, 1997.

> A leading scholar of urban and regional planning demonstrates how simulations are used throughout society as representations for what is being planned. Increasingly vital for decision making, simulations assist us in planning successfully in such wide-ranging concerns as medicine, the military, engineering, law, religion, business, government, and science and technology.

Brand, Stewart. *The Clock of the Long Now: Time and Responsibility.* New York: Basic Books, 1999.

> Innovator-futurist Stewart Brand discusses plans to build a 10,000-year clock—a slow computer that will keep perfect time during the "long now." This future-oriented project serves as the starting point for his insightful reflections on the future.

Braun, Ernest. *Technology in Context: Technology Assessment for Managers.* New York: Routledge, 1998.

> This comprehensive and accessible volume describes the role of technology assessment in the strategic management of business firms.

Brockman, John, ed. *The Next Fifty Years: Science in the First Half of the Twenty-First Century.* New York: Vintage Books (Random House), 2002.

Twenty-five visionary scientists foresee breakthroughs that will change the way we think, live, and learn. Contributors include astronomer Martin Rees, psychologist Mihaly Csikszentmihalyi, computer scientist Jaron Lanier, physicist Paul Davies, and biologist Richard Dawkins.

Broderick, Damien. *The Spike: How Our Lives Are Being Transformed by Rapidly Advancing Technologies.* New York: Forge, 2001.

Broderick, an Australian science writer, predicts that, by 2030-2050, developments in computers, genetics, and nanotechnology will produce a period of high-speed change on a scale that humans have never experienced. He expresses doubts, however, about an end-of-the-world "singularity." The author is a noted critic and scholar with an interdisciplinary doctorate in literature and science.

Brown, Lester R. *Plan B: Rescuing a Planet Under Stress and a Civilization in Trouble.* New York: W.W. Norton, 2003.

Using the earth's natural assets with little regard for the economic and environmental consequences is not going to work much longer. Soon the environment will burst, resulting in massive food shortages, rising global temperatures, and worldwide water deficits. Brown's rescue plan (Plan B) envisions deflating the bubble economy by rethinking taxes and subsidies, creating a market that accurately reflects the worth of natural commodities, and taking action at wartime speed to stave off accelerating degradation. Brown's many books—of which this is only a recent example—have consistently been perceptive and readable as well as solidly grounded in his long experience with global environmental and economic issues.

Bryson, John M., and Robert C. Einsweiler, eds. *Strategic Planning: Threats and Opportunities for Planners.* Chicago: American Planning Association Planners Press, 1988.

This is a book for people seriously interested in planning. It offers a critical examination of strategic planning approaches for public agencies and nonprofit organizations, and outlines concepts, procedures, and tools that can help planners, managers, administrators and policy makers cope with an increasingly complicated and interconnected world.

Bury, J.B. *The Idea of Progress.* New York: Macmillan, 1932.

In this celebrated book, a British historian describes the development of the notion of progress from its origins in Cartesianism to its efflorescence in the late nineteenth and early twentieth centuries. Belief in progress led writers such as the Marquis de Condorcet to try to anticipate what the improved future world would be like and thus opened the way for serious thinking about the future.

Capezio, Peter. *Powerful Planning Skills: Envisioning the Future and Making It Happen.* Franklin Lakes, New Jersey: Career Press, 2000.

This book offers excellent guidance on improving the specific steps in planning: developing a vision, defining project goals, brainstorming ideas, forecasting, contingency planning, reviewing progress, managing change, etc.

Cartmill, Robert H. *The Next Hundred Years...Then and Now.* Philadelphia: Xlibris Corporation (www.xlibris.com), 2002.

The first half of this book presents a review of the world of 1900 together with a critique of forecasts made at that time for the long-term future. The book's second half reviews a variety of forecasts made around 2000 for the twenty-first century.

Cetron, Marvin J., and Owen Davies. *American Renaissance: Our Life at the Turn of the 21st Century.* New York: St. Martin's Press, 1989.

Though now dated, this book correctly anticipated many of the developments seen in the years since, from the general prosperity of the 1990s to the continuing spread of evangelical Christianity in America. It remains a good example of systematic and successful trend analysis.

Cetron, Marvin J., and Owen Davies. *Cheating Death: The Promise and the Future Impact of Trying to Live Forever.* New York: St. Martin's Press, 1998.

In the years ahead, the human life span may be dramatically lengthened, with humans living to several centuries or even more. The consequences of "cheating death" could be devastating for society, the economy, the environment, and family life, the authors believe.

Cetron, Marvin J., and Owen Davies. *Probable Tomorrows: How Science and Technology Will Transform Our Lives in the Next Twenty Years.* New York: St. Martin's Press, 1997.

This look at near-term future advances discusses computers, telecommunications, high-speed railroads, planes able to fly around the world in four hours, extremely cheap production of consumer goods, and solutions to environmental problems.

Cetron, Marvin J., and Thomas O'Toole. *Encounters with the Future: A Forecast of Life in the Twenty-First Century.* New York: McGraw-Hill, 1982.

This first general-interest book by Cetron, a pioneer of modern forecasting, explored a variety of social and technological developments that seemed likely to occur in the coming decades.

Christakis, Nicholas A. *Death Foretold: Prophecy and Prognosis in Medical Care.* Chicago: University of Chicago Press, 1999.

Physicians need to predict the likely outcome of alternative medical treatments for patients and also answer many predictive questions such as "How long before this tablet relieves my headache?" A wrong answer may disappoint a patient or embarrass the doctor. Most feared of all is the question, "How long do I have to live?" This book offers an interesting perspective on forecasting from the standpoint of medical practitioners.

Claeys, Gregory, and Lyman Tower Sargent, eds. *The Utopia Reader.* New York: New York University Press, 1999.

This well-edited anthology includes excerpts from writers describing imaginary ideal conditions on earth or elsewhere. The authors range from ancient Greeks and Romans to modern Americans. The volume is noteworthy for the wide variety of its materials; however, the sources are limited to Europe, the Near East, and America.

Clarke, Arthur C. *Greetings, Carbon-Based Bipeds! Collected Essays 1934-1998.* New York: St. Martin's Press, 1999.

These essays reflect the long career of a futurist with many achievements, including the concept of communications satellites, the motion picture *2001: A Space Odyssey,* inspiring Gene Roddenberry's creation of the *Star Trek* series, and numerous books, such as the futurist classic *Profiles of the Future.*

Clarke, Arthur C. *Profiles of the Future: An Inquiry into the Limits of the Possible.* Rev. New York: Holt, Rinehart and Winston, 1984.

A slightly revised edition of a book first published in 1962. This is one of the classics of futurist literature. The author methodically explores the fantasies of science fiction, such as the obsolescence of gravity and the colonization of the solar system, to determine what is really and truly impossible and what may indeed be accomplished by determined technologists. Exceptionally well written and scientifically balanced, the book presents the author's imaginative forecasts for the next 150 years.

Clarke, I.F. *The Pattern of Expectation 1644-2001.* London: Jonathan Cape, 1979.

This is an excellent scholarly history of people's ideas about the future, focusing particularly on Europe over the past three centuries. The book emphasizes literary speculations, including not only those of Jules Verne and H.G. Wells but the works of many authors whose names have been long forgotten. Also included are illustrations showing how artists (mainly nineteenth century) envisioned the future.

Cleveland, Harlan. *Nobody in Charge: Essays on the Future of Leadership.* San Francisco: Jossey-Bass, 2002

A collection of fifteen essays by one of the most renowned thinkers and insightful writers on leadership of our time. Cleveland's exploration of what the accelerated spread of knowledge, enhanced by computers and global telecommunications, means for leaders in the twenty-first century is founded on more than fifty years' experience observing and participating in management and leadership. His essays are thought-provoking and inspiring—a must-have for tomorrow's leaders.

Coates, Joseph F., and Jennifer Jarratt. *What Futurists Believe.* Bethesda, Maryland: World Future Society, 1989.

The authors did in-depth interviews of seventeen futurists, including Daniel Bell, Kenneth E. Boulding, Arthur C. Clarke, Governor Richard Lamm, Dennis Meadows, and Peter Drucker, and then carefully analyzed and synthesized their views. One technique used in the book is to dissect out the views of all the interviewees on a given topic, such as energy, and then present them together so that similarities and differences stand out.

Coates, Joseph F., John B. Mahaffie, and Andy Hines. *2025: Scenarios of U.S. and Global Society Reshaped by Science and Technology*. Winchester, Virginia: Oakhill Press, 1996.

> Members of the Coates & Jarratt consulting firm in Washington, D.C., offer fifteen scenarios suggesting possible effects of science and technology on the world to come. Based on a three-year research project, these scenarios cover over fifty fields of science, technology, and engineering.

Condorcet, Marquis de. *Sketch for a Historical Picture of the Progress of the Human Mind*. 1795. Translated by June Barraclough. New York: The Noonday Press, 1955.

> An eighteenth-century French nobleman's forecast, which accurately predicted the abolition of slavery, the rise of the Americas in world affairs, and other events. Condorcet has been hailed as the most successful forecaster in history.

Conway, McKinley. *Three Tomorrows*. Norcross, Georgia: Conway Data, 2004.

> Mingling fact and fiction, this book offers numerous forecasts for the years out to 2050. It is particularly strong in discussing large-scale engineering projects that may be attempted in the years to come.

Corn, Joseph J., ed. *Imagining Tomorrow: History, Technology, and the American Future*. Cambridge, Massachusetts: MIT Press, 1986.

> A lively and informative look at the future as it was envisioned in the American past. Separate essays show how people thought radio, nuclear energy, plastics, homes, skyscrapers, computers, and electric lights would develop. One essay looks at the utopian visions that found expression in the world's fairs of the 1930s.

Corn, Joseph J., and Brian Horrigan. *Yesterday's Tomorrows: Past Visions of the American Future*. New York: Summit Books, 1984.

> This beautifully illustrated book shows past visions of the community of tomorrow, the home of tomorrow, the transportation of tomorrow, and the weapons and warfare of tomorrow. Included are nineteenth-century etchings of future apartment houses; an underground city envisioned in a popular magazine of the 1920s; scenes of the 1939 World's Fair, billed as "The World of Tomorrow"; and more recent visions of cities located in the sky.

Cornish, Edward. *The Study of the Future.* Bethesda, Maryland: World Future Society, 1977. (Out of print; replaced by the present text.)

This general introduction to futurism and future studies discusses the history of the futurist movement, ways to introduce future-oriented thinking into organizations, the philosophical assumptions underlying studies of the future, methods of forecasting, current thinking about what may happen as a result of the current revolutionary changes in human society, etc. A special feature of the book is five- to seven-page biographies of notable futurists such as Margaret Mead, Bertrand de Jouvenel, Herman Kahn, Arthur C. Clarke, and Daniel Bell.

Dash, Leon. *Rosa Lee: A Mother and Her Family in Urban America.* New York: Basic Books, 1996.

A *Washington Post* reporter tells the story of a mother living on welfare and petty crime in the slums of Washington, D.C. Six of her eight children followed her into welfare and crime, but two chose to make a different life for themselves—and did so. This Pulitzer Prize winning investigation showed how people in appalling circumstances can choose a better future for themselves.

Dator, James A., ed. *Advancing Futures: Futures Studies in Higher Education.* Westport, Connecticut: Praeger, 2002.

A collection of twenty-eight essays bearing on futures studies, with an introduction by the editor, a long-time professor of political science at the University of Hawaii. The contributors are almost exclusively professors who have been active in futures studies. The well-informed papers will mainly interest those teaching futures studies or interested in doing so.

Davidson, Frank P., with John Stuart Cox. *Macro: A Clear Vision of How Science and Technology Will Shape Our Future.* New York: William Morrow, 1983.

Though now dated, this book remains an excellent introduction to macro-engineering—large-scale engineering projects. The author, long active in the American Society for Macro-Engineering, served as the first president of the Institute for the Future, now located in Menlo Park, California.

de Jouvenel, Bertrand. *The Art of Conjecture.* Monaco: Editions du Rocher, 1964; Rev. New York: Basic Books, 1967.

This classic of futurist literature discusses basic concepts of thinking about the future. De Jouvenel rejects the notion that there can be a "science of the future," and calls for the study of ideas about what may happen in the future as a means of deciding what actions to take in the present.

Denning, Peter J., ed. *The Invisible Future: The Seamless Integration of Technology into Everyday Life.* New York: McGraw-Hill, 2002.

Eighteen chapters by such authors as Ray Kurzweil, Alan Kay, David Baltimore, and Michael Dertouzos on virtual reality, "ambient intelligence," and other technologies changing our lives in different ways.

Dewar, James A. *Assumption-Based Planning: A Tool for Reducing Avoidable Surprises.* Cambridge, United Kingdom, 2002.

Strategic planner James A. Dewar directs RAND's Frederick S. Pardee Center for Longer Range Global Policy and the Future Human Condition. In his book, he emphasizes the importance of identifying key assumptions in planning and hedging to prevent trouble if these assumptions prove vulnerable. Readable and authoritative, the book should be especially useful to practicing planners.

Diamond, Jared. *Guns, Germs, and Steel: The Fates of Human Societies.* New York: W.W. Norton, 1997.

Diamond argues that environmental factors are primarily responsible for history's broadest patterns, helping to explain such things as the development of agriculture in the Middle East, European colonization of the Americas, and the enormous diversity and primitiveness of cultures in New Guinea. In the context of this fascinating explanation for the technological and material success and/or failure of certain cultures, Diamond argues strongly that history can be a science, though he concedes that certain human personalities do play a significant role in shaping events.

Diderot, Denis. *Encyclopédie, ou Dictionnaire Raisonné des Sciences, des Arts, et des Métiers.* Paris, 1763. Selections edited with notes and introduction by Charles Coulston Gillispie. *A Diderot Pictorial Encyclopedia of Trades and Industry.* 2 vols. New York: Dover Publications, 1959.

The engravings in these volumes provide a fascinating look at what manufacturing was like before the Industrial Revolution.

Didsbury, Howard F., Jr., ed. *Frontiers of the 21st Century: Prelude to the New Millennium*. Bethesda, Maryland: World Future Society, 1999.

This collection of twenty papers presented to the 1999 General Assembly deals with such topics as the future of God, information technology, genetic engineering, utopias, and the next thousand years.

Didsbury, Howard F., Jr., ed. *21st Century Opportunities and Challenges: An Age of Destruction or An Age of Transformation*. Bethesda, Maryland: World Future Society, 2003.

Prepared for the Society's 2003 conference, this volume provides an excellent introduction to current thinking among leading futurists. The thirty authors (twenty-six papers) include Wendell Bell, Lynn Elen Burton, Vary T. Coates, Amitai Etzioni, Theodore J. Gordon, Jerome C. Glenn, Hazel Henderson, J. Østrøm Møller, Arthur B. Shostak, Richard A. Slaughter, David P. Snyder, Allen Tough, and Ian Wilson.

Diebold, John. *Technology and Social Policy: Meeting Society's 21st Century Needs*. Quincy, Massachusetts: Management Science Publishing Co., 1997.

A visionary leader in the use of technology to meet human social needs, the author here addresses such issues as getting innovation into politics, finances, railroads, organizations, and more. In 1952, Diebold published a book entitled *Automation* and thus popularized the word he invented for what was happening in leading-edge industries.

Dyson, Freeman. *Imagined Worlds*. Cambridge, Massachusetts: Harvard University Press, 1997.

A physicist-astronomer offers a wide-angle view of science and science-fiction speculation. He envisions humans spreading out over the universe, taking on different forms as they adapt genetically to different environments.

Easterbrook, Gregg. *The Progress Paradox: How Life Gets Better While People Feel Worse*. New York: Random House, 2003.

Life has improved in the past century, even in the developing world: more food, more money, better health care, etc. Yet many people feel life is getting worse, and the author asks why that should be. One problem is that prosperity does not necessarily bring happiness. But there's much more to be said, and the book makes an interesting and thought-provoking read.

Ellul, Jacques. *The Technological Bluff.* Grand Rapids, Michigan: William B. Eerdmans Publishing Co., 1990.

> A French Calvinist continues his long war against modern technological society. Ellul became famous for his 1954 book *La Technique,* translated into English as *The Technological Society.*

Emery, Merrelyn, and Ronald E. Purser. *The Search Conference: A Powerful Method for Planning Organizational Change and Community Action.* San Francisco: Jossey-Bass, 1996.

> The search conference is a participative approach to planned change that engages the collective learning and creativity of large groups, such as corporations, professional associations, or even cities. This book offers a wealth of illustrative examples for using search conferences to plan the future.

Fagan, Brian. *The Long Summer: How Climate Changed Civilization.* New York: Basic Books, 2004.

> Technological progress may be driving most change in human life today, but climate change, such as global warming, could become increasingly important in the future. Anthropologist Fagan explains how scientific discoveries in recent years have revealed historic climate shifts that have had enormous consequences for human life.

Fahey, Liam, and Robert M. Randall, eds. *Learning From the Future: Competitive Foresight Scenarios.* New York: Wiley, 1998.

> Practitioners of scenario methods describe their techniques. Twenty-five well-chosen and edited essays provide an excellent introduction to the contemporary use of scenarios. Authors include Peter Schwartz, Jay Ogilvy, Ian Wilson, and Stephen Millett.

Ferkiss, Victor. *The Future of Technological Civilization.* New York: George Braziller, 1971.

> A political science professor calls for a new world view, "ecological immanentism," in order to bring about the peaceful revolution needed for human development on a finite planet. He argues that "the essence of humanity's current crisis is that we have allowed our collective destiny to be determined by the political philosophy usually called liberalism,

which holds that the prime purpose of society is to encourage individual self-aggrandizement." In addition to liberalism, Ferkiss attacks other conventional ideologies such as Marxism, socialism, and anarchism. None of these ideologies, Ferkiss believes, can possibly cope with the crisis now gripping the world. But mankind can survive, he argues, through an "immanent revolution" that will involve a radical restructuring of society.

Ferkiss, Victor. *Nature, Technology, and Society: Cultural Roots of the Current Environmental Crisis.* New York: New York University Press, 1993.

A wide-ranging, historical study by a noted political scientist of people's attitudes toward nature and technology. Concisely written and highly informative, the volume serves as an excellent historical briefing for understanding the environmental issues that now face us.

Flechtheim, Ossip K. *History and Futurology.* Meisenheim am Glan, Germany: Verlag Anton Hain, 1966.

This collection of essays by a professor of political science who taught in the United States and Germany is now mainly of historical interest. Ossip Flechtheim published a prophetic article entitled "Teaching the Future" in a relatively obscure U.S. publication in 1943. In this article he called for the development of courses dealing with the future. Later he published other articles on what he called "futurology." This volume of essays, written primarily between 1941 and 1952, is about equally divided between history and futurology. During the late 1960s, the author founded the German journal *Futurum*, a scholarly journal devoted to studies of the future.

Fogg, C. Davis. *Team-Based Strategic Planning: A Complete Guide to Structuring, Facilitating, and Implementing the Process.* New York: AMACOM, 1994.

How to structure strategic planning, facilitate the process, and use teamwork smoothly and productively. Includes actual procedural steps, plans for facilitators, and extensive lists of *do*s and *don't*s.

Forrester, Jay W. *World Dynamics.* Cambridge, Massachusetts: Wright-Allen Press, 1971.

Jay Forrester, long-time professor of management at the Massachusetts Institute of Technology, developed a technique known as "system dynamics" to simulate the functioning of factories, cities, and the world as a whole. The simulation of world trends indicated that catastrophe looms if man does not drastically slow down the growth of population and industrialization. Forrester's colleague, Dennis Meadows, used system dynamics in the *Limits to Growth* study that was widely discussed in the early 1970s.

Fowles, Jib, ed. *Handbook of Futures Research.* Westport, Connecticut: Greenwood Press, 1978.

This collection of writings by forty-six futurists, including Arthur C. Clarke, Herman Kahn, Victor Ferkiss, and Theodore Gordon, is a treasure house of ideas about the future. Though now dated, this scholarly book has been skillfully edited and can be used with profit by almost anyone interested in the future.

Fukuyama, Francis. *Our Posthuman Future: Consequences of the Biotechnology Revolution.* New York: Farrar, Straus and Giroux, 2002.

The author worries that if we don't stop tinkering with human biology we may enter a "posthuman" future in which "freedoms" have run amok. What will happen as parents are free to choose the kind of children they have and entrepreneurs are free to pursue the technology for profit? Fukuyama also frets about human embryos, which now have "a moral status somewhere between that of an infant and that of other types of cells and tissues." To what extent are we willing to create and grow embryos for utilitarian purposes?

Gabor, Dennis. *Inventing the Future.* New York: Knopf, 1964.

Dennis Gabor, a Nobel Prize winning physicist, popularized the phrase "inventing the future." He argues that it is not possible to predict what will happen in the future, but it is possible to create the future through imagination and effort. In this book, Gabor argues that civilization faces three dangers: nuclear war, overpopulation, and "the age of leisure." Gabor suggests that man may be able to cope with the first two dangers more easily than with the third, because of its novelty. In recent decades, man has moved rapidly toward the abolition of work but has done little to prepare himself for leisure. Gabor argues for more creative imagination both in short-range social engineering and in long-term visions of the future.

Galtung, Johan, and Sohail Inayatullah, eds. *Macrohistory and Macrohistorians: Perspectives on Individual, Social, and Civilizational Change.* Westport, Connecticut: Praeger, 1997.

A compact and valuable introduction to macrohistory. Separate chapters discuss a score of macrohistorians (Hegel, Marx, Spengler, Toynbee, and others). These big-picture historians do not provide very usable guidance to the future, the editors decided.

Gardner, John W. *Self-Renewal: The Individual and the Innovative Society.* Rev. New York: W.W. Norton, 1981.

In this modern classic, Gardner explains why some individuals and societies atrophy and decay while others remain innovative and creative. Topics discussed include innovation, obstacles, commitment, and meaning; attitudes toward the future; and moral decay and renewal.

Gates, Bill, with Nathan Myhrvold and Peter Rinearson. *The Road Ahead.* New York: Viking, 1995.

After telling how his 1974 vision of the future led to his becoming the world's richest man, Gates gives his new vision of the future: Rapid progress in computers and telecommunications will produce good things for everybody. He admits to a few worries: power failures and the loss of privacy. (He envisions people using videocameras to document every moment of their lives to guard against criminal charges.) This is a readable and informative book by someone whose expertise is heavily credentialed by his wealth.

Gelernter, David, *1939: The Lost World of the Fair.* New York: Free Press, 1995.

"The World of Tomorrow" was the theme of the 1939 New York World's Fair. Yale professor Gelernter's vivid account of that Fair and its visions of the future includes an assessment of the subsequent success of the Fair's anticipations of what would happen in the following years.

Georges, Thomas M. *Digital Soul: Intelligent Machines and Human Values.* Boulder, Colorado, and Oxford, England: Westview Press, 2003.

An inquiry into the implications of machine intelligence and human values. The author explains how humans can make machines that are smarter than their designers, and analyzes such issues as: How will we distinguish "human" from "machine" in the future? What will happen if machines not only think but have emotions? What if machines become conscious? What rights will they have? A highly readable discussion of the profound questions that advancing machine intelligence is posing for human values.

Gibson, Rowan, ed. Foreword by Alvin and Heidi Toffler. *Rethinking the Future.* Naperville, Illinois: Nicholas Brealey Publishing, 1997.

This collection of essays by such noted business futurists as Charles Handy, John Naisbitt, Lester Thurow, Warren Bennis, Philip Kotler, and Peter Senge offers a cutting-edge look at the new paradigm. Businesses will need to rethink their basic principles as well as changes in competition, control and complexity, leadership, markets, and the world.

Gleick, James. *Chaos: The Making of a New Science.* New York: Viking 1987.

Though now dated, this may still be the best popular introduction to the science of chaos.

Gleick, James. *Faster: The Acceleration of Just About Everything.* New York: Pantheon, 1999.

The author of *Chaos* takes a hard look at today's quick-reflexed, multi-tasking, channel-flipping, fast-forwarding society.

Glenn, Jerome C., and Theodore J. Gordon. *Futures Research Methodology.* Version 2.0. Paperback, with CD-ROM. Washington, D.C.: American Council for the United Nations University, 2003.

Some twenty-five methods and tools for forecasting and analyzing global change are provided in the latest version of this comprehensive and internationally peer-reviewed handbook. Chapters cover each method's history, primary and secondary uses, strengths and weaknesses, applications, and potential uses. The chapters are presented in both MS Word and PDF formats. Order from the publisher.

Godet, Michel. *Creating Futures: Scenario Planning as a Strategic Management Tool.* London: Economica, 2001.

A general discussion of scenarios and other future-oriented issues by the head of a future-oriented group at the Paris-based National Conservatory of Arts and Professions (CNAM).

Halal, William E., ed. *The Infinite Resource: Creating and Leading the Knowledge Enterprise.* San Francisco: Jossey-Bass, 1998.

> Promising new concepts, lessons, and suggestions for leading the new organizational enterprise are here offered by some of the best minds in business and government. Among the contributors are Bell Atlantic CEO Raymond Smith, Indianapolis Mayor Stephen Goldsmith, and networking gurus Jessica Lipnack and Jeffrey Stamps.

Hammond, Debora. *The Science of Synthesis: Exploring the Social Implications of General Systems Theory.* Boulder, Colorado: University Press of Colorado, 2003.

> Systems thinking, well documented in this scholarly text, is an important strain in modern scientific thought. Systems thinking emphasizes the relationships and interconnections in biological, ecological, social, psychological, and technical dimensions of human life. These interconnections become extremely important in thinking about the future.

Harper, Stephen C. *The Forward-Focused Organization: Visionary Thinking and Breakthrough Leadership to Create Your Company's Future.* New York: AMACOM, 1999.

> Management professor Stephen Harper offers a readable, practical guide to creating a forward-focused organization. He has digested much of the best thinking of the management gurus on strategic management and leading changes, and he neatly sums up many of their most useful insights. He devotes a full chapter to futuring.

Harrison, Lawrence E., and Samuel P. Huntington. *Culture Matters: How Values Shape Human Progress.* New York: Basic Books, 2000.

> Two Harvard scholars present an excellent anthology of papers dealing with the influence of culture on economic progress. Thought provoking and readable. Harrison is the author of *Underdevelopment Is a State of Mind.* Huntington is widely known for his best seller, *The Clash of Civilizations and the Remaking of World Order.* Among the causes of underdevelopment are fatalism and negative attitudes toward the future.

Heilbroner, Robert. *Visions of the Future: The Distant Past, Yesterday, Today, Tomorrow.* New York: Oxford University Press and New York Public Library, 1995.

> Stretching 50,000 years into the past and "who knows how many into the future," this gracefully written volume explores

how humans have viewed the future. Heilbroner argues there have only been three ways to view the future: The first, which spans from the Stone Age to the 1700s, was that the future would be like the past; the second, spanning from the 1700s to about 1950, is that the future will be better than today; and the third, where we are today, is an ambivalent outlook.

Henderson, Hazel. *Building a Win-Win World: Life Beyond Global Economic Warfare.* San Francisco: Berrett-Koehler, 1996.

A provocative economist and futurist examines the havoc that the current economic system is creating globally. Even as new markets emerge worldwide, they are running on old textbook models that ignore social and environmental costs and that will inevitably lead to global economic warfare. Henderson shows how win-win strategies can bring stability and peace to our future.

Herman, Roger E., Thomas G. Olivo, and Joyce L. Gioia. *Impending Crisis: Too Many Jobs, Too Few People.* Winchester, Virginia: Oakhill Press, 2002.

The authors foresee a dangerously growing shortage of skilled workers in the years ahead as well as a widening gap in worker skills. The book is designed mainly to provide practical advice for business executives. Herman and Gioia are strategic business futurists concentrating on workforce and workplace trends. Herman is a contributing editor to *The Futurist* magazine. Olivo is a recognized expert in measuring factors that affect bottom-line performance in organizations.

Hesselbein, Frances, Marshall Goldsmith, and Richard Beckhard, eds. *The Organization of the Future.* Drucker Foundation Future Series. San Francisco: Jossey-Bass Publishers, 1997.

A collection of forty thoughtful essays on how organizations might reshape themselves for the coming years.

Hicks, David. *Citizenship for the Future: A Practical Classroom Guide.* Godalming, U.K.: WWF-UK, 2001

A resource book for teachers seeking to teach about environmental issues and the future.

Hicks, David. *Lessons for the Future: The Missing Dimension in Education.* London: RoutledgeFalmer, 2002.

This book by an outstanding British educator well-experienced in teaching young people about futuring is strongly recommended to educators.

Higgins, James M. *101 Creative Problem Solving Techniques: The Handbook for New Ideas for Business*. Winter Park, Florida: The New Management Publishing Co., 1994.

Highly readable, useful, and attractively presented descriptions of creative problem-solving methods, such as scenario writing, brainstorming, Delphi polling, use of analogies, role playing, etc.

Hoyle, John R. *Leadership and Futuring: Making Visions Happen*. Thousand Oaks, California: Corwin Press, a division of Sage Publications, 1995.

This short, readable book introduces the use of futuring and visioning mainly to teachers at the high-school level.

Hubbard, Barbara Marx. *Conscious Evolution*. Novato, California: New World Library, 1998.

This highly personalized vision of the human future describes humans evolving toward higher forms of being in which to express their creativity and life purpose. The author, one of the best-known visionaries of spiritual awakening, is founder and president of the Center for Conscious Evolution (San Rafael, California). Her book offers a five-stage plan for human salvation.

Hughes, Barry B. *International Futures: Choices in the Creation of a New World Order*. 2nd ed. Boulder, Colorado, and Oxford, England: Westview Press, 1996.

This book and the accompanying software help you to define and develop key concepts in demographics, economics, the environment, and other issues. You can use the software to develop alternative views of our global future.

Huxley, Aldous. *Brave New World*. New York: Harper Row, 1931.

A classic dystopian novel by a writer celebrated for social satires.

Inayatullah, Sohail, and Paul Wildman. *Futures Studies: Methods, Emerging Issues and Civilisational Visions*. CD-ROM. Brisbane, Australia: Prosperity Press, 1999.

What is the long-term future of humanity? Will civilizations violently clash, or are we on the verge of planetary governance? These and other critical questions about the future are addressed in this unique, multimedia CD-ROM. The presentation includes a Reader of methods, emerging issues, and visions; a Gallery of fractal images; a participatory Future Forum, and the Future Coffee Shoppe—an e-mail discussion group and hyper-archiving bulletin board through which you can e-mail authors, converse with other readers, and even initiate a collaboration for future editions. Completing the CD may also help you earn a diploma in futures studies.

Jensen, Rolf. *The Dream Society: How the Coming Shift from Information to Imagination Will Transform Your Business.* New York: McGraw-Hill, 1999.

The director of the Copenhagen Institute for Futures Studies argues that the future of business lies not in selling products but in selling dreams and emotions. He identifies six markets: (1) the market for adventures; (2) the market for love, friendship, and togetherness; (3) the market for care (e.g., pets); (4) the who-am-I market (products that proclaim their owner's identity, such as fashion, automobiles, and accessories); (5) the market for peace of mind; (6) the conviction market, which is also referred to as cause-related marketing ("green" products, worker welfare, etc.).

Johnston, William B., and Arnold H. Packer. *Workforce 2000: Work and Workers for the 21st Century.* Indianapolis, Indiana: Hudson Institute, 1987.

This study, prepared for the U.S. Department of Labor, examines the forces shaping the American economy, such as the integration of the global economy, the shift from goods to services, and the proliferation of advanced technologies. Challenges for policy makers include finding ways to accelerate productivity increases in service industries, maintain the dynamism of an aging workforce, and reconcile the conflicting needs of women, work, and families.

Jones, Glenn R. *Free Market Fusion: How Entrepreneurs and Nonprofits Create 21st Century Success.* Denver, Colorado: Cyber Publishing Group, 1999.

Educational entrepreneur Jones, creator of Knowledge TV and the University of the Web, argues that the recipe for a strong economy in the twenty-first century will be to mix the unique capabilities of for-profit and nonprofit organizations. The book includes interviews with futurists Theodore Modis and Alvin and Heidi Toffler.

Jungk, Robert, and Johan Galtung, eds. *Mankind 2000.* London: Allen and Unwin, 1969.

This volume contains thirty-five papers from a 1967 conference on the future in Oslo. It is now mainly of historic interest for what it shows about futurist thinking when the movement was getting started.

Jungk, Robert, and Norbert Müllert. *Future Workshops: How to Create Desirable Futures.* London: Institute for Social Inventions, 1987.

Jungk ran his first "future-creating workshop" in 1962. Ideally, he decided a workshop lasts three days. Day 1 is devoted to a critique of the situation to be addressed. Day 2 focuses on fantasizing about ways to solve the problems being addressed. Day 3 reviews suggested solutions for practicality and getting action started. The editors conclude that the workshops are a remarkable tool for harnessing the creative forces within society.

Kahn, Herman, and Anthony J. Wiener. *The Year 2000: A Framework for Speculation on the Next Thirty-Three Years.* New York: Macmillan, 1967.

This volume summarizes the thinking of Herman Kahn and his Hudson Institute colleagues concerning the world of the future. At the time of its appearance, many futurists regarded the book as possibly the most impressive work then available in terms of its disciplined and penetrating attempt to identify and describe the major trends in Western society. The book describes the "basic, long-term multifold trend" in Western civilization, and projects economic and other trends to the end of the twentieth century.

Kahn, Herman, William Brown, and Leon Martel. *The Next 200 Years: A Scenario for America and the World.* New York: William Morrow and Company, 1976.

A highly optimistic view of America's future: America will become increasingly wealthy, and the problems associated with shrinking supplies of fossil fuels and increasing pollution can be overcome.

Kaku, Michio. *Visions: How Science Will Revolutionize the 21st Century and Beyond.* New York: Doubleday, 1997.

Physicist/science writer Kaku bases his book on interviews with more than 150 top scientists in many fields. He expects major research projects already under way to yield dramatic results between now and the year 2020, and these new findings should make possible wholly new technologies in the decades to 2050 and beyond.

Kelly, Kevin, Peter Leyden, and Members of the Global Business Network. *What's Next?* Cambridge, Massachusetts: Perseus Publishing, 2002.

Selected quotes from twenty-two visionary scientists, business leaders, and futurists at a computer conference are organized into topic areas, including geopolitics, values and belief systems, science, technology, environment, civilization, and more.

Kiernan, Matthew J. *The Eleven Commandments of 21st Century Management.* Englewood Cliffs, New Jersey: Prentice Hall, 1996.

Tomorrow belongs to the smaller, more agile companies. Managers who are not already working in one had better start now to position their companies to succeed in a new business environment demanding constant innovation and creativity. Among the new commandments for managers are: Get innovative or get dead; use all of your people, all of their skills, all of the time; and turn organizational learning into a corporate religion.

Kindleberger, Charles P. *Manias, Panics, and Crashes: A History of Financial Crises.* Rev. ed. New York: Basic Books, 1989.

This book is an excellent investment in your financial future. Read it before you start investing. (See Chapter 10 of *Futuring* for more on Kindleberger's book.)

Kressley, Konrad. *Living in the Third Millennium.* Mobile, Alabama: Factor Press, 1998.

A professor of political science offers a readable, straightforward vision of probable futures, with an emphasis on helping readers develop skills for managing their own futures. Topics include the art of forecasting, planning your career, preparing for financial security, becoming proactive about your health, and more.

Kuhn, Thomas. *The Structure of Scientific Revolutions.* Chicago: University of Chicago Press, 1970.

This book popularized the concept that science progresses by means of repeated "paradigm shifts," such as when the Copernican view of the solar system replaced the Ptolemaic view. Since then, the term "paradigm shift" has become a catch term in business, the social sciences, and elsewhere.

Kurian, George, and Graham T.T. Molitor. *The Encyclopedia of the Future.* 2 vols. New York: Simon & Schuster Macmillan, 1996.

Graham Molitor, vice president of the World Future Society, spent five years recruiting distinguished futurists and other scholars to produce this monumental work. Probably never before had so many scholars collaborated on a future-oriented project. The result was an enormous assemblage of ideas and insights about the future. The 400 separate articles discuss the future of everything from comic books to capitalism, from dentistry to demography, peace keeping and the performing arts. Though now dated, it contains an enormous amount of material that is still useful and interesting.

Kurian, George, and Graham T.T. Molitor. *The 21st Century. Macmillan Compendium.* New York: Macmillan, 1999.

This one-volume edition of the *Encyclopedia of the Future* (above) condenses the contents of the two-volume set.

Kurzweil, Ray. *The Age of Spiritual Machines: When Computers Exceed Human Intelligence.* New York: Viking, 1999.

A noted inventor describes likely advances that will result in computers exceeding the memory capacity and computational ability of the human brain by the year 2020; relationships with automated personalities who will be our teachers and companions; and information fed directly into human brains along direct neural pathways. Eventually, the differences between humans and computers will be so blurred that we will believe the machines are conscious when they say they are.

Lee, Laura. *Bad Predictions.* Rochester, Michigan: Elsewhere Press, 2000.

A compendium of erroneous forecasts from many sources. Covers transportation, technology, medicine, arts, business, history, and more. Demonstrates that anyone can make a mistake when trying to predict, and many forecasts are highly amusing in hindsight. Includes introduction but no commentary on individual forecasts.

Linstone, Harold A. *Decision Making for Technology Executives: Using Multiple Perspectives to Improve Performance.* Norwood, Massachusetts: Artech House, 2000.

The author, a veteran of many years in technical planning for the Hughes and Lockheed corporations, astutely analyzes the problems of making decisions concerning technology: Specific examples discussed include such disasters as the Maginot Line, the Exxon *Valdez,* and Three Mile Island. Though somewhat technical, this well-informed text requires no deep knowledge of technology or mathematics to appreciate its important insights into decision making.

Lippitt, Lawrence L. *Preferred Futuring: Envision the Future You Want and Unleash the Energy to Get There.* San Francisco: Berrett-Kohler, 1998.

The Preferred Futuring concept, developed by Ron Lippitt (the author's father) and Ed Lindaman in 1968, focuses on getting all the stakeholders together to develop a vision that is clear, detailed, and generally understood. The vision then is translated into action goals, a series of planned steps with accountability identified, together with a structure to implement the action plan. *Note:* This approach resembles the Future Search approach described by Marvin R. Weisbord and Sandra Janoff. See entry for their book.

McGuire, Bill. *A Guide to the End of the World: Everything You Never Wanted to Know.* New York: Oxford, 2002.

An authoritative yet highly readable book that will open readers' eyes to the dangers posed by our natural environment including climate change (global warming vs. a new ice age), super-volcanic eruptions, giant tsunamis, earthquakes, asteroids, and comets. The author, a professor of geophysical hazards at University College London, provides much eye-opening new information that scientists have developed. An exceptional book on this topic.

McNeill, William H. *Plagues and Peoples,* 1976. Rev. ed. New York: Anchor Books/Doubleday, 1998.

AIDS, SARS, and Mad Cow Disease demonstrate the continuing importance of epidemics in shaping events. McNeill's classic text traces the impacts of epidemics on human life through the centuries.

Maddox, John. *What Remains to Be Discovered: Mapping the Secrets of the Universe, the Origins of Life and the Future of the Human Race.* New York: Free Press, 1998.

A former editor of the British science journal *Nature* takes a serious look at what scientists don't know. "The record of previous centuries suggests that the excitement in the years ahead will spring from the answers to the questions we do not yet know enough to ask.... The problems that remain unsolved are gargantuan. They will occupy our children and their children and so on and on for centuries to come, perhaps even for the rest of time."

Marien, Michael, and Lane Jennings, eds. *What I Have Learned: Thinking About the Future Then and Now.* Westport, Connecticut: Greenwood Press, 1987.

Leading futurist authors of the 1970s and 1980s report how their thinking about the future has changed. Contributors include W. Warren Wagar, Kenneth E. Boulding, Willis W. Harman, Victor Ferkiss, Irene Taviss Thomson, Robert T. Francoeur, Jim Dator, Amitai Etzioni, Walter A. Hahn, Joseph F. Coates, Vary T. Coates, Harold A. Linstone, Bertram Gross, Kusum Singh, and Hazel Henderson. The varied contributions demonstrate the wide diversity of views among people sharing a common interest in the human future. This diversity may be frustrating to people expecting to be told exactly what the future will be like by a knowledgeable expert, but the diversity of the contributions also shows the creative strength of the futurist community, which provides an opportunity for futurists with strongly opposed ideas to come together and share their often-radically different ideas in a friendly and mutually respectful venue.

Marsh, Nick, Mike McAllum, and Dominique Purcell. *Strategic Foresight: The Power of Standing in the Future.* Melbourne, Australia: Crown Content, 2002.

An Australian perspective on introducing strategic foresight into organizations. The book also discusses national foresight programs in New Zealand, Finland, Brazil, and elsewhere.

Masini, Eleanora. *Why Future Studies?* London: Grey Seal Books, 1993. (Out of print. Copies still available through the World Future Society.)

> An Italian futurist and professor examines the history, principles, concepts, philosophy, and ethical elements of the futures field. Masini spent many years working for the World Futures Studies Federation and teaching at Rome's Pontifical Gregorian University. Her long experience is reflected in this thoughtful book.

Mason, Colin. *The 2030 Spike: Countdown to Global Catastrophe.* London and Springfield, Virginia: Earthscan Publications, 2003.

> This is a recent example of a "doomsday" book anticipating global calamity unless action is taken immediately. The author, a well-known Australian journalist and politician, believes that depleted fuel supplies, massive population growth, poverty, global climate change, famine, growing water shortages, and international lawlessness will converge in the 2030 decade and may smother civilization.

Masuda, Yoneji. *The Information Society As Post-Industrial Society.* Bethesda, Maryland: World Future Society, 1981.

> A principal architect of Japan's $65 billion computer-usage plan offers a vision of the society of the future when computers will free people to live more creative and happy lives. He discusses computer-controlled vehicle systems, automated supermarkets, etc. Though it is now dated, Masuda's visionary book excited many in the computer world when it first appeared, and his ideas are still interesting.

Matathia, Ira, and Marian Salzman. *Next: Trends for the Near Future.* Woodstock, New York: Overlook Press, 1999.

> Trend watchers for a New York advertising firm offer a host of predictions for business, technology, and lifestyle changes in the years just ahead. The book is packed with facts and forecasts but lacks references to the original materials. The text seems largely aimed at marketers, and the authors are not shy about advertising their research services.

May, Graham H. *The Future Is Ours: Foreseeing, Managing and Creating the Future.* Westport, Connecticut: Praeger, 1996.

> A lecturer at Leeds Metropolitan University in England explores such questions as why we forecast the future despite the likelihood we will be wrong, how people relate to the fu-

ture, and other issues. This is a college-level text for use in future-oriented courses in business, management, urban planning, and other areas.

Mazaar, Michael. *Global Trends 2005: An Owner's Manual for the Next Decade.* New York: St. Martin's Press, 1999.

Mazaar, a fellow of the Center for Strategic and International Studies in Washington, D.C., offers a general overview of the transformations to be expected in the near future. He also considers a few surprise scenarios, such as a media-savvy demagogue who rises to power offering alienated millions an authority figure to replace traditional institutions that have been undermined by information overload.

Meadows, Donella H., Dennis L. Meadows, Jorgen Randers, and William W. Behrens III. *The Limits to Growth.* New York: Universe Books, 1972.

This volume summarizes the Club of Rome report prepared at MIT by Dennis Meadows and his colleagues, using the computerized system dynamics approach developed by Professor Jay Forrester. The pessimistic report created a sensation in intellectual circles, especially in Europe, with its contention that, if present patterns of rapid population and capital growth are allowed to continue, the world faces "a disastrous collapse."

Merriam, John E., and Joel Makower. *Trend Watching: How the Media Create Trends and How to Be the First to Uncover Them.* New York: AMACOM, 1988.

This how-to book deals with understanding, analyzing, and anticipating trends based on what is being reported in the media.

Michalko, Michael. *Cracking Creativity: The Secrets of Creative Geniuses.* Berkeley, California: Ten Speed Press, 1998.

A clear and lively discussion of creativity techniques.

Miller, James G. *Living Systems.* New York: McGraw-Hill, 1978.

A mammoth volume presenting an overview of the author's theory of living systems at both high and low levels of complexity. He creates a hierarchy of seventeen components of systems.

Millett, Stephen M., and Edward J. Honton. *A Manager's Guide to Technology Forecasting and Strategy Analysis Methods.* Columbus, Ohio: Battelle Press, 1991.

A short, well-informed, and practical guide to the use of forecasting and strategy analysis methods in corporate planning. It provides forthright and detailed critiques of their strengths and weaknesses.

Mintzberg, Henry, Bruce Ahlstrand, and Joseph Lampel. *Strategy Safari: A Guided Tour Through the Wilds of Strategic Management.* New York: Free Press, 1998.

A primer on business strategy with a critique of different approaches.

Modis, Theodore. *An S-Shaped Trail to Wall Street: Survival of the Fittest Reigns at the Stock Market.* Geneva: Growth Dynamics, 1999.

In his earlier books *Predictions* (Simon & Schuster, 1992) and *Conquering Uncertainty* (McGraw-Hill, 1998), physicist/ futurist Modis showed how scientific theories about seasonal change and cycles of behavior in plants and animals might be used to explain—and forecast—changes in human society. This newer book uses this approach to explain events in the stock market. The book offers fascinating insights into parallels and between completely unrelated areas of nature and human society.

Molitor, Graham T.T. *The Power to Change the World: The Art of Forecasting.* Potomac, Maryland: Graham T.T. Molitor, 2003.

A spiral-bound presentation of the "Molitor Model of Change: Basic 22 Signature Patterns of Change." The book features more than 200 charts showing trends of many varieties. The patterns of change include litigation, random phenomena, subtle impacts, catalysts, voluntary accommodation, and much more. An unusual and stimulating presentation of material. Provenance of the original data is not indicated.

Moravec, Hans. *Robot: Mere Machine to Transcendent Mind.* Oxford, England: Oxford University Press, 1998.

A former Carnegie Mellon University robotics expert believes robots will model themselves after successful biological forms. He anticipates that robots will become "intelligent machines" that will learn our skills, share our goals and values, and become our evolutionary heirs.

Morrison, Ian. *The Second Curve: Managing the Velocity of Change.* New York: Ballantine, 1996.

> Help for managers preparing for future growth and change. "The second curve" is a revolutionary business model that allows companies to anticipate the rate of change, identify new directions, and know when to jump onto the second curve of change.

Mulhall, Douglas. *Our Molecular Future: How Nanotechnology, Robotics, Genetics, and Artificial Intelligence Will Transform Our World.* Amherst, New York: Prometheus Books, 2002.

> A readable, imaginative survey of cutting-edge technologies and their implications for human life. Discusses such things as transhumans, the possibility of a "singularity," molecular weapons, and scenarios for what may happen in the future.

Naisbitt, John. *Global Paradox: The Bigger the World Economy, the More Powerful Its Smallest Players.* New York: William Morrow, 1994.

> The author argues that both nations and individuals are now breaking up into smaller and smaller units, because the telecommunications revolution is simultaneously creating a global economy and empowering its constituent parts, with power flowing particularly to small units. Goods and services can be sold all over the world with increasing ease, so the small nations and businesses are finding that they can compete more successfully than in the past.

Naisbitt, John. *Megatrends: Ten New Directions Transforming Our Lives.* New York: Warner, 1982.

> Naisbitt describes ten major trends affecting our society today. For instance, we are moving from an industrial society to an information society, from a national economy to a world economy, and from institutional help to self-help. Though now dated, this book was a best seller that got many people thinking about trends.

Naisbitt, John, and Patricia Aburdene. *Megatrends 2000.* New York: William Morrow, 1990.

> Modeled on the best-selling *Megatrends*, this book focuses on a new set of perceived macrotrends, including the rise of the Pacific Rim countries, a religious revival, etc. This volume like its predecessor can be described as a "newsbook"—a book-length text designed to help time-short people understand the forces that give rise to news events. Despite critics sneering at

this "millennial megababble," thousands of readers like Nais-bitt's information-rich, readable presentation and have put his books on best-seller lists.

Naisbitt, John, with Nana Naisbitt and Douglas Philips. *High Tech – High Touch: Technology and Our Search for Meaning.* New York: Broadway Books, 1999.

This highly readable and informative but loosely organized book argues that people need "high touch" experiences—the non-technological joys of living—to set off the high tech aspects of their lives. The book includes a strong chapter on the social and ethical consequences of genetic technology.

Nanus, Burt. *Visionary Leadership: Creating a Compelling Sense of Direction for Your Organization.* San Francisco: Jossey-Bass, 1992.

This timely book explains what visionary leadership is all about and why it is important to develop the skills necessary for leading organizations into the future. Leadership expert Burt Nanus, co-author of this best-selling book shows you how to develop a vision, implement it, and know when it's time to "re-vision." A participant's workbook is also available.

Nanus, Burt. *The Vision Retreat: A Facilitator's Guide.* San Francisco: Jossey-Bass, 1995.

A leadership expert offers a logical, step-by-step process for creating and implementing a new direction for your organization.

Nirenberg, John. *Power Tools: A Leader's Guide to the Latest Management Thinking.* Englewood Cliffs, New Jersey: Prentice Hall, 1997.

A guide to 100 of the latest management "tools," with an assessment of just how useful they are.

Ogilvy, James A. *Creating Better Futures: Scenario Planning as a Tool for a Better Tomorrow.* Foreword by Peter Schwartz. New York: Oxford University Press, 2002.

A co-founder of the Global Business Network argues that we today "suffer from a lack of sufficient idealism." Popular images of the future tend to be grim. Ogilvy takes "an unabashedly hopeful" view but says there is nothing inevitable about better futures. We must create them, and we can help people do so by framing alternative scenarios customized to their particular situations. This is not a how-to book for scenario planning but rather a general discussion of its usefulness in improving organizational futures.

Organisation for Economic Cooperation and Development. *21st Century Technologies: Promises and Perils of a Dynamic Future.* Paris: OECD, 1998.

OECD's secretariat prepared this report for the World Exposition in Hannover, Germany, in 2000. The report consists of seven articles by experts writing on such topics as biotechnology and the macro conditions conducive to realizing technology's potential.

Orwell, George. *Nineteen Eighty-four.* New York: Harcourt, Brace and Company Inc., 1949.

A classic dystopian novel. The atomic wars Orwell refers to as occurring in the 1950s never occurred, but his portrayal of a totalitarian state remains of lasting interest. The book can best be viewed as a satire rather than a serious attempt to forecast the future. Orwell wanted to attack the totalitarian tendencies by means of a satire, so he showed them in exaggerated forms. But the tendencies remain alive and well today, and may be seen in such phenomena as the vilification of enemies, the terrorization of non-conformists, and the rewriting of history to fit current political dogmas.

Pearson, Ian, ed. *Macmillan Atlas of the Future.* New York: Macmillan Reference, 1998.

Full-color maps and graphics provide a vivid overview of where we are headed in the new millennium. An international team of leading analysts predicts developments in such areas as space exploration, economics, life expectancy, biodiversity, democracy, and more. Though dated, the book's approach is eye-catching and still interesting.

Pearson, Ian D., and Chris Winter. *Where's IT Going?* New York: Thames & Hudson, 1999.

Two British Telecommunications experts offer a forecast for future developments in information technology. Specific topics include computers, communications, financial systems, and social institutions and behavior.

Petersen, John L. *Out of the Blue: Wild Cards and Other Big Future Surprises.* Lanham, Maryland: Madison, 1997.

John L. Petersen, president of the Arlington Institute in Arlington, Virginia, examines the potential impacts of such "wild card" events as an asteroid collision, the collapse of the U.S. dollar, a shift in the Earth's axis, and the perfection of techniques for cloning humans. This rapid ride through scores of scenarios is designed to get you to think "out of the box" and learn how to manage surprises.

Pirages, Dennis Clark, and Theresa Manly De Geest. *Ecological Security: An Evolutionary Perspective on Globalization.* Lanham, Maryland: Rowman & Littlefield Publishers, 2003.

The senior author is a professor of international environmental politics at the University of Maryland with years of distinguished scholarship and numerous books to his credit. This book is a well-organized, systematic discussion of the ecological issues of the near-term future, with lucid analyses and many suggestions for solving the problems of a globalizing world.

Pirages, Dennis, ed. *Building Sustainable Societies: A Blueprint for a Post-Industrial World.* Armonk, New York: M.E. Sharpe, 1996.

This collection of twenty previously unpublished essays by noted scholars analyzes the implications of economic development as part of the search for an economic system that can be sustained over time.

Polak, Fred L. *The Image of the Future.* New York: Elsevier, 1973.

A Dutch scholar prepared this study of the role of images of the future down through history. Translated by Elise Boulding, a sociologist and futurist.

Prantzos, Nikos. *Our Cosmic Future: Humanity's Fate in the Universe.* Cambridge, England: Cambridge University Press, 2000.

Billions of years from now, the sun will run out of fuel and grow dark, making the earth uninhabitable. Engineer Prantzos of the Swiss Technical Institute in Zurich offers an escape plan for humanity—in plenty of time to prepare for the crisis.

Prehoda, Robert W. *Designing the Future: The Role of Technological Forecasting.* Philadelphia: Chilton Books, 1967.

Technological forecaster Robert Prehoda presents a rationale for man's potential ability to foresee accurately the future capabilities and results of applied science. The book defines technological forecasting as "the description or prediction of a foreseeable invention, specific scientific refinement, or likely scientific discovery that promises to serve some useful function." Prehoda describes several approaches to technological forecasting; his primary technique is through what he calls "the Hahn-Strassmann point." The name comes from the Hahn-Strassmann experiments in 1938, which showed the possibility of uranium fission. His method is to look for analogous situations; i.e., laboratory achievements that show the possibility of some major advance on a practical scale, then forecast the practical results that could be based on this laboratory achievement.

Rees, Martin. *Our Final Hour.* New York: Basic Books, 2003.

The Astronomer Royal of the United Kingdom takes time from his cosmological work to issue a bleak warning to earthlings: "I think the odds are no better than 50-50 that our present civilization on earth will survive to the end of [this] century." He offers a long list of worries, from black holes to unstable individual buildings, but he also suggests reasons why many of his horrors may not prove as horrible as he fears.

Reibnitz, Ute von. *Scenario Techniques.* New York: McGraw-Hill, 1987.

Scenario techniques are suitable for all projects dealing with complex, interrelated problems. This book clearly shows how scenarios may be used in strategic planning, individual planning in organizational departments, and personal planning.

Renesch, John. *Getting to the Better Future: A Matter of Conscious Choosing.* Foreword by Anita Roddick. San Francisco: New Business Books, 2000.

Humans have hardly reached full maturity as a species, the author contends, as evidenced by conditions throughout the world. The present course suggests that the future of our world will unfold by default—the result of haphazard and random decisions based on short-term expediency. However, the author offers an alternative future—one created by conscious intention with the longer term in view.

Rescher, Nicholas. *Predicting the Future: An Introduction to the Theory of Forecasting.* Albany, New York: State University of New York Press, 1998.

The author, a professor of philosophy at the University of Pittsburgh, provides a thorough discussion of the nature and problems of prediction. The volume discusses the ontology and epistemology of the future, predictive methods, evaluation of predictions and predictors, obstacles to prediction, and other aspects of prediction. Rescher also focuses on the theoretical and methodological issues of prediction, but does not attempt to make predictions of his own for the future.

Ringland, Gill. *Scenario Planning.* Chichester, United Kingdom: Wiley, 1998.

A comprehensive guide to using scenarios in business. It can function well both as a general primer and as a detailed textbook. The author, an executive with the London-based information technology firm ICL, notes that people in business sometimes confuse scenarios as forecasts. Rather, they are ways to understand the total environment in which business operates.

Rischard, Jean-François. *High Noon: 20 Global Problems, 20 Years to Solve Them.* New York: Perseus Books, 2002.

A vice president of the World Bank argues that current ways of dealing with complex global issues are not up to the job. He argues that "each global issue should have its own problem-solving vehicle" and proposes twenty global issues networks.

Rubenstein, Herb, and Tony Grundy: *Breakthrough: High Growth Strategies for Entrepreneurial Organizations.* Harlow, England: Financial Times/ Prentice Hall Pearson Education Ltd., 1999.

This book by two business consultants, focusing on how companies can grow rapidly, discusses trend analysis and other futurist techniques.

Sale, Kirkpatrick. *Rebels Against the Future: The Luddites and Their War on the Industrial Revolution.* New York: Addison-Wesley, 1995.

A long-time critic of technology recounts the famous Luddite uprising against the new manufacturing equipment powered by steam or water engines in the 1790s. The British parliament dispatched an army of 14,000 men to put down the rebellion. Viewing the Luddites as martyrs to the cause of halting the technological juggernaut, Sale proposes a wholesale dismantling of industrial technology as we know it.

Salmon, Robert. *The Future of Management: All Roads Lead to Man.* Translated by Larry Cohen. Oxford, United Kingdom: Blackwell Publishers, 1996.

> The former vice-chairman of the cosmetics giant L'Oreal offers business executives a visionary guide to the coming decades. Salmon believes a new economic order is emerging on the basis of human dynamics and aspirations rather than short-term financial gains achieved at employees' and customers' expense. It is devotion to human potential that will unlock the future, Salmon believes.

Schnaars, Steven. *Megamistakes: Forecasting and the Myth of Rapid Technological Change.* New York: Free Press, 1989.

> A marketing professor at the City University of New York argues that 80 percent of business forecasting has been dead wrong. His analysis focuses on the past three decades in which entrepreneurs, managers, and forecasters have repeatedly anticipated great success for such developments as the videophone only to have them fail in the marketplace. In this entertaining volume, Schnaars explores the question of why consumers repeatedly reject the new products they are offered, thereby invalidating the forecasts of the developers.

Schrage, Michael. *Serious Play: How the World's Best Companies Simulate to Innovate.* Foreward by Tom Peters. Boston: Harvard Business School Press, 1999.

> A discussion of business innovation by means of models, simulations, gaming, and prototyping.

Schwartz, Peter. *The Art of the Long View: Planning for the Future in an Uncertain World.* New York: Doubleday/Currency, 1991.

> A former leader of the Global Business Network shows how composing and using scenarios can help people visualize and prepare for a better future. Oriented largely toward business rather than individuals.

Schwartz, Peter, Peter Leyden, and Joel Hyatt. *The Long Boom: A Vision for the Coming Age of Prosperity.* Reading, Massachusetts: Perseus Books, 1999.

> An optimistic vision of the first two decades of the twenty-first century.

Sherden, William A. *The Fortune Sellers: The Big Business of Buying and Selling Predictions.* New York: Wiley, 1998.

Sherden launches a frontal assault on futurists, economists, stock market gurus, weather forecasters, technology prophets, and others who make forecasts for money. The gravamen of his indictment is that forecasters are frauds because the future is unknowable: When forecasters do manage to get something right, it's simply by chance. This is a highly readable exposé but so one-sided that it's hard to take seriously. Futurists do not need to be told that forecasts often prove wrong, but they may find it useful to hear what a critic has to say.

Shostak, Arthur B., ed. *Viable Utopian Ideas: Shaping a Better World*. Armonk, New York: M.E. Sharpe, 2003.

A collection of forty-seven original essays exploring pragmatic reform possibilities of special interest to futurists. Features ideas by such leading forecasters as Wendell Bell, Joseph F. Coates, Lane Jennings, Michael Marien, and many others.

Slaughter, Richard A. *The Foresight Principle: Cultural Recovery in the 21st Century*. Westport, Connecticut: Praeger, 1995.

Why is foresight useful? How much does it really cost, and who should support it? What are the real megatrends?

Slaughter, Richard A. *The Knowledge Base of Futures Studies*. 3 vols. Hawthorn, Victoria, Australia: DDM Media Group, 1996.

This three-volume set provides an in-depth, authoritative, and truly international overview of futures studies. Volume 1, *Foundations*, considers the origins of futures studies and discusses some of the social, cultural, and historical reasons for their emergence. Volume 2, *Organizations, Practices, Products*, begins with case studies of five very different futures organizations from different continents. Volume 3, *Directions and Outlooks*, describes recent developments and innovations in futures studies itself. This set of volumes will aid anyone working in any of the emerging futures professions. *Note:* A fourth volume is included in the CD-ROM version.

Stableford, Brian, and David Langford. *The Third Millennium: A History of the World: AD 2000-3000*. New York: Knopf, 1985.

Fanciful scenarios for possible developments in the centuries ahead.

Stewart, Hugh B. *Recollecting the Future: A View of Business, Technology, and Innovation in the Next 30 Years*. Homewood, Illinois: Dow Jones-Irwin, 1989.

Where growth is involved, scientist/engineer Stewart believes it is possible to "recollect" the future—that is, apply laws of growth similar to those in biology to the development of new industries, energy use, and the economy. Stewart believes that if his arguments are correct we will see the dawn of a very important new industrial, energy-use, and economic surge beginning before the year 2000. The book should appeal strongly to people interested in ways to anticipate future technology.

Stock, Gregory. *Redesigning Humans: Our Inevitable Genetic Future.* New York: Houghton-Mifflin, 2002.

An expert on recent advances in reproductive biology discusses the ethical dilemmas occurring as we gain the ability to choose our offspring's genes. Biological enhancements of human abilities may challenge what it means to be human. The author has served as director of UCLA's Program on Medicine, Technology, and Society. Compare with Fukuyama's *Our Posthuman Future.*

Tenner, Edward. *Why Things Bite Back: Technology and the Revenge of Unintended Consequences.* New York: Alfred A. Knopf, 1996.

New technologies are likely to produce "revenge effects"— bad consequences that were not intended. Advanced safety systems can lead to overconfidence, as in the case of the *Titanic* sinking. This popularized, largely anecdotal discussion also notes that technology's "bites" have often had good effects: The sinking of the *Titanic* led to new measures to deal with the hazards of icebergs and ocean travel in general.

Thomson, Sir George. *The Foreseeable Future.* Rev. ed. Cambridge, England: Cambridge University Press, 1960.

Nobel Prize winning British physicist Sir George Thomson published this book in 1955. The author focused on sources of energy, transportation, communication, meteorology, natural resources, food production, and intellectual development. Two decades after his book appeared, a reviewer in *The Futurist* reported that Thomson's twenty-year-old forecasts had generally turned out to be remarkably accurate. Thomson had correctly foreseen the energy crisis in the 1970s and the triumph of the computer.

Toffler, Alvin. *Future Shock.* New York: Random House, 1970.

This international best seller argues that increasing numbers of people are suffering from the impact of too rapid social change. Toffler believes that the problem may become increasingly severe in the years to come. A final chapter, "The Strategy of Social Futurism," proposes a number of ways in which society can learn to cope with future shock. The author outlines his ideas about how to make democracy more anticipatory in its character.

Toffler, Alvin. *Powershift: Knowledge, Wealth, and Violence at the Edge of the 21st Century.* New York: Bantam, 1990.

Powershift is the third and final volume of a trilogy that began with *Future Shock* (1970) and continued with *The Third Wave* (1980). Toffler examines three forms of power: (1) knowledge (information, communications, and media), (2) wealth (business, financial), and (3) violence (government, politics). He, argues that power is now shifting from violence and wealth toward knowledge and provides a highly browsable compendium of fascinating anecdotes and insights.

Toffler, Alvin. *The Third Wave.* New York: William Morrow, 1980.

The author describes a new civilization that he believes is emerging from our present industrial civilization, but the best part of the book may be the author's ability to provide numerous fascinating insights, useful perspectives, and plausible anticipations concerning current trends.

Toffler, Alvin, and Heidi Toffler. *War and Anti-War: Survival at the Dawn of the 21st Century.* Boston: Little, Brown, 1993.

A readable but disturbing discussion of what war may be like in the future, including widely dispersed nuclear weapons available to small groups such as Asian warlords or Mafia families. A nuclear bomb may explode in Washington or other big city without anyone knowing who is responsible.

Vision Center for Futures Creation. *A Tale of the Future.* E-book. Göteborg, Sweden: Visionscentret Framtidsbygget, 1998.

This electronic book offers an extended scenario or "social science fiction," based on a study conducted by a group of twenty-six Swedish young people. The electronic book is available in either Swedish or English.

Wagar, W. Warren. *Good Tidings: The Belief in Progress from Darwin to Marcuse.* Bloomington, Indiana: Indiana University Press, 1972.

The belief in progress is sometimes viewed as "the religion of modern man." In this book, Wagar analyzes how this belief changed during the period from 1880 to 1970. A good companion volume for J.B. Bury's earlier work *The Idea of Progress.* (See above.)

Wagar, W. Warren. *The Next Three Futures: Paradigms of Things to Come.* Westport, Connecticut: Praeger, 1991.

A historian and futurist based at the State University of New York in Binghamton identifies three major camps of futurist thinking: technoliberals, radicals, and counterculturalists. The book as a whole provides a vital introduction to the diversified field of futurist inquiry.

Wagar, W. Warren. *A Short History of the Future.* 3rd ed. Chicago: University of Chicago Press, 1999.

Historian/futurist Wagar offers a detailed scenario for world developments during the twenty-first century.

Weiner, Edith, and Arnold Brown. *Insider's Guide to the Future.* New York: Boardroom Books, 1997.

Two veteran futurists specializing in analyzing trends for business clients offer insights into the new "Emotile Society," which blends emotions and mobility. Knowledge will be the greatest economic asset, but it will be limited by time: Information that is incredibly valuable one moment may be worthless the next.

Weisbord, Marvin R., and Sandra Janoff. *Future Search: An Action Guide to Finding Common Ground in Organizations and Communities.* San Francisco: Berrett-Koehler, 1995.

The future-search process focuses on resolving conflicts, generating commitment to common goals, and taking responsibility for action. This practical guide offers techniques for running successful future-search conferences.

Weldon, Lynn L. *The Future: Important Choices.* Boulder, Colorado: University Press of Colorado, 1995.

This introductory text for college-level courses in futures studies is also useful for general readers, offering a succinct summary of major world issues and differing views.

Wilson, Edward O. *The Future of Life.* New York: Knopf, 2002.

Wilson, a Harvard biology professor, warns of an "armageddon" due to humanity destroying the earth's living environment.

World Future Society. *The Futurist Directory: A Guide to Individuals Who Write, Speak, or Consult about the Future.* Bethesda, Maryland: World Future Society, 2000.

A listing of nearly 1,400 individuals including specialization, employment, publications, street and electronic addresses, and telephone numbers. Geographical and subject indexes.

Worldwatch Institute. *The State of the World.* New York: W.W. Norton. Published annually.

This annual volume has been published every year since 1984. Lester R. Brown, the Institute's founder and first president, led the development of these reports, and their readability and high quality has continued under the leadership of the Institute's new president, Christopher Flavin. The reports offer authoritative information on current world trends, with special emphasis on the environment. Readable and trustworthy information. Specific topics vary from year to year.

Worzel, Richard. *The Next Twenty Years of Your Life: A Personal Guide Into the Year 2017.* Toronto: Stoddart, 1997.

Clear, concise discussion of how technologies and other changes will affect your family, your work, your health, and your lifestyle. Among author Worzel's forecasts: the end of retirement, the end of television, the biggest stock market boom in history, and life spans extended beyond age 100.

Zey, Michael G. *The Future Factor: The Five Forces Transforming Our Lives and Shaping Human Destiny.* New York: McGraw-Hill, 2000.

A general discussion of the human future, with emphasis on the new possibilities opened by emerging technologies. Topics include nanotechnology, cloning, genetic engineering, smart machines, space settlement, and general human progress. The optimism of this book's view of the human future is extreme: Probably no previous book has suggested that humans might someday save the universe from eventual death in a "Big Chill" or "Big Crunch," as augured by cosmology's Big Bang theory.

This bibliography is accessible online and continuously updated. Please visit *Futuring* at wfs.org/futuring.htm.

Glossary

backcasting. A method of forecasting or planning in which an event is posited as having occurred in the future. The question then becomes, How did this event come to be? For example, one might posit that, in the year 2050, the cost of a year's worth of electricity for either a car or a home will be less than $10. The task then is to develop a scenario to explain how the posited future might actually come about. Backcasting offers a way to get a group to envision a desirable future and then determine what must happen in order for that goal to be reached.

bellwether. A leader or forerunner. (Originally, a belled wether or male sheep that leads the flock.) The term is often applied to a jurisdiction or class of people who are among the first to adopt a new technology, product, or practice that will later be adopted by others.

brainstorming. A method for getting a group to generate a lot of ideas on a specified topic. A key part of the method is to withhold all criticism of the ideas that are offered so that people will freely offer unexpected and unconventional but potentially useful ideas. All ideas are recorded for later review to see which if any might be useful.

butterfly effect. A metaphor to illustrate sensitivity to initial conditions. The metaphor was popularized by MIT's Edward Lorenz with his 1979 paper, "Predictability: does the flap of a butterfly's wing in Brazil set off a tornado in Texas?" The metaphor illustrates how a very small event may have very large effects.

chaos. In general usage "chaos" connotes random, unpredictable behavior. In chaos theory, chaos is deterministic behavior that is so complex as to appear random. Chaos theory deals with the irregular, seemingly unpredictable behavior of nonlinear dynamic systems.

cross-impact analysis. A matrix method for identifying the effects that future developments may have on each other. This can be done by creating a matrix and identifying two sets of factors, listing one set of factors from top to bottom on the left side of the matrix and the other across the top. *See* **"Matrix Power"** in Chapter 10.

cycle. A regular recurrence of some condition, such as the coming of night after day. Forecasts can often be made on the basis of knowledge of cycles. *See* **Chapter 4.**

Delphi technique (or method). A method of polling people in order to produce a group judgment. Typically, this might involve soliciting individually the judgments of experts on a possible future event. The judgments of the different experts would later be combined to create a consensus view. The Delphi technique keeps individual responses anonymous so that social influences (prestige of a certain participant, shyness of certain participants, etc.) are minimized. However, the Delphi administrator can re-pose questions to the group to refine the consensus judgment.

discontinuity. A relatively abrupt change in the nature or direction of something. If the growth of a city's population suddenly stopped and population began declining, we could say that a *discontinuity* has occurred. Another example would be the sudden end of the Age of Reptiles (Cretaceous period).

discounting the future. Reducing the perceived value of a benefit because it will not be received until sometime in the future. The more distant the anticipated reward or punishment, the more the benefit (e.g., a large sum of money) will likely be ignored in deci-sion making.

dystopia. An anti-utopia or an imaginary society with many unde-sirable features. George Orwell's novel *Nineteen Eighty-four* de-scribed a dystopia. *See also* **utopia.**

expert forecasting. Having knowledgeable people make informed guesses about possible future events.

fatalism. The belief that future events are determined by external forces rather than human choices. Fatalism often leads to mystical or magical efforts to influence the arcane. Even today, in high-risk situations, people may carry a lucky talisman—any object believed to avert danger or bring good luck.

force. A persistent cause of change. In thinking about future possi-bilities, futurists may identify a number of ongoing develop-ments that are likely to produce further change. For instance, high birthrates may produce growing poverty and environmental destruction.

forecast. A statement that something will probably happen in the future. *Forecast* implies less certainty about the event's occurrence than *prediction*, but the terms are often used interchangeably.

forecast, self-fulfilling. A forecast that tends to make itself come true. For example, a forecast for rapid growth of a certain city may encourage businesses to locate there, thus causing the growth that was predicted.

forecast, self-negating. A forecast that tends to reduce its own likelihood of coming true. For example, a forecast of a shortage of teachers in five years may encourage many college students and others to seek teaching certification, thus negating the forecast of a shortage.

forecasting, judgmental. Forecasting based on the forecaster's personal knowledge or expertise rather than a special forecasting methodology. Such forecasts are constantly made in everyday thinking and conversation (e.g., "Hernandez will almost certainly be here tomorrow morning, but Schmidt is unlikely to come.") Judgmental forecasting is also expected of physicians, lawyers, accountants, and other professionals functioning as experts in particular areas of concern.

forecasting, technological. The forecasting of the future potential characteristics of a new or upgraded technology, device, procedure, or technique. A technology forecaster is generally called on to forecast the *feasibility* of a certain technology, not whether it will actually be developed, because that would depend on non-technological factors such as anticipated profitability and governmental regulations. Example: We might predict that a new chemical compound could be developed, but not whether it would be an effective and profitable drug.

foresight. The ability to anticipate and assess future events as well as to strategize to avert future dangers and grasp future opportunities. A person demonstrates foresight by being able to develop successful long-term strategies and by being well prepared for likely contingencies. In a famous fable, an ant shows foresight by storing up food for the winter, whereas an unprepared grasshopper starves to death. Similarly, many people quickly spend whatever money they have and are quite unprepared for a financial crisis.

future (adjective). Belonging to that part of time that has not yet occurred but that will occur.

future (noun). This term may refer to any of the following:

1. The period of time following the present moment and continuing on indefinitely. "The polar ice caps may shrink in the future."
2. The situation or condition of someone or something in the future. "The future of biotechnology looks bright."
3. One of a plurality of possible future conditions or situations. These are sometimes described as *alternative futures* or just *futures*. For instance, three futures may be envisioned for the giant pandas: extinction, revival in the natural environment, or domestication and continued existence in zoos and private preserves.

future (verb). *See* **futuring.**

future, alternative. One of a number of *futures* that may be envisioned for a person or thing. The term *alternative futures* stresses that there is not a single inevitable future toward which people move through time, but a number of possible futures that are yet to be decided. In our thinking about the future of something, it is often useful to describe several mutually exclusive scenarios. These *alternative futures* help to clarify the options available to the decision maker(s).

future shock. The disorientation caused by rapid social change. The term was popularized by Alvin Toffler in a 1970 book with that title.

future(s) studies. The study of future possibilities. The term is one of many that are used for what futurists do and is most popular in academia. *See also* **futuring.**

futures. Possible future events or developments.

futures research. The study of future possibilities. This term is popular among researchers in or outside of academia.

futurics. The study of future possibilities. *See* **futuring.**

futuring. The act, art, or science of identifying and evaluating possible future events. *Futuring* is a very broad term and can be used in future-oriented discourse in both professional and personal affairs. It is less popular currently in academia than *futures studies,* which tends to be misleading in nonacademic settings. Other terms used include *futures research, futuristics, futurics, futurology, prognostics,* etc.

futurible. A future event or development that is deemed possible but not necessarily probable. This term, developed by Bertrand de Jouvenel and his organization, is one way to indicate that a prediction or forecast is not intended where one is discussing a possible future event. An alternative term having much the same meaning is *scenario.* However, a scenario is generally thought of as a sequence of events rather than a single one.

futurism. Futurism is the doctrine (or movement) that emphasizes the importance of rational, scientific, or commonsense thinking about the future. The ultimate goal in futurism is generally to improve the future through better decision making. Futurists try to identify and assess the possibilities and probabilities of the future as a means of making better choices regarding alternative actions. Note: *Futurism* also refers to an artistic movement started by the Italian writer Filippo T. Marinetti in 1909, which had waned by the 1920s.

futurist. A person who engages in a great deal of futuring or otherwise demonstrates a serious rational or scientific concern for the future.

futurize. To orient toward the future. An institution may futurize by reorganizing its activities so as to meet future challenges. An educational institution may offer courses in futures studies (or futuring), or introduce the future into a regular course. Warren Wagar, a historian as well as a futurist, developed a future-oriented world-affairs course that became one of the most popular at the State University of New York at Binghamton.

game. A game may be developed as a way to test alternative strategies and to train personnel. War games, for example, may involve actual soldiers and mock battles, or they may be fought by means of computer simulations of conflict situations. A game helps decision makers to anticipate how various "players" would respond to challenges in a real-world situation.

gaming. The use of a game that simulates a real situation. For example, games have been developed to represent the operations of a city government. Different players may play the parts of the mayor, city council, real estate lobby, tenants' association, etc. By playing the game, the players can get a clearer understanding of the dynamics of a situation.

heuristic. Serving to stimulate research or discovery. A number of methods may be used because of their heuristic value; that is, their ability to encourage people to learn a variety of new things. For example, students may be asked to design a model community; in the process, they are led to acquire wider knowledge about how communities operate, what values are important to different people, etc.

holistic. Emphasizing the entirety of something. (*Holon* is Greek for "whole.") In dealing with complex systems, such as a human being or a city, researchers will often look at individual elements rather than the system as a whole, but it often is essential to consider the system as a whole.

ideation. The process of forming ideas and relating them to other things, including other ideas. Ideas can emerge from brainstorming and other heuristic techniques. *See also* **heuristic.**

image. A mental picture or concept of a person, object, institution, or other thing. A politician, for example, may try to create in the minds of voters desirable or undesirable images of future events—e.g., a future rise or decline in taxes—as a means of attracting political support.

indicator. A statistic or measurement used to gauge the condition of something. Economic indicators include figures for the GNP, freight loadings, stock prices, etc. Social indicators include crime rates, divorces, high-school graduations, etc.

indicator, leading. A variable whose change generally precedes some other event or situation, or an event with a similar characteristic. For example, an increase in economic activity is typically preceded by a rise in the prices of stocks; thus, stock prices are a leading indicator of economic activity. There also are *lagging indicators*, such as the increase of jobs during the later stages of an economic recovery.

indicator, social. A statistical variable relating to the state of society. The crime rate, the level of literacy, and the incidence of alcoholism are social indicators. Social indicators give policy makers a measure of the quality of life in a city or area. Social indicators allow us to grade or rank such things as cities or universities according to the quality of life they offer.

lead time. The time required for a development to move from conception to completion. In some cases, lead times are very long: Building a new electric power plant, for example, may take ten years or more because of the time consumed by planning, legal obstacles, construction, etc.

linear. Following a straight line or having a single dimension. A *linear* relationship is one that is straightforward and direct, in contrast to a *nonlinear* relationship, which is complex and may involve feedback. A *linear thinker* might hold that a 20 percent increase in a tax rate would result in a 20 percent increase in tax collections, but such an increase is unlikely because taxpayers would be motivated by higher taxes to do more things to avoid being taxed at all, such as moving to a jurisdiction where the taxes are lighter.

Malthusian. Referring to the gloomy views of Thomas R. Malthus, an English clergyman and economist (1766-1834). Malthus expounded the theory that world population tends to increase faster than food supply and therefore must be controlled by famine, disease, or war. Modern-day Malthusians, sometimes styled *Neo-Malthusians*, advocate measures to restrict population growth to avoid the unpleasant results that may otherwise ensue.

model. Something made to resemble something else, such as a miniature automobile or person (doll). A model has some features of the thing it represents but lacks others. As a result, it can be smaller, cheaper, more convenient, or otherwise more suitable for a certain purpose than the "real" object. In addition to physical models, there now are mathematical or computer models of complex phenomena, such as a business, a city, or a national economy. These computer models can be used to simulate actual or potential developments in the real world, and such simulations can guide policy makers in deciding on actions to take.

model, mathematical. A series of equations for describing a real-world system, such as an economy. The equations can be entered into a computer and a variety of simulations made, using various assumptions. This enables policy makers to ask "what if" questions: For instance, if tax revenues rise by $30 billion, how would that affect the government's budget?

modeling. Representing significant aspects of something so that they can be evaluated in some fashion. A model may be either physical or symbolic, such as a computer program.

modeling, global. The use of computer programs containing sets of mathematical equations and other (logical) algorithms that describe problems of global scope.

monitoring. Continuous (or ongoing) observation of certain aspects of something. Nurses monitor the vital signs of patients. Arborists monitor the condition of trees. In futuring, monitoring typically focuses on selected features of the environment in which one operates, such as economic and governmental indicators.

morphological analysis. *Morphology* refers to the study of the structure or form of something. By breaking down something into its components or aspects, we can systematically think about each one in turn. Without a morphological analysis, we may easily overlook certain factors when we try to solve a problem or understand what is happening in a particular situation. *See in* **Chapter 10, "Mapping Our Thoughts."**

nonlinear. *See* **linear.**

planning. The preparation of *plans,* that is, a set of tentative decisions about what we will do in the future. A plan may include the identification of goals that one wants to reach, as well as reasonable strategies about how to achieve the goals. Planning, unlike futuring, is sharply focused on making immediate decisions about what one should do. In contrast, futuring focuses on developing a better understanding of *possible* goals and strategies as a preliminary to making decisions and plans.

precursor (noun). Something that commonly happens in advance of something else and therefore can be used to anticipate the later event. *See also* **bellwether.**

precursor (adjective). Referring to some group, jurisdiction, or thing that normally changes in advance of the others. For example, Scandinavian nations often adopt social policies in advance of other nations.

prediction. A statement that something will happen in the future. The term *prediction* connotes a greater degree of precision and certainty than does *forecasting*. Today's future-oriented scholars generally avoid making predictions and deal more in terms of forecasts or conjectures.

proactive. Oriented toward dealing with possible problems before they become crises or with opportunities before they are seized by competitors. After proactive managers identify a significant challenge or opportunity, they prepare for it. *Reactive* managers ignore emerging problems and opportunities until they become obvious, when the time for dealing with them effectively may have passed.

prognostics. The field that deals with forecasts or study of future possibilities. From *prognosis,* meaning "foreknowledge" in Greek. In his book *Prognostics* (Elsevier, 1971), the Dutch scholar Fred L.

Polak writes: "In the broad sense prognostics covers all the variants and methods of scientific future thinking."

progressionism. The doctrine that the human race or society is making continuous progress. Progressionism developed in Europe in the seventeenth and eighteenth centuries, along with the idea of progress, and reached its zenith in the late nineteenth and early twentieth centuries. However, progressionist views were discredited by intensifying world wars, economic depressions, the Holocaust, new weapons of mass destruction, and other negative factors. *See* **Chapter 13.**

projection. A forecast developed by assuming that a trend will continue into the future. For example, if the population of a city has recently been increasing 2 percent a year and the number of inhabitants is now 1 million, we might assume that the population one year from now will be 1.02 million.

quality of life. The noneconomic aspects of a human life, such as the purity of the air, security from crime, effective cultural institutions, availability of leisure and recreation, and general feelings of satisfaction and well-being. By contrast, the term *standard of living* emphasizes the economic aspects, such as salary, size of home, retirement benefits, vacations, etc. *See also* **indicators.**

reductionism. The tendency to explain a complex phenomenon by analyzing and measuring its individual parts or aspects. Whatever cannot be measured satisfactorily may be ignored as unimportant or even considered nonexistent.

relevance tree. A diagrammatic technique for analyzing systems or processes in which distinct levels of complexity or hierarchy can be identified. A relevance tree for a new drug might start with Biomedical Objectives, under which would be listed Prevention, Diagnosis, Treatment, etc. Under Diagnosis, the tree might branch into Structure, Function, Composition, Behavior, etc. A relevance tree enables an analyst to identify the various aspects of a problem or a proposed solution and thus arrive at a more complete understanding of something. This technique is also useful for identifying unintended side effects of innovations. *See* **Chapter 13.**

risk assessment. The identification and characterization of the quality and quantity of potential adverse effects of an event, such as an investment decision, a new technology, or a natural phenomenon.

scanning. The initial and continuing process of reviewing and analyzing current literature, Web sites, and other media to identify and describe noteworthy trends and their possible development and future impacts.

scenario. A description of a sequence of events that might possibly occur in the future. A scenario is normally developed by: (1) studying the facts of a situation, (2) selecting something that might happen, and (3) imagining the various ways for that development to occur and the sequence of events that might follow. For example, a person charged with protecting a city might first seek to identify the various threats that might occur and what responses the city's agencies might make; he could then get ideas about specific challenges to the city's current security system. In this way, the scenario writer can try to identify potential weaknesses in a city's security system and suggest ways to improve them.

simulation. The use of models, including computer and physical models, and/or role-playing exercises to test the effects of various developments or events on the system being studied. *See also* **model, gaming.**

singularity. A postulated time in the future when technological progress and other aspects of human evolutionary development becomes so rapid that nothing beyond that point can be reliably conceived.

social experiment. A small-scale test of a social policy or system. Carefully monitored social experiments can help policy makers find more effective ways to deal with social problems.

stage. A distinguishable condition in the development of something as time passes. In human development, a fertilized egg develops into an embryo, then a fetus, then an infant, then a toddler, etc. A new product may move from conceptualizing to prototyping, to market testing, to full-scale production, etc. *See* **Chapter 4.**

synergy. The combined action of a number of parts so that the result is greater than would be produced by the parts operating independently. In brainstorming, people freely express their ideas, thereby stimulating other members of the group to get ideas. The result: A larger number of original ideas may be produced than if everyone worked on the problem independently.

systems theory. A theory that seeks to explain the behavior of systems, which are aggregates of interacting units. One important aspect of a system is the existence of feedback; that is, when one part of a system is acted upon, the results of that action, propagated through other parts, cause the original one to be affected, as when a drop in a stock's price frightens investors, thereby causing a further decrease in its value. *See* **Chapter 5.**

thought experiment. The test of a concept through the use of imagination and logic. Typically, the thinker posits a certain state or situation as being true, and then asks the question, If that is true, what might result?

threshold. The point at which a change produces some new effect. Certain types of change proceed without noticeable effect, but at a certain point a notable reaction occurs. Example: When water reaches 100° C, it begins to boil.

time frame. The period of time that one is assuming for the purposes of decision making and planning. For instance, a planner might think normally in three-month segments.

time horizon. The farthest distance into the future that one considers in forecasting and planning. A company may be viewed as having a "short time horizon" if it rarely gives serious consideration to events that are forecasted to occur more than two years into the future.

utopia. An ideal society or a description of such a society. A utopia normally exemplifies desirable things that might happen in the future. The things judged desirable may reflect the period of history in which the utopia is conceived, as well as the author's own preferences. *See also* **dystopia.**

visioning. The process of creating a series of images or visions of the future that are real and compelling enough to motivate and guide people toward focusing their efforts on achieving certain goals.

wild card. An unexpected event that would have enormous consequences if it actually occurred. The term often refers to a future event that is unlikely during the period of time being considered but would have great consequences if it did.

This glossary draws from the online futuring dictionary, which is continuously updated. Comments and suggestions are welcome. Please visit *Futuring* at wfs.org/futuring.htm.

Index

About the World Future Society

The World Future Society helps individuals, organizations, and communities see, understand, and respond appropriately and effectively to change. Through media, meetings, and dialogue among its members, it raises awareness of change and encourages development of creative solutions. The Society takes no official position on what the future will or should be like. Instead it acts a neutral forum for exploring possible, probable, and preferable futures.

Founded in 1966 as a nonprofit educational and scientific organization in Washington, D.C., the Society has some 25,000 members in more than eighty countries around the world. Individuals and groups from all nations are eligible to join the Society and participate in its programs and activities.

The Society's annual conferences provide opportunities to hear and meet many outstanding thinkers and to take one- or two-day courses dealing with the future.

Chapters of the World Future Society are active in cities around the globe. Chapters offer speakers, educational courses, seminars, and other opportunities for members in local areas to meet and work together.

The Society's Web site (wfs.org) features unique resources such as the online Futurist Bookshelf—brief summaries of new and noteworthy books, reviews, and links to order—and Web Forums such as Future Generations, Utopias, Social Innovation, and Global Strategies.

Membership Benefits

- *The Futurist*, a magazine of forecasts, trends, and ideas about the future. Every member receives a subscription to this exciting bimonthly magazine. Experts in various fields share their insights and forecasts in articles directed at a general audience.
- A monthly e-mail newsletter, *Futurist Update*.
- Special rates for all annual conferences. These conferences provide members with the opportunity for face-to-face meetings with distinguished scholars, leaders, and experts from around the world.
- Access to your local chapter. More than 100 cities in the United States and abroad have chapters for grassroots support of futures studies. They provide a way for members to get

involved in their local communities through workshops, discussion groups, and speakers.

• Extended membership privileges for those professionally involved in the field of futures studies, including subscriptions to *Future Survey*, a monthly digest of abstracts on future-relevant literature, and *Futures Research Quarterly*, a professional journal providing information on more technical future-oriented topics.

For additional information, or to apply for membership, please contact the Society or go to the Society's Web site.

Contact information

World Future Society
Membership Department
7910 Woodmont Avenue, Suite 450
Bethesda, Maryland 20814, USA
Telephone: 301-656-8274
Web site: www.wfs.org
E-mail: info@wfs.org

Future Generations Fund

The World Future Society's Future Generations Fund enables young people and others to acquire the knowledge they need not only to manage their personal futures but also to preserve and enhance the world's natural and human resources for future generations.

Donations are used to support student memberships in the Society, scholarships for students at Society conferences, resources for classroom teachers educating young people about global problems and potential solutions, and other programs designed to encourage youth to become effective stewards of the human future.

Donations to the Society are tax deductible on U.S. income tax returns. The Society is classified as a 501 (c) 3 tax-exempt organization under the U.S. Internal Revenue Code.

World Future Society

Additional Praise for
Futuring: The Exploration of the Future

"The best general introduction to futures studies by far."

Michael Marien, editor, *Future Survey*

"This book could not come at a better time. Assisted by the promises and perils of a revolution in technology, globalization, and other historic upheavals, the world badly needs this trove of wisdom Edward Cornish has cultivated over a long career. *Futuring* will equip us all for the challenges ahead."

William E. Halal, professor of management, George Washington University; author, *21st Century Economics*

"*Futuring* is magnificent... An engrossing and important book...Read it. It could change your future."

Wendell Bell, Yale sociology professor; author, *Foundations of Futures Studies*

"I really enjoyed reading the book and find it a constant source of interest and information."

Thomas S. Foley, former Speaker, U.S. House of Representatives

"*Futuring* by Edward Cornish is recommended...The book is an insightful introduction to the art and science of the future... Students are highly encouraged to become acquainted with the content of this book."

Felipe Korzenny, professor of marketing, Florida State University